the secret music at tordesillas

Winner of the Tuscarora Award in Historical Fiction

Hidden River Arts offers the Tuscarora Award yearly for an unpublished book-length work of historical fiction. The award provides $1,000 and publication by Hidden River Press.

Hidden River Arts is an interdisciplinary arts organization dedicated to supporting and celebrating the unserved artists among us, particularly those outside the artistic and academic mainstream.

the
secret music
at
tordesillas

a novel by

MARJORIE SANDOR

HIDDEN RIVER PRESS
Philadelphia 2020

Library of Congress Control Number: 2020930514
ISBN 978-0-9994915-3-9

Cover design by Andrea Marks
Interior design and typography by P. M. Gordon Associates

Cover illustration: detail, *Ritratto di il suanatore di chitarra*, Giulio Campi,
used by permission of the Uffizi Galleries, Florence, Italy.

This is a work of fiction. While the author has made every effort to honor the
historical record of the period, the names, characters, places, and incidents of this
novel are either products of the imagination or used fictitiously.

Grateful acknowledgment is made to *Jewishfiction.net*, in which Chapter Two
appeared, in slightly different form, under the title "The Secret Music" (September
2018 issue).

HIDDEN RIVER PRESS
An imprint of Hidden River Publishing
Philadelphia, Pennsylvania

*Dedicated to the memory
of my brother David*

1942–2019

author's note

Juana I of Castile, the Spanish queen known to history as "Joan the Mad," died on Good Friday, the 12th of April, 1555, at Tordesillas, after forty-seven years in forced seclusion. Whether she was genuinely unfit to rule or simply politically inconvenient has long been a source of controversy.

We do know that Juana was a gifted Latinist, a great reader, and a skilled musician. Her brightly painted clavichord still stands in the convent of Santa Clara in Tordesillas, and in the inventory of the queen's possessions, among the plain linen gowns and rotted roundlets of Asturian lace, are listed several songbooks and musical instruments, including a monochord, a clavichord, and a plucked vihuela. On the queen's household payroll, until quite late in her life, we find a few chapel singers and an instrumentalist, this last a player of the vihuela.

The vihuela is a small plucked instrument that looks, to the modern eye, like an early guitar, but which has the double courses of the lute, and a deep, melancholy timbre not unlike that of the lute's Arabic ancestor, the oud. The rise of the vihuela's popularity in Spain coincides with the first decades of the Spanish Inquisition, an era in which Juana's parents, the Catholic Kings Fernando and Isabel, sought to purify their realms of other religions, other cultures. They began with the order, in 1492, for all Jews to convert to Christianity or depart their realms. A similar order followed for Muslims in 1502.

What happens to music in such a time as this? Might music itself have undergone a forced conversion? After all, the oud, revered as the most princely of instruments in Moorish Spain, would have no place in the Christian monarchs' court, except as a curiosity in pageants portraying the conquered Moors and Jews, and mocking their antiquated customs.

And what became of musicians who played it? What about the oud player who takes up the vihuela in service of the Catholic Kings and goes on to serve their descendants, repressing the now-forbidden traditions, musical and otherwise, of his own lost childhood?

When you tell someone your secret, your freedom is gone.
Fernando de Rojas, 1499

*We are always looking for the missing part of the
tune; and all we've ever heard is in there somewhere,
all we've witnessed, buried in the memory.*
Ciaran Carson, 1996

one

I promise to confess everything. But first set down how the snow is to blame. If not for the snow I would have been at San Antolín this morning, saying Mass and mourning the death of our sovereign lady. You may safely believe I am sorry to be here and not there. That said, I am ready to answer our good commissioner's questions in full—more fully, perhaps, than he would wish. Accuse me of theft, or some heresy of my own. Murder, if you like. But look at me. Surely I am too withered and dry to harbor a flea, let alone a secret Jew.

And if I am not at church, it is not for any dark reason. It is only because last night a rare Easter storm came through, and this morning, between the bells, water fell from the palace eaves, one paltry beat at a time. I have always had a weakness for small sounds. My fellow musicians, were they still here, could bear witness: how, in our long years together, such trifles distracted me at the most inopportune times. Even the instrument I played for the queen produces only a quiet tone. The vihuela was never meant to compete with trumpet and shawm, those instruments so necessary for state occasions, triumphant entries into towns.

No—it is best suited to the small chamber, played alone, or accompanying a single voice. A female voice if you ask me. Not necessarily royal. An alto, softly burred by kitchen smoke.

The last time I heard such a voice? Years ago now. Only stay, and I will remember.

But church. Church is why you find me here. Everyone else left the palace yesterday after the queen's body was removed, among them our last chamberlain and his wife, the cobbler and the poulterer, the cook and kitchen helpers, the washerwoman and the master of the wax. A few singers, yes. She kept a few singers to the end.

What matters is my pious intent. There is, of course, the problem of moving—my knees, you see, and sometimes the feet. And yesterday in particular, with snow on the way, there was a mineral tang on my tongue, the pale blue taste of mountain air. A memory lay hidden in it, but wouldn't come out.

I'll just stay, I told the singers. You children go on.

After they left, I felt drowsy and sat down here in this passage and closed my eyes, and for this I am truly sorry. I failed to see if they took mules or went on foot, or if they set out to the north or south. I am afraid I am very little use to you. But for all that, I hope you stay. Solitude is one thing. Loneliness, another. Have either of you children? No? Not even the good commissioner here, so robustly made?

A shame for him. But this scribe is still young, I see, and not bad-looking. Young man, may you be fortunate.

But listen, do you know that earlier this morning, when I should have been at Mass, I heard laughter over my head? I was astonished: Queen Juana still lying in state at San Antolín, and already it seemed we had thieves. I was sitting here, in this very passage, near these doors. This old thing was in my arms then too, but I didn't have the heart to play.

Morning is my melancholy time.

It's a kind of vihuela, yes, let us call it a vihuela despite its odd shape. And even if it bears only a slim relevance to the crime you hope to expose, let me keep it here, for it will help me remember other things. That said, I must say I am surprised the Judaizers are still of such great interest to the Holy Office. I thought we were well shut of them, and onto more devious heretics: those who secretly read the Quran, for instance, or those who follow Erasmus. You are surprised to hear me speak of such matters, but in fact we have had the Holy Office here in the palace before today. The queen herself caused no small panic earlier this year by refusing to hear Mass or make confession. Even when she was on her deathbed, they had such a time getting her to say the right thing.

But about these Judaizers. I sympathize with the need to ferret out the last of them. For if there is one thing I have learned in my long life, it is that there is no alien population so weak, its ranks so thinned, that it might not still have the power to infect our nation's pure blood. I admire what you do. It must take constant vigilance, attention to the smallest detail, to keep after them.

I will commend your diligence with my final breath.

But the laughter: it wasn't the roaring kind. Small, uneasy, though the voices were deep. I must have drowsed and missed them as they came in through the great doors. Over my head the floorboards creaked under great boots. Then we had the long, grating howl of a cupboard on the move, or, God help them, the marriage bed the queen insisted on keeping, carved from the finest holm oak and hauled through Castile, along with the beautiful dead man who once lay in it. It is heavier than it looks. How her servants got that bed up those stairs in the first place—nearly fifty years ago—I cannot recall. I only know that it will never come down in one piece.

Then came a clattering, followed by another weak fit of laughter.

Did you drop that?

No. I thought you—

They say she hoarded treasure up here.

They say her ghost—

I plucked two strings. Not to frighten the thieves; only to stop them stealing. I was, in fact, all this morning trying to make myself invisible by a method taught me by the singer whose voice I mentioned, whose voice I have not heard for years, for her soul slipped your fetters long ago.

It was she who once told me that if I ever needed to vanish I should simply picture something that brought me peace.

"You," I said, reaching for her waist.

She only laughed and leaned away. "Peace is the last thing I brought you," she said. "Think of something else. Before me."

But I was a young man at the time, and my mind was on other things.

Yes, she had a name. A small, unimportant one. It is sewn, in large letters, on a yellow tunic that hangs in San Antolín. Come to think of it, you can find it on another of these *sanbenitos*, in the church at Benavente, two days north and a little west, if you keep a good pace.

A stubborn Judaizer. Nearly a legend. I understand the urge to commit heresy comes down through the generations. Three or four rinsings, I've heard it takes, to dilute the dirty foam of a family like hers.

Where was I? Yes, the thieves, and my plucking of two strings. How they heard such a little sound I will never know. But down the stairs they came—possessed of neither trinket nor bedpost—and in their boot-falls I heard not only panic, but the weight and nature of their grief. Where, cried the boots, are the legendary gold coins, the jewel-encrusted crucifixes, the hair ornaments from our sovereign lady's joyous entry into Antwerp? Where is the famous jewel casket with the false bottom, sworn to exist by Catalina, the queen's last washerwoman? I suspect all the two fellows could have turned up were a few bundles of lace roundlets, some still in their papers. Several plain linen gowns. Too many books—over a hundred—missals, breviaries, songbooks, and her mother's copy of *Tirant lo blanc*, the one great romance she managed to keep. A monochord and clavichord. Nothing worth taking. And they would need to come back with more men for that bed.

Quick, think of something that brings you peace, said the singer with the little waist.

Before me.

And this, gentlemen, is what kept me from church this morning. This and nothing more. I listened to the snow-water dripping off the roof, and the little memory flitted near once more, bringing its mountain taste of cool dark earth. A window square of such pale blue—

Forgive the poetry. I only meant to say, it is not a memory from here. I promise a full confession, if only we might conduct it here, and both of you stay—especially this young fellow who writes so well. What a fine hand he has, and a tender, serious eye—I am confident that he will understand me well, and miss nothing. Conduct the interview here, and I will tell you everything you want to know, and more. I will tell you some things about our late sovereign lady, too—things no one else knows. They may shed light on her occasionally alarming behavior, and be of use to the Holy Office in years to come.

She had her own peculiar notions of spiritual life. Of faith.

Think of all you have to gain, far beyond what the Holy Office expects. A tale inside a tale. You may peer behind every door and molest every cupboard—who knows but there are many false and hidden ones, and treasures still hidden within. Nor will you risk losing valuable words should I die in the cart on the way to some more official place. For I must tell you, I have not eaten or drunk for a few days now. It is a marvel I have lasted this long.

First, observe this trick: you can put your fingers just here, on the neck of this odd vihuela, and slide them just so, and the human ear will miss almost all of what is held within.

The thieves? Gone for now. Down the stairs they came, their boots making the floorboards tremble. I had to press my palm over the central rosette to keep the strings from sounding again, this time by themselves.

Too late. The strings sang out.

The men stopped, inches away. One laid a hand upon the sleeve of the other.

Jesu. Did you hear that?

The mad queen's ghost—still here, I knew it.

And with that, they made for the great doors, scattering sunlight everywhere. No looking back for them. The passage went dark again, quiet but for the snow-water dripping from the eaves. You can't hear the river from this side, no. Later, I will send you there to look. You shall see it all.

Of those thieves—I knew they'd come back, their courage swollen by numbers and noise. In fact, when you arrived, I was sure it was them.

But for the moment, all was quiet. And into that interval, a memory dropped. And then another.

Inés.

There now, you have it all: Inés de Castro. Is that the name you want? She is long gone, gentlemen, and I am to blame. I will tell you how.

But first I have something else to report. There are a thousand kinds of silence on this earth, not one of them pure. Take the velvet black humming deep in the ear after a long night of playing. Or that pale blue I mentioned before. A mere cupful of sound, to fit into the hollow just beneath the collarbone, where you can see the flicker of a lover's pulse. I chase it in the dark.

two

Inside one note, many more are hidden.

I learned this long before I met Inés de Castro—learned, but did not fully understand. I learned it from my father, who played the oud, that antiquated "lute" of the Moors, as did his father before him, and so on, all the way back to the time of Alfonso the Wise. I hereby state that my name is Juan de Granada. I was baptized in the spring of 1492, at the age of ten, and you find me now in my seventy-third year. In all this time, I have been as good a Christian as any.

I am the last leaf of my father's tree, ready to fall and be done with it.

Of my family, I have only a few things to tell. We lived in Granada's dwindling Jewish quarter until, in the days following Fernando's triumph, our neighborhood was branded a nest of criminals and the sadly misguided. But well before this, my parents had made sure my brother and I were circumcised, and bestowed upon each of us two names: one to carry into the world, and one to keep hidden in the heart.

Naïve, defiant, or simply exhausted—it is not for us to judge. After all, for ten years, rumors of Christian conquest had come and gone every day; who could keep up with them? To be on the safe side, our mother had taught us the Castilian of her own northern childhood, while our father taught us to play the oud and sing in the Arabic of our native place. He still held out hope that one of us would succeed him in his playing, both at the caliph's palace inside the Alhambra, and at the many *zambras* in the city below.

Suffice it to say that our father was an innocent: a quiet, slender, brown-eyed man, and after he vanished one night in March of that momentous year, our mother told us that his only crime was to have carried his talent so openly in the world.

"Are you listening to me?" she asked.

We said we were.

No matter. The thing to remember is that until he disappeared, our father played. His fingers moved swiftly up and down the neck of his oud, and when he came home, he wore like a badge the scent of whatever place he had performed. Sometimes his good shirt gave off little breaths of jasmine and myrtle, which our mother could not scrub out. He liked to joke that he could never hide anything from her: she could tell from sniffing his clothes precisely how near a court lady had drawn.

He played late most nights, but when he was home, he told us stories about the age of peace and music both, when the greatest oud player of all time escaped his enemies in Baghdad and arrived in Spain with ten thousand songs held safely in his ears. This man's skin was so dark and his voice so clear that he was given the nickname Ziryab: blackbird. It was Ziryab who raised the number of courses on the oud from four to five, thereby giving it a soul, and who taught the caliph and his courtiers to eat elegantly and to love poetry. There were stories of Granada as it had been in our great-grandfather's time, the heyday of the Moors, its Jewish quarter still pulsing with life, of the silk markets, the importers of myrrh and calamus, the great baskets of saffron, of pomegranate and peach. Its songs, which carried at least three languages with ease.

If we weren't sleepy yet, our father went still further back in time, to the tale of the Jewish musicians called to the court to play for the Sultan on the Ninth of Av. This was the anniversary of the destruction of the two Temples and the Great Dispersion, when the rabbis forbade the playing of any music at all. But the ruler was so hungry for their music that he ordered these musicians, on pain of death, to play. When at last the musicians complied, their song came out as a lamentation so deep that even the Sultan wept to hear it.

From that day forward, they were called the Singers of Affliction.

And so it is, our father said, that to this day, a musician who carries even a little bit of our ancestors' blood will find that in the last days of summer, it hurts to put one's fingers to the strings. They stiffen at the knuckles, as if God holds them fast, and no matter what you do, the melody comes out as a lament.

In the final days of the old kingdom, our father told all his stories in a hushed voice, as if he were afraid that Christian soldiers or envious musicians already waited just beyond our front door. His voice was as steady and low as a pipe's drone. I could never keep my eyes open, but fell asleep a full century before the riots and bloodshed began in earnest, and in the morning, it seemed I had only dreamed the old Granada of the Jews with its bright noisy streets. There was nothing now in our city to suggest such a place, nothing except a few stars cut in the synagogue walls, where our father sometimes took us to sit among the last handful of worshippers and hear the old chants.

On the second day of January, 1492, I woke early. It had snowed the night before, and the streets were still quiet. Then someone started beating a tin pot—or so it seemed—far away on the Vega. A dog began to bark.

I sat up beside my sleeping brother, and at that moment, from the hill above, came a dark iron clanging, fat and sour. Birds burst from their eaves and swung through the sky; every small creature began to howl.

The bells rang all that day and into the night. They rang to proclaim many things, but most of all the entrance of the Catholic Kings Fernando and Isabel, their children and courtiers, their priests and armies, from their encampment on the plain below. A city entering a city. A procession that would make its way past our own house later that morning, the royal parents and their five children dressed in the robes of the caliph they had conquered, winding up the hill on which the houses of the last Jews of Granada crouched. Up they went, into the Alhambra and deeper still, into its royal gardens and palace. Later it would be said that all the alarm bells of Granada had been melted down and recast as church bells, purely to oppress the ear of the conquered Moor.

That winter a saying arose in those bruised streets: *the kings can ring their cowbells, but they have no cows.* I was ten years old, and did not understand. I only knew that no muezzin's call could be heard under all that iron howling.

Then it was March, and the tight pale buds of myrtle and olive unclenched, until one day it wasn't snow but almond blossoms that lay on the shoulders of those who stumbled, weak and exhausted, into the streets, their faces carved into new shapes by famine and sickness, by so much impossible news. Town criers sang out: it had been decreed by the Catholic Kings that the Moors might stay and practice their religion, but the Jews had until the end of July to depart Spain, or convert to the One True Faith.

One night, as my brother and I lay down to sleep, our father came and knelt beside us. He put a hand on each of our heads and let his fingers drift down our faces in the old way of blessing, soon to be forbidden.

"Life is not so terrible," he said, "if I can still do this."

I must have fallen asleep, because I remember waking later, to see the moon shining through the high window. I heard the comforting rustle of my father's robe, the crunch of his slippers on packed earth as he stepped outside, as he always did at that hour, to make water under the fig tree. Then I dropped back to sleep.

In the morning, he was gone, and our mother could not lift her hands from her face. "If only it had been half a moon."

"Why half a moon?" I asked, but she only shook her head.

"There is a time to shine your light," she said. "And a time to hide it."

What did she mean? Our father had only gone outside to relieve himself, not to perform in some musical competition. His oud was still in the house, leaning against the wall. Beside it lay his little coin pouch, tipped heavily to one side.

"Don't worry," she said. "He'll make his way back. We'll wait."

What she couldn't tell me was that she was afraid for me, too, not only because I had my father's ear for music, but because I was beginning to resemble him. When my brother and I stood side by side, all eyes came to rest on me. I felt it, and wished they wouldn't; all those eyes, hungering and lapping. But what even my mother didn't realize—and what I was only beginning to grasp—was that the greater danger lay between myself and my brother.

She didn't see it. She was too busy watching as her neighbors packed, as every other husband but her own locked his front door and put the house key in his pocket.

"Maybe they're leaving because the bells hurt their ears," I told her one morning not long after, and this, at least, made her smile.

"Truly, you have your father's gift," she said, and held my shoulder firmly, as if the merest breeze could take me, not knowing that in the house, her elder son was awake and waiting for her to proclaim his talent, too. Together we watched as a neighbor boy rushed down the street in his nightshirt, only to be caught by his father and pinned under the arm like a goat bound for the butcher. A grandmother squatted in the dust and dung of the road, forcing donkeys and carts and all those on foot to part around her, so much water around a rock. And through all of this, the bells kept ringing, as if to push the people all the way to the port at Cadiz, and into the sea itself.

Cadiz, Cadiz, it sounded fine to me. There would be talking birds and platters heaped with fish, and a sea captain who asked me to climb to the top of the rigging and help him watch for pirates.

"Shouldn't we be leaving too?" I asked my mother.

She didn't answer, but her hand tightened on my shoulder as if I'd already leaned too far out into the street.

But a mother's fear only makes a child restless, and it's worse when she has lately lost the husband who used to balance her endless list of terrors with his reasonable hopes, stroke her forehead with his callused thumb, and ask her to sing. And it's worse still if that husband arose one moonlit night in March to visit the fig tree, and never came back. From then on, even the hour before dawn brought her no rest. She stayed up all night, consulting a piece of oak carved in the shape of a child holding a staff. "Put this in your frying pan," a neighbor had explained to her. "It will tell you if your love is safe, and on the road home." But how to read the piece of oak? Which way should the child face for good news? This the neighbor had failed to say.

So each morning in our doorway she held me close. "God knows what will become of you. You could be stolen from me like a loaf of bread."

And she pulled me back inside the house.

By May our father had not yet returned. The kings' soldiers paid a visit to the quarter with catapults and stones. A hospital goes here, they said. A tournament field there. The old synagogue will be the Church of St. Cecilia—the patron saint of music and the blind. Was this what convinced my mother it was time to leave? Because one night shortly after, she began to fuss around the house in a different way, rolling all our clothes into bundles and singing her old Castilian songs. I lay awake listening.

"Go to sleep," she said. "Some things are hard to pack, but we carry them anyway." Then she started singing again.

Nani, Nani, sleep, my sweetheart,
Sleep, sleep, apple of my eye.
Your father is coming and his spirits are high.
"Open the door, wife.
Open the door because I'm coming
And I'm tired from plowing the fields."

I must have drifted off, because now the mother in the song wouldn't let the father back into the house. *You have a new love*, she sang.

"What's a new love?" I asked my mother.

"Never mind," she replied. "Just pay attention to the melody. Give it a home inside your ears." And she sang it again, this time without the words. Her voice leaped once, rose a little higher, then began to fall in the smallest of steps. She squinted as she sang, as if trying to hear a deeper secret tucked inside the notes, until I saw a little scene: I saw my father, dragged off by other musicians jealous of his gift, away from the fig tree and up into a fine palace. There he was sold to a rich Christian lady who kept him captive and made him learn to play other instruments, never his own. He lived in her chamber, never out of her sight.

So a mother is driven to fill her child's heart to the brim with love ballads and other fanciful tales, leaving no room for a darker, simpler truth: that an ordinary man can be dragged off in the dark for humming an old prayer in his own street.

And so I lay abed, willing my father to slip out of the pudgy fingers of a bejeweled Christian lady.

"What should we do with his oud?" I asked my mother that May night as she bundled our clothes and sang.

"You'll carry it. Keep it safe for him. Think how proud he'll be when he sees you again."

"But if we leave, how will he find us?"

"By the manner of your playing," she said.

"But you said it shouldn't stand out."

She nodded. "Modesty above all," she said. "Don't worry, it will stand out to him."

The next morning I woke early and went out to play a balancing game on our doorstep. I rolled my bare soles to and fro on the threshold, catching the beat of two tuneless bells that sounded like a pair of fools—one fat, one thin. How I loved the thin bell, so sad and funny and left behind.

A moment later my mother stood beside me. Her warm hand rested on my shoulder. It felt so heavy—I felt stifled, high in my chest, and could not get my breath. I began to squirm.

"Stay here," she said. And as if to anchor me there, she put two things into my hands: my father's oud, and the key to our front-door. She couldn't find the plectrum, the eagle's quill for plucking. It had a habit of disappearing, even in good times.

She gave me one last thing: a small cloth bag on a string. This she tied around my neck, tucking the bag well-down inside my shirt. "An amulet," she said. "Good words are hidden inside, with your name, to protect you from the evil eye. Your father wears one all the time, sewn inside his sleeve."

"Where are you going?"

"Only up to Ana's for bread."

Still she stood there, balancing between the lintels with me, rocking to and fro, watching the forlorn parade trickle down our street. Three girls sang a Moorish dance-tune as they walked; a grown man beat a tiny drum.

"We'll leave too," she said. "As soon as I get back."

My father's coin pouch dangled from my mother's wrist. She held her wedding band up between thumb and forefinger. "A loaf of bread for a ring of gold," she said. Then she kissed her fingers and pressed them to the mezuzah on the wall beside the door. "Your brother's awake. Don't fight. What's out there is much worse." Then she said, "If soldiers come, you don't know what they're saying."

If only she hadn't given me the oud to hold. If only she hadn't said, "Don't fight," and gone off like that, up the street toward that mass of trees that ended, according to my father's stories, in the gardens of the Nasrids, tucked inside the red fortress itself.

No sooner was she gone than my brother's warm breath lifted the small hairs of my neck.

"When we are on our way," said he, "a fat bishop all in red will ask, 'How much for the pretty little Jew,' and Mother will let him have you for a second loaf of bread."

Nani, nani, I sang in my head. One small leap up, and then another, then a little series of half-waterfalls, down and down. The song was a green vine twining up, then down again. The sort of vine you wouldn't be able to safely sing in the days to come; every eye would narrow, every tongue wag with the old accusations: *Aren't you singing that song in the manner of the Jews?*

But not yet. Not in Granada, anyway.

That morning I had the song by heart, and wove it through my brother's iron voice like a thread of gold.

But what was taking our mother so long? Ana's was uphill, and the whole world appeared to be moving down it in a clatter of hoof and wheel. I understood that her errand might take longer than usual, but time seemed to have stopped. I was trapped in the doorway with my brother, while our mother might be in trouble, fighting to get down the street again with her loaf of bread.

"Let me look," said my brother, nudging me aside. "Which way did she go?"

That's how it started. I lowered the oud to my side to make it smaller in my brother's eyes, and its back struck the doorframe, giving out a hollow boom.

"Give it here," cried my brother. "You're going to break it." He narrowed his eyes. "And what's that around your neck?"

"Nothing," I said, holding the oud tight—and then I made my next mistake. "Besides," I added. "She asked *me*."

He held very still, his face a perfect mask. Then he spoke. "Nothing," he echoed. "Besides, she asked *me*." And he reached for my neck.

I flushed hot and twisted away.

"You're going to break it," he cried. And gave me a second push.

I confess it now: as my brother's hand came off my shoulder, I was filled with pride and rage. Let all the world see how it is with us! I sprang out so hard that the amulet flew out ahead of me on its little string. Let my brother come fetch me, I told myself. Let him beg my forgiveness. And if he doesn't, let our mother blame him, and hate him forever.

But something was wrong with the street. It had disappeared,

turned into an ocean of angry brothers, of too many voices and sting-
ing dust. At the edges of this ocean were other voices, singing and
clapping a lively tune. "Hey Jews, pack up your things," they sang,
"for the kings are sending you across the sea!" I craned my neck to see
these singers, but a bundle of clothes smacked me in the face, and I
only knew I couldn't let go of my father's oud, even as I felt my feet lift
off the ground, felt myself float up and out on a tide of rough cloth.
Higher and higher I rose, until at last I found myself perched on a pair
of bony shoulders. A low, gruff voice said, "Only as far as the river."

When at last I was set down, there was, in fact, a small river.
No houses. Just a low stone wall, a few scrubby trees, and a place
where clutches of people crossed very slowly on clattering stones, then
waded into the stream, holding their children on their shoulders. On
the other side, a cloud of dust stretched away across the Vega.

Later I would understand: this was the road to the port at Cadiz.
Later I would hear stories of that late spring and summer, my country's own endless Ninth of Av, though I never knew who or what
to believe. The Christian tales were full of mercy, offering baptism
to deluded parents, saving children from certain death at the docks.
And those who left Spain, surviving the rewards prepared for them
in other lands only to return and take the sacrament, would speak
only of the horrors of the places they'd gone, never of what happened
before they left. Once in a while someone whispered a tale of a young
man, his head shoved into a basin and smeared with chrism, then in a
great act of mercy stabbed to death on the spot so he might go out of
this life a Christian. Or of a girl squatting in the weeds, then handing her newborn, smeared in filth and blood, to a passing stranger,
so that she herself could lie down and go to sleep in the birth matter.
Old men and old women curled up, too. They put their faces to any
wall, or lacking that, the trunk of a tree. There were stories of Cadiz,
too. Stories of a fever that cut children down where they stood, their
feet already touching the pier. Stories of men who shrugged, grabbed
your food and bundle, and pointed you overboard with their swords.

All this is long past, of course. All the Jews are gone, and our
good scribe here is probably too young to have known a single one; a
little history will not harm him.

As I waited by the river, a strange girl walked toward me. Her
brown arms and legs were dusted white as flour at elbow and knee

and she leaned on a staff, patting the air with one hand. I was afraid her hand would find me, and she would beg my help, and I would never get away, so I stepped to one side, and watched her grope in the empty air, watched as she crouched and crawled to the river's edge, where she began to drink the muddy water. Still I didn't move. I noticed how the creases in her neck glistened, silver on the dark, and here is a thing I have told no man until now. I imagined putting my tongue there to taste the salt. My skin tingled and I felt a sweet dark thrill.

Then the girl crawled backward, away from the stream. She felt along the bank for her staff, stood and turned to face me. I felt as if she knew everything about me: my cowardly hiding and my urge to touch—oh, even that I had run away from my family in a vain rage.

That's when I remembered what my mother had said about the evil eye. Surely this was it. Should I touch the little bag at my neck, or was I supposed to know its words by heart, and recite them now? My mother hadn't told me what was written there beside my name. So I simply looked down into the river and listened to its gurgling voice. I waited until I heard the soft scrape of her feet on the gravelly bank. The soft pelting. Fading. Gone.

I stayed a while longer, watching the passing groups for any face that would soften when it saw mine. But no one more than glanced. It seemed as if no one would ever look my way again; that in the moment of hiding from the girl I had cursed myself, hidden myself forever from all eyes.

As the people passed by, some sang, and others played on pipes and drums. Other groups went past in silence, and it was in one of these that a man stopped. Surely this man knew my family's name and would point the way home. But the man only shook his finger, and frowned at my father's oud. "By the waters of Babylon, we hanged up our harps," he said. "Silence is the only just reply."

There was nothing to do but walk back uphill, against the tide, back the way I'd been carried. Yet I recognized nothing I passed. I felt the house key in my pocket. Maybe my mother and brother were still at home, waiting. I pictured my mother standing by the door, holding her frying pan with its child carved from oak—the child with its staff—asking it to tell her not only where her husband had gone, but now her younger son, too.

I saw again, in my mind's eye, the girl by the river. Was she not all brown with a staff of wood? Heat flooded me, a sudden dizziness. What if she was the child in my mother's frying pan, come to life to point the way? What if it was *I* who should have held out my hands to her, led her to drink, and asked the way home?

I stumbled on. Soon there were more houses, with only a few lamps lit in the windows. It was like the evening of a market day, with rotted vegetables and straw scattered everywhere, but other things, too, that didn't belong: a delicate birdcage, its door standing open; a white tablecloth for Shabbat; a tiny casket full of silver forks. People were in the streets, carrying torches and shouting.

Once that evening I was asked to play my father's oud—by a group of Christians and their ladies in a mood to dance. The men wore crimson hose and the softest boots; they had clean-shaven faces and slaves to bear their lights. Their women were not properly covered; their shoulders gleamed under those small circles of light, and one of them winked at me, then kept on looking. I chose quickly, the tune I knew best, though it came out slowly without the plectrum, and I was sure, the whole time, that the lady would see my fingers trembling, and pull me to her breast. But my father had said that this tune, "Calvi vi calvi, calvi arabi," came from the time of Alfonso the Wise, a Christian king from long ago who loved music no matter who made it. The gentlemen and ladies swayed a little to it, and smiled, and as they left, one of them gave me an orange. This, the winking lady said, will do you more good than a coin.

After they were gone, I kept walking uphill. Sometimes my legs went to jelly and I stumbled over nothing at all, but by dusk I found myself in a ravine, with trees rising up on either side, a good place to wait for morning. A moment later my fingers brushed against the trunk of a tree so small that I felt its saddle just at shoulder height. I leaned the oud against the trunk, settled myself in the saddle, and reached down for the oud. Once its belly was snug against my own, I peeled and ate my orange, down to the bitter pith. I promised myself that in the morning I would ask the first passerby to point the way home, even if I had to be baptized first.

That's when I remembered that my mother had only gone up the street to Ana's for bread—was it still the same day?

Tomorrow, I told myself, you will hold that sharp crust in your mouth until it melts clear away, crumb after tiny crumb. *But child, that's yesterday's bread*, my mother would say, still angry, and rightly so. She'd be in a terrible hurry, too. But I wouldn't fight or squirm. If she insisted, I would even let her hold me, very tightly as she used to do, when I was a little child.

I touched the amulet on the string around my neck.

The sky was black and there were no bells. No wind or human voices or even birds. Only a silence so immense that I heard the faint ringing we carry in our own ears, as we carry the stars beneath the lids of our eyes.

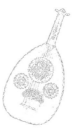

three

Picture a young lady of royal birth in a garden: small birds watch her from the lemon trees, petals drift through the air. A *bower*, she might call such a place, since she loves poetry, and, at thirteen, has already discovered, in her mother's traveling library, Aesop's fables and the great knightly romance *Tirant lo blanc*. And now, at last, in this garden, an adventure has come to her. She has found a wounded boy. A nightingale, she tells her ladies, its wing broken and askew. It seems to have fallen out of this little tree.

Any other infanta would have been content to carry the story home to her parents: the story, mind you, and not the wounded thing itself.

She should have called for her mother's guards and had me thrown back to my filthy street. Then she could have gone back to the conquered palace of the Nasrids and made a poem of me, perfectly shaped, wittily rhymed. Dazzled everyone with verses but left a mystery at the heart. As the wrongheaded Hebrews of old used to say, *Dayenu. Lord, had you only brought us out of Egypt, and not given us manna in the desert, it would have been enough. Had you given us manna in the desert, but not the two tablets of the Word, it would have been enough.*

Dayenu—such blasphemy!

I only meant to say that even as a young girl, our sovereign lady had trouble letting go of things.

So I lay there beneath a tree, my shoulder singing out, all heat and bright pain.

"Don't touch it, Inés!" cried a high thin voice, in the language of my mother's songs.

A hand reached out, and a girl in green lifted up my father's oud and carried it away. I swore I saw a bruise—or some black smudge—on its back as it floated off. Then my shoulder sang again and I closed my eyes.

Another girl stepped forward, this one all in crimson and cloth-of-gold, her face small and pale and somber beneath a broad-brimmed hat. A ribbon lay against her throat, and from it, a gleaming stone swung out and struck my forehead once. "Oh!" she cried, and a damp-faced lady tugged her away.

"Wait, a poem," said the girl in red. It was she who had the high thin voice. I strained to catch her words. "A nightingale," she recited, "has fallen from the branches of our sacred holm oak, our own *encina*. Look how it lies there, panting its last breaths, one wing bent and broken. A lyre hangs from the branches of the tree, caught there, saved from death by its own strings."

There was a small chorus of applause, and now I saw there were other young ladies all around.

"That will please Master Encina," she said.

"May I speak frankly, Infanta Juana?" That was the girl in green, no oud in her hands now. Where had she put it? "First, it is your brother's tutor who should please *you*. Second, it is *not* a lyre. It is not even a vihuela. It's one of the Moors' old lute-things, and it fell out of the tree."

"Inés," said the one in red. "For the poem it *must* be a lyre, and still hanging from the tree."

Infanta. I pushed myself up on two watery legs, only to fall back down again. A tall shoe hovered above my hand. "Stay down," said Inés.

This I could do.

"Inés," said the damp lady. "Go to the place where we left the mules. Bring two pages, or three. They can inspect him."

I heard the reply—"I can do it myself"—and opened my eyes just in time to see a long twig waver above my breeches like a divining rod. With this, Inés lifted the cloth at my hip. Her eyes flicked down and up.

"Doña Beatriz, I believe it is a Jew," she said. "Although, it is true, the Moors also practice this disgusting rite of—"

"Inés," cried the damp lady again, rapidly touching her brow and chest.

The other young ladies hid their faces in their hands. Among them were three dark-skinned slaves, all in white.

"I want to keep it," said the infanta. "An act of compassion, since I forgot to give away any clothes this year. He will be baptized this day and I will choose his name. He may well turn out to be gifted. Orpheus, they say—"

"Someone find a priest," said the lady, sighing. "And a surgeon." She pointed at a slave. "You, give me that cup there."

Everyone did as they were told, that is, all but Infanta Juana and the girl called Inés. Inés had her eye on my throat. My amulet-string. "Your lute-thing is gone away," she sang.

"*Al 'ud*," I croaked.

"The lyre hung in the *encina*," recited the infanta. "Saved from death by its own strings."

And as if that were some signal, Inés reached out. For a moment, the world held still and I felt cool fingertips touch my collar bone. Then a tug, and the amulet bag lay in her palm. She nipped a little paper out—the blessing I had never seen. She looked at it, then leaned close, and whispered my own name in my ear. "Keep it to yourself," she said. "Never say it aloud. Ever." Just before she made to hand the paper to the infanta, her fingertips crumbled it to dust. "Oh, beg pardon," she cried. "It must have been old and rotten."

"Did you see what was written there?" asked the infanta.

"I couldn't make it out," Inés replied. "It was in their abominable language."

"I thought your mother taught you—"

"My mother never learned Hebrew," she said. "Nor my father. Not even my grandmother learned it."

"Of course not," said the infanta.

A boy my own age, all in dark blue, stepped forward. "Come along, worm," he said cheerfully. Two more boys emerged and began to tug at my feet, until a deeper voice shouted for them to stop. "Lie still," said this voice, in clumsy Arabic. Someone knelt and cradled my arm, then offered me a pain so deep I lost both breath and sight.

I awoke slumped over a saddle, on a mule so swathed in crimson and cloth-of-gold that only its brown ears stood free. My arm was bound in a silken sling, and did not hurt. A hand steadied my back, and the deep voice spoke again in rough Arabic. "Pretend it still hurts. Pretend you understand nothing."

And that, gentlemen, is how I entered the Alhambra in May of 1492: slumped on a mule, deprived of my mother's amulet and my father's oud, but still possessed, somehow, of the key to my family's house, which no one had bothered to take from me. That is how I entered the very gardens and palaces of the Nasrids, a place I had never seen, but where my father, with his legendary gift, used to play. Where was he now? I tried to picture him safe in the mountains to the south, playing in the exiled court of Boabdil himself—perhaps he had been kidnapped to keep the caliph in music.

We went, in mock procession, the Infanta Juana, Inés, and the other young ladies at the front, from fine gardens into finer ones, and from there into great stone yards where men worked and shouted in whatever tongue they pleased. Along the way, the gentleman who fixed my arm fed me a few dusty almonds, and twice held up a water-skin. We traveled along the rosy walls to a place where three brown-robed men waited at a great basin.

I was lifted from the mule. The basin made no sound; there was no running water above its lip. Cold droplets ran down my face, and something thick and cold and rancid was thumbed against my brow. Words spilled and rose around the sullen stone. Whispers followed, then the sweep of robes.

"Juan de Granada," said a voice. Then more words fell.

Hushed laughter. "Her own little Moses-Orpheus," someone whispered.

Silence—laced with more laughter—as all bowed their heads.

The next moment I was back on the mule, the kind gentleman walking alongside. Once in a while I fingered the house key in my pocket: nothing else seemed real. The clatter and clang of iron boomed out and the language of the Catholic Kings swelled around me. We rocked forward, and with each step, there fell fewer tatters and shreds of my city's tongue.

Ahead of us, the infanta and Inés had halted by a gate, and waited on their mules. I heard the play of water just beyond. As we approached, the infanta spoke to Inés. "Do you remember 'The Nightingales,'" she asked. "That old lullaby your mother used to sing to us when we were young? About the nightingales in the trees, so sad for love?"

Inés shook her head.

"I know you remember it," said the infanta. "*The nightingales sing in flowering trees. Underneath sit those who suffer from love.* It's beautiful. I don't care if the Jews sang it. It's our song too."

But Inés would neither speak nor sing. I wasn't sorry: I didn't want to hear her voice stealing one of my mother's songs. I held the verses close, and imagined a little cave deep in my left ear, a place she could never lay her fingertips.

My mule was just behind theirs now, but they ignored it.

"With all respect," said Inés. "Your mother the queen would not approve—"

The infanta sighed. "You *have* to say that."

Inés put her finger to her lips, and at last the infanta turned to look at me.

"Juan de Granada," she said sternly. "Listen to me. You are blessed beyond measure. Here is your new master. He will teach you to play a true Spanish instrument and to honor the One True Faith."

Inés laughed. "Save your fine words. He doesn't understand."

But I did understand. And now I saw who they meant: a new gentleman stood beside my mule. This one was younger, with bright hazel eyes and a slender, clean-shaven face, dark hair curling beneath his cap. He wore a scholar's robes, and kept silent as he lifted me from the saddle and set me on the ground.

The infanta and Inés went quiet and gazed at their animals' bright trappings. It was Inés who, without ever looking up, leaned forward and urged her mule through the open gate, the infanta following. The moment they reached the other side, they fell to chattering again, like little birds.

The scholar watched them go. A sigh escaped him, but not till the gates were closed did he speak. "What did they tell you about me?" he said.

I shook my head.

At last the scholar put his palm to his own chest. "I am called Juan, too. Juan del Encina. From now on, you are called Juanico, and do what I say."

four

Juan del Encina. Surely this is a familiar name. I understand the Holy Office has nominated his comedy, *Placida y Vitoriano*, for inclusion in the next *Index of Prohibited Books*—surely a sign of its lasting worth. I imagine a few other works will wind up in there in the years to come—music as well as literature. For it is true that we might hear, in some of his tunes, a sinuous and disturbing interval so common in the music of the Levant and rightly banned for its power to infect the limbs with shocking and ruinous desire.

An interval, yes.

Did Juan del Encina have Jewish blood? Did it taint his music, his poetry, his plays?

Musicians cannot help what enters their ears. How then, can we help what is created by our fingers? May God save us from the persistence of wrong music. Really it is as stubborn as a mad old queen or a dead convert. It might not hurt, here, to invoke the infamous case of Diego Arias, the tax collector, who was some thirty years gone when his descendants drew your scrutiny and found themselves held accountable for the faint sounds that fell, now and then, from his tongue. It seems he was singing one night, keeping himself company on a dark road, and was heard by three shepherds who chanced to pass him there. These shepherds swore they heard, in his voice, some stain of an ancient chant, though they allowed, too, he had a fine tenor voice.

Poor voice, to be enclosed in such misguided flesh. This is indeed a vexing problem, as the music we hear in childhood is the most difficult to scrub out. Is it possible that this noble gentleman and tax collector was himself the victim of some memory he was powerless to erase, try as he might? Let us give him that, for I confess I have experienced it myself: a single childhood moment in a synagogue of old. Consider the child, only eight or nine years old, into whose ears there comes the sweet rattle of two branches held high to make the sound of rain. That a rabbi holds those branches is something the child did not arrange. Blasphemous, we can all agree, and something I barely recall myself. But if that wretched heretic was only a boy at the time, perhaps we can forgive him: he cannot help what he heard.

Apart from an old folk tune or two, I can attest Juan del Encina was not plagued by memories of any rituals or rites he might have witnessed as a child. Other things troubled him, as you will come to learn, but not these. I swear no Judaizer is to be found in his family, nor does he have descendants that I am aware of. Indeed, the family, as I would come to know it later, was a model for others to follow in learning the right way to kneel, to make the sign of the Cross, to say the right words at the right moments, to always be where it was supposed to be. No stain or blot or question could fall on it. Like water on a frying pan, it would bubble and shrink to nothing. I promise to explain. For now, what matters is that Encina himself was concerned enough to take the precaution of changing his name before he arrived at court. A few years later, when I met the family myself, I saw for myself how deep this concern went. It was perfectly reasonable: the father was a cobbler, that ancient trade of the Hebrews, and the family name was Fermoselle—a village near Salamanca—and it takes but a little to rouse suspicion.

At any rate let us accept the poet's likely intent: to invoke, with his new name, the very image of the *encina*, the sacred holm oak that stands alone, sturdy and small, on the Castilian plain.

Yes, Encina was ambitious. And yes, it's true he found some freedom in Granada that triumphant year. He was young and brilliant and if not handsome, I know not what. Men did not always trust him, but women—oh, he drew them.

I wish my mother had known him. She would have treated him as tenderly as a son, and called him Blackbird. She would have taught him when to shine his light and when to hide it.

But who knows how to hide his light at twenty-four? That was Encina's age in 1492 when he came to Granada; all faith and brilliant fire. He was a scholar of Salamanca, and he had come to court bearing an introduction to the queen's own chapelmaster, Juan de Anchieta. He believed his talent would conquer the Catholic Kings as they had conquered Granada. Ambitious, yes. But he was patient with me, and as kind as he could safely be. He took me from the gate to his own curtained sleeping place, gave me clean clothes, and washed my face. It was not his fault that as he scrubbed my brow, a tiny crust of baptismal chrism fell away. He never meant to remove it. He looked alarmed and crossed himself and looked around.

I stayed close, wanting to hear him speak again. For in his low voice with its gravelly edge, I caught a hint of my father's bed-time drone. In that brief paradise, I was Encina's dedicated flea; no matter how he scratched and slapped at the place on his arm, I always jumped back on. He must have marveled: one day he was a free man, a gifted poet and composer newly sprung from the greatest university of the land, and already the favorite tutor of the prince; the next, chosen to play nursemaid to a broken bird who—according to that prince's little sister—might be Orpheus himself.

He had three weeks to teach me to play the vihuela. At the end of this time I would perform for the queen and her ladies. If I played well, Encina said, we might be invited to stay on.

And if not?

It is not worth thinking of, he said.

He found me a faded blue doublet and clean hose and set me small tasks: carry away this dish, fetch that shirt, wait near this lady's door, but not too near. And here, he'd say, in his free moments here and there, this is how you play the vihuela. We don't use a plectrum, and the fingers don't slide. Hold your right hand so. Take good care of your hands, and fingernails always clean. How I hated the vihuela's little shape. Its back was flat, its sides came in like a small girl's waist. A narrow strip of black wood was trapped there, running all along; it made me sad. Yet like my father's oud, the vihuela's courses were tuned in unison; its melancholy voice spoke, almost, of home.

Encina said, "You were made for each other. She fits you very well."

I scowled, and he cocked his head in surprise. "You understand my words?"

I shrugged.

"Well, well," he said. "Our Infanta Juana is right. You are blessed beyond measure."

Such prophecies didn't stop me from hunting for my father's oud. Wherever we went in those great halls, if I saw cupboard or trunk of any size, I veered toward it like a wobbling wheel, squawking *bywlh*, *'ud*. Encina sighed and tugged me back. "Watch yourself," he said, in the language of the kings. "They'll think you a thief."

"Inés took," I said, in the most halting Castilian I could produce. "Inés thief."

We were standing in a dim hall, and I could not see his face. But his laugh was warm, and brighter than before. "I believe you," he said. "She has stolen something of mine, too."

The hall felt suddenly close, the air too thick. I stumbled and caught at his sleeve.

"What, are we already in love?" he said, laughing.

I let him go, and slumped against the stone. He sighed, and put his cool palm to my head.

"Not love," I said. "Hate." I could not seem to say her name.

"The fever burns the same for both," he said.

At night—or what little of it my master saved for rest—I slept at the foot of the bed he shared with the queen's chapelmaster. This gentleman, Juan de Anchieta, was a great friend of Encina's eldest brother, the great Diego de Fermoselle, himself a professor of music at Salamanca. For Anchieta, Encina had only praise: "A great composer in his own right," he said. "I sleep at the foot of his bed, as you sleep at the foot of mine."

"Is he a hundred years old?" I asked.

"Thirty," he said, frowning.

"Then why does his stomach sing, and why does he have no hair?"

To this Encina made no reply at all, only smiled and ruffled mine. "You have excellent Castilian, and a sharp little heart," he said. "Keep both to yourself. And if, in the night, you wake to find me gone, do not go looking. I am only playing for Prince Juan, or singing to some lady."

"Where?" I said, my voice all crumbled. "What lady?"

"It doesn't matter. It is certainly no cause for tears. Now sleep."

So began my new life, conducted under the fat sour bells and a dark blue sky, while far below, the city of Granada groaned and shook; later I understood she was being baptized: her wrong buildings plundered, razed or reshaped into right and proper ones. But all this happened far away. Up on the hill, I awoke each morning to find Encina's bedclothes tossed aside, and Anchieta sorting papers and grumbling as he moved about. Our sleeping place was no true chamber, but a curtained alcove in one of that palace's great halls. But the ceiling was fine—a dome of deepest blue, into which the Nasrids had carved one line from the Quran again and again—I remember wondering if the Christians knew what it meant, and if I might, sometime, be asked to tell them. I remembered my mother's warning, and that of the man who fixed my arm. Pretend you don't understand. Encina seemed to say it too.

Keep your Castilian to yourself. Especially with the queen's chapel-master.

I was glad to do so. I feared and hated Juan de Anchieta with all my spiny heart. Each morning it was Anchieta who gripped my bad shoulder, then went through a dumb-show. First he'd point to the passage just beyond, then cradle his cheek in two hands to signify a sleeper, then make a hundred other awkward gestures, all by way of telling me what I already knew: that my young master Encina had been out carousing all night, and had gone straight from his revels to the chambers of Prince Juan, to tutor him in math and science, and that this wild life could come to no good end.

Then a boy named Roderigo—the one who'd called me "worm" in the gardens, and helped put me on the mule—came to fetch me to Mass, where I sang in a great chorus of boys and repeated what I did not know. After this we had our bread, and a century of Latin, during which Encina returned from the prince's quarters. He leaned against a wall, and I saw how his tired eyes shone.

Back in our alcove, he unwrapped a fine napkin, in which were nestled two tiny pots of stewed chicken, and a third of quince.

"He gave me lemon-blossom candies, too," he said. "He has no appetite, and nothing tempts him." He paused. "Nothing but music. If he could eat music, he would thrive." Then he held up two copy-books. "He has trouble giving away his old clothes. But he gave me these."

To my eye these copybooks seemed very dull. But Encina pointed out, with the same awe, the prince's writing—a Latin phrase copied out again and again. As he turned the pages to show me more, I saw a bit of verse, a line of musical notes. "Go back," said I. "What was that?"

He laughed and refused. "Those are only my scribblings, forget them."

I remember them still. Those scribblings would become witty verse, elegies, tributes to the kings. "Tan Buen Ganadico" in seedling form. "Amor Con Fortuna," with its lilt that will not get out of your ears. There might even have been the first shiver of another tune, composed a few years later at Salamanca, in a minor key: "Triste España sin ventura," in memory of Prince Juan, that sickly lad who loved music, and on whom so much care was lavished, to so little end.

My master had a way of seeing ahead, though never for himself.

Those were good nights—the nights Encina, like my father, did not go out. Above on the high bed, his cloak folded behind his head, he scratched away at the prince's copybook. Sometimes he took up the vihuela quietly, the way my father used to take up his oud, late at night. And like my father, Encina had shadows beneath his bright eyes. The face of a dreamer with no time to dream.

One such night, he let me draw on a page with a bit of charcoal. He was in a softened mood; something—either of writing, or some little conquest—had gone well that day.

"Show me," he said. "What your house looks like, and where it is."

I made a rough picture. I was about to tell him about my family when he spoke again. "Do you know how to get from this hill to the hill of the Moors? El Albaicín?"

I nodded. My story could wait. I wanted to please him.

He smiled. "Some night soon. Before the court moves north. How do you say 'music' in your tongue?"

When I told him, he ruffled my hair again. "Good," he said. "When we go, we will take your little map." He paused. "In Salamanca I have five brothers and a sister. There is one your age named Pedro. Someday you will stay at my house, and meet them all."

I stowed this promise away like a lemon-blossom sweet.

For a precious hour each day he gave me lessons on the vihuela, and taught me how to read music. Then he went to the Prince, who hungered for music all afternoon. Evenings, we made our way to a great hall. The noise in that place was deafening, and Encina frowned, and put me up on his shoulders to keep me from being swept away. It was my duty to hold the vihuela aloft.

At the end of that jostling, heaving crowd, on a small platform, sat a small group of men. Encina bade me stand between two of them, each dressed in somber black. One had a long gray beard and held a clutch of pipes. Another, as bald and sallow as Anchieta, kept one drum on his knees and another tucked up against his chest. There were three others, each with an instrument stranger than the last. I started to ask, but Encina handed me a small cloth, and took the vihuela.

"Wait here for me," he said.

He stepped down, and settled himself on a stool some distance away, before a canopied dais, and after a moment, a figure joined him there.

At first, she was nothing but a figure in a bright cage of crimson and cloth-of-gold. Then I saw why: her skirts stood out like great hips. It was the Infanta Juana herself. She held her slim arms out over this strange tableland as if it were part of the earth, and she might the next moment ascend. Her head was uncovered and I saw, for the first time, her dark red-gold hair. She curtseyed before the dais, then turned to Encina and lifted her chin. He began to play for her, and to his music she moved her feet and slender arms. But was this dancing? Every move careful and stiff. Still, her face was lovely, somber, absorbed by her task.

Then, at the side of the crowd, my eye caught a streak of green. Only one girl wore green—Inés. I remembered what Encina had said. *She has stolen something of mine, too.*

Encina didn't see her, so intent was he on his playing, and I was strangely glad. I forced my own gaze back to him just as he finished and bowed his head. Juana sank to her knees, and as if on signal, the mass of bodies jostled and shifted and began to surge about. Inés had disappeared, but a pink-faced fellow wriggled forward and made straight for the royal dais. The crowd of courtiers, like a river current, eddied and swept him to a wall. He tried again, and was forced back. Juana stepped up to the dais edge. A hand appeared, small and plump and adorned with two small rings. Juana kissed the hand, and it withdrew.

When Encina knelt there, next, no hand appeared, but as he made his way back to us, his face was flushed and his eyes shone as they had when he showed me the prince's copybooks. He took the cloth from me and wiped his palms.

Even Anchieta looked happy. He put a hand on Encina's shoulder, tapped it once, twice.

The pink-faced man was still pinned against a tiled wall, breathing hard.

Encina turned to the others. "That's Hieronymus Munzer," he said. "The Emperor's Austrian tailor, come to measure the infanta's hips for a wedding gown."

The other musicians on the platform laughed—though Anchieta frowned. Then the group struck up a tune with pipes and drums, and the crowd below formed itself into orderly quartets. Encina took up a drum himself, and gazed down at the dancers as he beat it. A steady eye, a hunter's eye. I followed his gaze—he was watching Inés.

After the tune was done, Encina leaned down to me. "There's your thief," he said. "If she's got your oud, she's hidden it very well."

His voice, so light and jesting, made my face go hot.

"Poor Juanico," he said. "You are doomed to learn a thing or two from her."

This made my face burn hotter still.

We played for hours that night, and when we were done, Encina beckoned me outside. Out of his bag he brought a local workman's shirt, and then, to my great wonder, my own old tunic, mended and fresh, but no longer smelling of home.

"Stop mooning and take this torch," he said. "Follow me. This is the guard I know."

I did not, in fact, know the way—and even if I had, my city was so changed I could not have found it. Do you know this feeling? Maybe it is night, or maybe it is because a place you once knew has been razed to the ground, and the skeleton of something else stands in its place. But let us say that as you pass the spot, you recognize it by some small unimportant thing they carelessly forgot to remove—a fig tree, a fountain—and you think, *When I round the next corner, I will find my old house.* But the young man who is eager for music won't let you pause, won't let you round that corner. Come, hold the torch this way, not that, and without warning—because in fact you are moving too slowly, halting where you should not—he picks you up and sets you on his shoulders, and grips your ankles tight, lest you leap for some rat-infested corner, some gaping door where—where, if only he'd give you a little more time, you might find your mother's *mezuzah* still fixed to the lintel, and where, with shaking hands, you would take the house key you still keep in your pocket, and fit it into the lock of your own front door.

We came to the place where the Darro runs beneath a little bridge, and he pointed up the other hill. That was the way to el Albaicín, where my father sometimes played. I must have squirmed on Encina's shoulders, and twisted my neck.

"Little brother," he said softly. "Don't look back."

My heart thrilled and I obeyed. *Little brother.*

Up we went, along narrow lanes, past gates through which, sometimes, a little light shone. "Good, good, we are there," he said, although I had helped in no way. At last we heard the pulse of a drum and followed it to a carmen door. Encina knocked and said "Music?" as I had taught him, and the man let us in. There was a wall of vines, neatly tended, little white trumpets with a scent I knew. Jasmine. The one my mother could not scrub from my father's shirt.

Encina set me down.

Listeners sat in a long row against a wall, fruit and wine within easy reach. The musicians sat across, along with three female singers all in robes and veils. Also a fellow arranging his pipes, a player of the oud, and a drummer whose long beard drifted across his drum.

A pure pleasure shone in Encina's face, as if all this time he had been in a foreign land, and only now was home. I basked in that glow, though every now and then the stony silence of my hill crept in from the side.

One of the women began to sing. Her voice rose and fell, slipping into hidden countries between notes. Encina stared, he leaned forward. Even though she remained seated, and was wrapped in white from head to toe, she moved more freely than the infanta Juana at her dance.

Encina took a sip of his wine and leaned back, closed his eyes. But it was impossible for me to close mine. It was the oud player. If I kept my eye on his left hand, those fingers as they slid up and down the neck, I could imagine he was my father.

The man who had brought us in leaned close to Encina. "Calvi vi calvi, calvi arabi," he said.

Encina opened his eyes, startled from some luxurious dream.

"'Inside my heart is the heart of an Arab,'" I whispered.

"Listen well," the man went on. "Because if those kings of yours have their way, you'll never hear this again—not even here in Granada."

This too I translated, and Encina put his hand to his own heart, and shook his head. "Tell him," he said to me, "that the kings respect your ways."

But the man only shrugged; his smile was gone.

The singer finished, and bowed her head. She leaned back against the courtyard wall, her hands hidden beneath her robes, her eyes closed in a tender sleep like Encina's. But Encina's eyes were open now. He was watching her the way he had watched Inés, so steadily that when she opened her eyes, her gaze snagged on his like silk on rough bark.

"Now is a good time to leave," said our host. He looked sternly at me. "Take your master home," he said in Arabic.

Encina put his hands together and I begged for him, too, but it was no use. The man waved us away; we were cobwebs now, or buzzing flies on meat.

Out in the lane again, Encina frowned up at the high white wall. A cruel little breeze blew the scent of jasmine our way. She began to sing again.

He knelt beside me, gripped me tight about the arms. "Wait for me here. Keep this torch." His voice was pure thirst.

That night, time refused to pass. Sometimes two men, or three, stepped outside the carmen gate and looked about, then went back in. Other listeners came along the street, and paused, leaned against the wall with me, waiting, until someone either let them in or sent them on their way. And all that time the music never stopped, and in the midst of it was the singer's voice, rising and falling, a river too pure to cross. In my misery, I was glad to hear it. It meant Encina could only be listening. What else he would have been doing I could not say; I only knew that when I pictured him beside the singer, holding her hand, I could not breathe, and my limbs felt wrongly weak.

Still I waited, and still he did not come out. My eyes stung; I decided he had gone back to the fortress by some back way, leaving me to my fate on this hill. He could easily say he'd woken in the night to find me gone, ungrateful wretch that I was. Anchieta, for one, would be glad to be rid of me.

Well, then, wasn't I free to run away? But to where? I saw myself: a wretched waif, dumb and unmoving in a narrow street. I flung out an arm, and moved one foot, and shook myself. One step down and then another. Soon enough I was squinting into the small black wash of the Darro, its low, soft gurgle. Beyond was the dark of my own old hill. A few more steps would take me there. In any case, Encina would have to return this way himself.

At last, turning the corner on my hill, I heard the sound of a fountain I knew. From there I knew my way home, and found our door where a door should be. I slid my fingers along the lintel where my mother always pressed hers, to touch the *mezuzah*. There was a small dent there. It was like touching, with your tongue, the place where a tooth once was. The tongue dips and probes and seeks in the absence; it will not stop. I took the key from my pocket, and found the keyhole, but before I could fit the key into it, a cry broke through the air. A high-pitched human cry, full of fear and very close.

My hand trembled as I put the key back in my pocket. I was soaked in my own water.

A new silence gripped the neighborhood now, a tall and pompous silence. I shook myself free and ran back down the hill, across the Darro's little bridge and back up into el Albaicín, until I stood shivering at the carmen door, on the spot Encina had left me. I had no torch, nor any memory of where I had left it. I stood as before, but empty-handed, my head bowed.

His voice rang out in the dark. I don't remember what he said, only how glad I was to hear it.

I babbled something about a lady's cry, and he knelt down. "It was cruel of me to bring you here." He bound a handkerchief about my eyes, and gingerly lifted me to his shoulders. "Anything you saw or heard tonight, you must now forget."

Sudden light after darkness. Candlelight, a mother covering her eyes with her hands, then opening them once more to take in the full Sabbath glow. It was something like that when Encina removed the cloth from my eyes and I saw the flank of the Sierra and the fortress walls gone rosy gold. And then, as if time were repeating itself, there came a tinny bell from the plains, and the answering deeps from the high tower above.

At the palace gate the guards let us through with a wink and a shove, and we slipped back into the hall. We were nearly to the alcove where, I am sure, Encina hoped to scribble down what he had heard. But as we approached, we saw a sliver of light between the curtain and the floor.

Inside, Anchieta stood over an oil lamp that sputtered and died. When he lit it again, we saw a second shape, tall and upright, in heavy robes.

"Doctor Soto," said Encina. "Is it the prince? Is he ill?"

The man gave out a small sad bark of a laugh. He shook his head and clapped Encina on the back. Encina murmured an apology, but the man waved it off, and as they spoke, I understood that Doctor Soto was the man who'd mended my arm in the garden, and told me to pretend it still hurt. Now he waggled it, and felt my fingers, and they murmured together, and he told me to rest, in preparation for that afternoon, when I would play for the queen.

Then we all lay down in our places, and for a long time Anchieta was quiet, by which we knew he was awake and full of righteous anger. But Encina pretended to be asleep, and at last the chapelmaster's stomach-tune began.

Then Encina called softly down to me on my pallet. "What's written on the ceiling here?" he said. "I meant to ask."

"There is no conqueror but God," I said.

"And tell me again the other words, what we heard last night."

"Calvi vi calvi, calvi arabi," I replied. "In my heart is the heart of an Arab."

I heard the scratch of his quill in the prince's old copybook.

I remember the afternoon of my first performance very well. There was a courtyard with musicians at one end, and the queen and her women at the other. The ladies had arranged themselves on cushions near a narrow pool, swathed in Granadan silks, mulberry-red and the gray-blue of doves. All except for one: a solitary lady cloaked and hooded in black who would not sit down, but paced alongside the pool. Encina whispered, "Young Isabel, her mother's favorite, already widowed." It seemed she would only eat thin soup and bread, and kept her hair shorn, and wore only rough black, even when the queen herself begged her leave off for a single day, to honor her father's victory at Granada.

No matter how beautiful the music, how soft the colors all around, it was the black figure I kept seeing.

Anchieta was already there, with the other musicians. Encina nodded at him, but he only frowned; he was still angry. Encina's hand stayed firmly on my back, pressing me forward. I felt the damp of his palm through my shirt.

He brought me forward, and Queen Isabel held out one hand— these were the small plump fingers I'd seen beneath the canopy in the great hall. Encina put the vihuela in my hands.

After I played, she nodded once, and addressed him alone. I caught just enough: *It pains us to lose you, but you will be welcome at the Duke of Alba's house.* Encina was being dismissed from court.

Then her gaze shifted to me, a mother's tender gaze. "Tell us your name again," she said. I looked up at my master. His face was brightly flushed, as when he had been insulted. But he nodded.

"Juan de Granada," I said. "Juanico."

She folded her hands. "Juanico. You are very young. Yet I understand you have already heard our Lord Jesus Christ's voice in your ear."

I bowed my head and nodded. From whom did this understanding come? Was it Soto? Surely it was neither Encina nor the chapelmaster Anchieta. She kept her solemn face. "And are you ready to make music in His service?"

I looked at Encina again. But his head was bowed, his face hidden from me.

In all this time, Juana had barely moved her head from her mother's knee. Now she raised her face and looked at me. She lifted her chin as she had before her dance, to bid Encina play.

"Yes, Sovereign Lady," I said.

The queen sighed, and placed her hand on my forehead. "The infanta practiced perfect Christian charity in saving you," she said.

And the queen gave Encina a brief nod, his signal to lead me away, out to the edge of the courtyard, where, I now understood, I was to join the consort. Between Encina and myself, there was only one vihuela, and it was still in my hands.

He left me there among them, and walked away, and as soon as I sat down, they struck up a cheerful little tune—by God it was one of Encina's own—and as they played, a wrong sound came from the figure in black on the pool's rim. A harsh dry sob. The strangest thing, though, was Juana, who, still at her mother's knee, gazed up at her unhappy sister with a glowing face, her eyes alight with admiration.

The consort stopped abruptly, and a murmur went around. They started again but this time played something sad, a short lament to honor young Isabel's sorrow.

And my master Encina? He had vanished. The garden looked false to me now. Everything looked false except the grieving woman in black, skirting the long blue pool.

I did not see Encina again until later that night. He spoke to me gently—too gently, I thought—and I could not catch his eye for long. He joined the consort as a singer for the evening, and did all he should, and I kept his vihuela and played till my fingers ached. But the longer the night went on, the less I found I could catch his eye. When it was at last over, I waited for him but he slipped away. The others saw me start, and one said, "Let him go. Let him nurse his wounds the way he knows best."

"Anchieta is making him leave," I said.

They looked at me, and at each other. "No," they said. "It is not Anchieta's fault."

I was sure they lied. And I was sure I knew where he would go to heal his wounds. I went to the alcove and put on my old shirt, and hid in one sleeve the scrap of paper bearing my map and his scribbled notes of the Moorish tune, "Calvi vi calvi, calvi arabi." I took a small torch from a wall and went out. The guards at the last gate were the same ones as the night before, and I fought my trembling. "I am sent to fetch my master," I said.

"And where has he gone so late this night, little man?" one asked.

"In search of music."

They burst out laughing and one guard squinted at my sleeve. "What do you have there? Let's see it."

"It is nothing," I said. "My own scribbling."

"Very well-taught," he said, all asquint. He would not give it back. "No one has gone out these gates tonight. Do you know why?" The other guard bent low. "Tonight, even *your* master can find the music he craves within these walls. Tonight all the shops are open late!" They laughed until the tears came. "Go back, little man, you will find him playing a Jew's harp at the last turning."

What could I do? He had the paper now. I followed where he pointed, where it seemed I should not go. For I was nearing the walls wherein the queen's daughters and their favorites slept. Was this not the last turning? And *Jew's harp*, this could not be right.

I heard a sound, as of a dove rustling and burbling in a hedge, and pressed myself to a wall. A lower voice, a murmuring drone I wished would sing in praise of me, and keep me near.

I forced myself to turn away. To go back to a turning I knew, and find, from there, my way to our alcove. Two steps, maybe three, and the dove gave out a little low trill of alarm, a faint echo of the cry I'd heard the night before, so close to my old house. I couldn't help myself. I turned back to look.

A dimming torch, a sliver of shadow: a male figure and a smaller, female one. He pushed back the girl's hood and pressed himself to her. His hands touched her hair—hair as dark as my own. He ruffled it so tenderly that a black knife split my chest. He bent and held her, and she took in her breath, and he gripped her waist and bent to her again.

I stepped forward, not knowing what I meant to do.

There are places in a story we do not like to go. Sudden turnings, shadowed places where we don't like to say what we've seen, either of others or of ourselves.

"Oud," I said. "You have. Where is?"

They stepped suddenly apart, and Inés put up her hood. She made no reply, but looked wildly up at Encina, whose face was turned my way now, all asquint like the guard's.

"Wait nearby," Encina said to her. "Just wait for me—"

Quick as a bird from a branch, Inés was gone.

Encina and I were alone. He held my shoulders firmly. "Still at my heel?" he said, so quietly I could not catch his tone. "That is curious. What more could you possibly want?" Now I heard it now: the buried note, taut and sharp. But he was squinting past me, into the dark. Men were coming. Men and lights.

He bent down. He looked at me with a terrible steadiness, as if it was the last look he would ever waste on me.

"She doesn't have your old oud anymore, you little wretch." He let go a short mocking laugh. "Inés took. Inés threw away."

"I don't care about her. I want to go with you. To the Duke of Alba's house!"

He looked at me in amazement. A crowd had gathered, and at the edges of this crowd stood the night watch I'd tried to trick.

"Here is the great Master," cried one. "But where is the little Jew's harp he is wont to play?"

The other smiled. "A wise man to get rid of it. But Sir, you forgot this." He held forth the paper.

Encina looked down at me. Then to the guard he said, "Let me see it," and the guard looked confused, but handed it over. Encina studied it, then said, in a voice supremely bored, "It's only a bit of filth, I don't know where he got it." And before they could stop him, he lifted the paper and touched it to the flame.

We must have gone back inside that night. I must have watched him pack his meagre things for the journey to the Duke of Alba's house. I remember nothing of it. I only remember how, the next day, the great city of Queen Isabel's court was loaded onto wagon and horse, and off we went into the August heat. For days you could imagine we were all going to the same place—and maybe it was Hell, for as the organ carrier observed, "The heat burns us all like heretics." We had great storms, too, sudden deluges, after which you might find that a royal tent looked no different than a peasant's hut. Along the way my master Encina spoke to me only to pass the water-skin, and looked at me seldom. He had decided to forget me.

Nor did my father's oud appear, though I watched the backs of wagons for a rounded shape, a darker sound than my vihuela made. Even Inés seemed to have vanished, though I think she was only keeping herself quietly hidden among the ladies.

One day we came to the crossroads where Encina would go north to the Duke of Alba's house, and where I would go east with the court to the city of Toledo. Encina rode a fine chestnut mare the queen had given him by way of recompense, along with a mule to carry his clothes and food.

He put his hand on my head as he had done the day we met, and I lifted my face for the blessing. I waited. Then he took his hand away.

"No," he said. "You are too blessed as it is. The musical talent alone, in one so young—" He stopped and shook his head.

"What do you mean," I whispered. "Is there something else?"

But at that moment, Anchieta rode up, coated in dust and sweat. He touched Encina's arm, but Encina spurred his horse and was away.

Anchieta's face, patched as it was with dust, shone damp beneath the eyes.

"A chestnut mare and a mule," he said to the air. "Our sovereign lady has been more than generous."

"It is not enough," I said. "She should have kept him at court."

Then Anchieta's hand moved, so swiftly it was no more than a blur, and a hundred hammers sang in my ears. The pain should have blotted out everything. But I cradled my head and heard, in that secret world, Encina's voice, its rumbling, stony edge for daylight and men, its quietness with me. *Give it a home in your ears*, my mother once said about an old song. And so I tucked Encina's voice away, too, in the place I hid her melodies and words.

To remember it now pulls me back again to the shadowed corner of the Nasrid palace where everything went wrong; that corner to which the night guard directed me, to find my master "playing a Jew's harp." I was too young to understand, but the scene is before me again. Once more Inés lifts her head, and once more Encina pushes back her hood, and lets his fingers drift in her dark hair. Once again I step forward like a sleepwalker and make my foolish complaint. Inés covers her head and runs. And Encina? Encina burns his poetry and his music for all to see. But there's one last thing he must do to make certain everyone sees his loyalty to the Crown and the One True Faith.

"Long live our most holy Catholic Kings," he shouts, and the little crowd cheers, and the paper floats easily up into the black night, first the charred bits, then those still bright. All of it full of lost music and maps.

five

I have never been one for burning things. I would prefer to take a sharp little knife to the years, such as an oud maker uses to carve the intricate design of the central rosette. Only give me such a knife, and I would gladly carve away many things, but none so delicately as the five years I will now relate. I would carve them so that you were pleased with their symmetry, and felt you had missed nothing at all. I would make you forget the story you came to hear, and begin to dream another. But I am determined to confess it all, and since my history in those years—my first journey north with the court—contains details of certain adventures undertaken by Inés de Castro, I suspect you will stay to hear. I have never been good at concealing things, and Inés herself seems to want her story told. In life, as you may imagine, she sometimes fell into a mood, and said things, sometimes in the wrong company, or at the wrong time. And it might have been witchcraft, but sometimes I saw a strange gleaming all about her, and sometimes I see it still. Forgive my clumsy telling: when she lived, she seemed to be astride an invisible horse, riding swiftly through a landscape I wasn't given to see. Sometimes she halted, and I happened to be near.

But surely, gentlemen, your bladders are set to burst—particularly that of the commissioner, who must be nearing his fiftieth year—am I right? Sir, I truly sympathize. Before I began this little fast of mine (did I mention that I have had no appetite since Queen Juana's death?) I was just like our good commissioner here, rushing off to the privy every quarter-hour.

In both our professions, it is an awkward business, growing old.

Well, I am glad to accommodate, and you need only give me a signal—don't stay and suffer! Fortunately our young scribe is, by my guess, near the age of twenty, and has both an excellent capacity for holding his water and a great respect for his elders—and of course for the institution of the Holy Office. Therefore, at any time, dear commissioner, feel free to step outside and relieve yourself. I swear I will say nothing of importance while you are gone, as I know very well that a scribe must never take testimony when there is no overseeing inquisitor or officer to bear witness.

Don't be alarmed—I only know this as the common man knows it, not from special experience.

Speaking of water, we might, for the moment—and only if it does not bring discomfort to the commissioner—consider our river here, and how different it is than the roaring Tagus at Toledo. The Duero is not navigable this far north, as I believe Fernando knew when he chose this place for his daughter Juana's health and safety; did he have visions of her rising in the dead of night to escape, by secret boat, from her palace-prison? Well, she could make you fear it; she had that kind of faith in herself, though so long-buried and so rarely exercised it only showed itself in failed gestures. And as she got older, of course, and her various mayordomos learned how to manage her, she stopped dreaming of escape, and took consolation in smaller acts of defiance. She was, in particular, excessively fond of long conversations with the lowest servants here at Tordesillas: her cobbler, her washerwoman, and the last of the young kitchen maids. This was, I think, a form of escape—one her governors had great difficulty preventing.

But rivers, rivers. We were contrasting the sluggish Duero below with the rushing Tagus at Toledo. Let me lower myself once more by rope and hook onto that unforgiving rock, the river taut around its throat like the bright collar of a favorite slave.

Three things I carried into that city of stone: the useless house key that no one ever took from me, Encina's gravelly voice, and the vihuela he gave me that day in the Court of the Lions. No more would I watch him scribbling, a melody taking shape beneath his hands. No: in Toledo, it was Anchieta who slept in the high bed above me, slept like a king carved from its stony ledges, except for his soft belly, which sang and gurgled all night long.

Toledo: that city I still think of as *without Encina*. A place I could never get warm. I closed my eyes and tried to bring him back: his scholar's cloak a cushion for his back as he scribbled in a princely copybook, my map still safe beneath his hand.

But in the bishop's house, in whose far corridors we were lodged, I heard no scratching of Encina's quill, nor any other comforting sound. One by one all the sounds I knew were stolen, replaced by echoes caught in stone, the sour tolling of cathedral bells, trumpets, choirs full of boys, their songs a thin boasting. Sometimes in my sleep I dreamed the scrape-and-tap of my mother's spoon against her kitchen pot, but when I awoke, it was only Roderigo, scratching and scraping outside the chapelmaster's door. "Did you hear the demon again last night?" he'd whisper in the morning, as we knelt together in the dark at Matins. "He smells your eggplant smell, and knows how to find you. He was crouched right outside your door; I saw his tail." He reached up into my sleeve and pinched, and while he pinched I closed my eyes and saw Encina. I saw myself on the gray mule, heading north at his side.

"Where is the Duke of Alba's house?" I sometimes asked the other players. They smiled and shook their heads.

"Forget the Genius, he's done with you," they'd say. "And besides, we hear he's away to Rome before the year is out. To see if the pope will acknowledge his brilliance though the kings did not." I didn't trust the way their lips curved when they spoke.

But for all their gossip and slippery talk, those players saved me from the perils of the choir, whispered to the kings that I played better than I sang. Some of them had dark skin and black eyes, and all were as startled as I, each time our Christian names were called. And in their music I swore I heard things I knew. Little amulets of song, faded or broken so you couldn't read the words.

I didn't believe Encina about my father's oud—that it was gone forever. I still thought to find it; I thought Inés knew where it was. I pictured the whole thing at night, how I'd press my hand against her mouth until she gave me the key to whatever cupboard or trunk kept my soul, then I would lift away my hand, and steal a horse, and flee this place like Ziryab, the great Blackbird himself, and make my way north. The next time I fall from a tree, I told myself, that tree will be in the garden of the Duke of Alba's house. Let them baptize me again, if they like, but under Encina's hand. Let them re-christen me, and call me Pedro this time, after my master's younger brother. I hereby promise I will never make another map.

One morning Anchieta got up very early and paced, gazing at a sheaf of music paper now and then. He scribbled and marked, and at last he said, "It is done." And we were off to church for a special Mass, in honor of the prince's birthday.

Do you know the feeling—something at first familiar, but you don't know from where, or when? An hour later, I stood to the side in the choir, half-asleep and still hungry, when I heard, in the voices around me, a phrase from a folk song I knew very well. My *body* knew it, my stomach most of all, for it clutched and shrank. Then my ears went hot, as if Anchieta had boxed them again, and the world tipped all to one side. I saw my old street at dusk, heard laughter and singing voices again: *Hey Jews, pack up your things, for the kings are sending you across the sea!*

From this melody, the words of the Mass—*Te Laudemas*—rose sad and smooth.

The king's eyes were closed, but the queen sat upright and wide-awake. One eyebrow went up by itself. And then she smiled, more fully than I'd ever seen, and nodded at Anchieta.

I made myself small and slithered out, to heave out my guts as far from the church as I could get.

Not far enough.

"Get away from these walls," said a voice—it was my shadow, Roderigo. "Heave away, but further from the church. You'll never get rid of it all."

I only half looked up. Had our eyes fully met, I would have leaped and clawed like the demon he said was in me, and being half his size, I'd be on the ground, scraped raw. I pressed my palms to the ground, and pushed away, slipping past my shadow, making myself a worm too low for him to chase. Let him think me a coward, I thought, so long as I can be alone—to be sick alone seemed, just then, the finest luxury. Surely no one would miss me, least of all Anchieta, who would be dining near the king and queen, warm in their favor after his splendid new Mass. So I let myself stumble downhill. The lane narrowed under lowering clouds, and I thought of Granada, how, at noon, a hot white silence used to touch our streets.

As I went, house shutters opened here and there, and children's voices leaked out against the light clash of pots and silver. But soon it fell quiet. No one walked or sat in a doorway; house upon house was locked up tight. I passed a synagogue, a bright silver cross planted high on its roof.

Thank God for the cliffs of that city, where a different silence held. I reached them, and crouched there. If I closed my eyes, I could pretend I was home, the roar of the Tagus a distant mountain wind. Swallows and doves launched themselves from those cliffs, and each time one let go, my own feet tingled, wanting to lift away.

After a time, I began to worry about Prince Juan's birthday, to picture Roderigo sent to search for me. I forced myself to climb uphill again, but gave myself the gift of a different street, that I might not see that synagogue again. That's how I wound up at a fine wooden gate that stood open, just enough to show a garden there. I had learned, since Granada, to mark my place by some little thing: here I chose a blue jug on a balcony just across the way. Blue jug, I commanded, stay where you are, and I pushed on the gate, making such a creak that all the dead of that place should have awakened at once. I held my breath, but no one came.

Old gray cistern, cat in the grass, fig, persimmon, pear. It was to the pear I turned for solace—the fig rustled too sadly; any minute it would sprout a moon, and speak my father's name, my mother's. I turned my back on it, and ate a pear. The grass was perfectly cropped, as though someone let his goats graze there; in every other way, it was an abandoned place. A broken pot lay on its side in the grass; there was a splintered silvery bench. The light felt old and clean, and glinted off the leaves. Warmth seeped up my arms and legs; it took me into the grass. I lay down, and let the bees wreathe and hum around my head.

I thought, at first, that the new sound came from the bees. But the more I listened, the more it seemed to come from below. From my own ribs, or a mumbling in the earth. It sifted up my ankles and calves, wound between my legs, rose the way water should, drawn up from caves. We had all heard the legends of Toledo sung out: there were caves beneath the city, among them the very cave of Hercules, ancestor of Queen Isabel. Was I lying right above it? The place was old enough, with its ancient fig and pear, its cistern and bench.

I turned onto my side and put my ear hard to the ground, imagined it traveling down and down. Voices. Voices—not water—rose like smoke from a candle just blown out, and in them, I heard a sound like the old clean light, some remnant of home. I smelled it, too: the high, sharp scent of lye, the shushing of a broom, softer slough of hands in water, scrubbing, squeezing, rinsing. Lifting up a man's good shirt with a sigh. My father's Sabbath shirt, kept clean, no jasmine in its threads. The sound was of chanting; a melody I knew and didn't know. That is, when I heard it, I pictured men waving branches as I myself walked to the place where they held the great scroll. The men made the brushing sound of rain.

Something bit, or stung; kept probing the soft flesh under one arm. I sat straight up, tugging at my ear, which itched from grass and dirt. A melody was caught in there too, curling and spiraling up and down, with intervals too small to play on the vihuela, let alone write down. A melody their majesties wouldn't want to hear.

A breeze touched the leaves above me, prickled my arms. The sky had gone leaden with cloud. I listened for the rumble of the Tagus below, but even the river's voice had changed, swelling with trumpets and single shouts that leaped up, only to fall back into the tumult. And were those drums? The day's pulse felt uneven; it made my own skitter and thrum. There was no telling how late I was, or who had noticed. I didn't think of my shadow, Roderigo, tugging on Anchieta's sleeve, but of Inés, whispering my own name in my ear just once, her fingers on the neck of my father's oud. Inés, who might, at this moment, be saying to the infanta Juana: *Watch out for him. He is still an infidel. He hides who he is and what he thinks.*

Is that what made me stand up, my heart pounding hard? Or was it a shift in the sound of the world: sudden spikes of noise that I understood now didn't come from the Tagus at all, but from the plaza above.

The blue jug was gone, but I didn't care. I could hear well enough where I should be, and as I made my way uphill, men and women—whole families—toiled with me, all in their feast-day clothes. I had only to follow, to be pulled along with the crowd. Bells rang out now too, from above and below, and with each tolling, more people stepped out of their doorways and began to stream uphill; a noisy, happy, crowd, come to celebrate the prince's birthday, as they should.

The smell of market day had bloomed while I was in my dream, garnished this time with frying oil and something burnt and sweet. Vendors cried out, and a lady handed me a little sack of yellow sweets all dusted pale.

"To a new day," said her husband, smiling down at me. "What better way to begin," he added, "than to rid this town of their eggplant stink."

A sweet was in my mouth; suddenly it cloyed, my tongue heavy as stone. The lady bent down, and touched my arm. "What a pretty child! Are you lost?" I shook my head, but they were looking at me now as if I were their own son, prone to fever, to falling out of bed. "It's the crowd," she whispered to her husband. "Here, lift him up so he can see," and hands were hoisting me up. Now I saw where we were: the plaza Zocodovar, where mules were sold on market days. But instead of mules, there were men everywhere, all holding staves, one every few feet to hold back the surging crowd.

Two great wooden platforms rose above our heads, above the heads of the guards. One was empty, but on the other, men in heavy robes sat at tables, solemnly at work with great ledgers and pots of ink. More guards stood at each end of this, too, frowning into the plaza below, shaking their heads. The crowd had hushed, by turns quiet and murmuring, only once in a while leaping into a roar, though I couldn't see what caused it. Plump ladies in veils leaned out from fine iron rails, and under the arches were children my age, and younger, too, all on the shoulders of men, shouting out whatever they saw.

It is a curse of old age that that long-ago day is so clear, that all memories fall back to the first stone in the well, the first tolling. And my first action—or lack thereof. You will say I was but a child and cannot be responsible. You will even say that I did right to say nothing, do nothing.

One thing I know: all things repeat themselves in time, making you think you are right. Until one day, something turns, or lifts, and you cannot look away.

The condemned came from one corner of the square, and a smell came with them, but not of eggplant, no. That was not the smell. Bare legs like sticks, speckled with mud and rivulets of rotted yellow, rusted red. As the procession wound through, people moved back without the help of staves. Women put their shawls against their noses. Some put their hands over their children's eyes. Others held their children's shoulders so they had to look.

"It's really true, about the smell," the lady beneath me said.

There passed a long dirty ribbon, a ribbon that cried and shook and shuffled as in a weakened dance—that was the sound of their linen soles, held by one strap onto blistered, bleeding feet. Each wore the yellow shift, a name in great black letters on the back. Some came silently, with dead eyes, and some came crying, arms outstretched to the crowd. One came a-muttering, pulling out tufts of her own hair, her voice a dark wavering, but of such a height, and familiar shape, known to me all my life so far, that my eyes began to sting, my gut to clench. But my mother had gone to Cadiz. It could not be her. I could not calm my trembling: the man who held me on his shoulders reached up to steady my legs, and asked if I were ill.

I thanked him, and closed my eyes until I judged she had passed. I opened them in time to see the name on her shift. Not our name, and I could breathe again.

Castro, it said.

The ribbon made its way, shuffling and shaking, onto the empty platform, and a guard helped each one up. That's when I realized the Bishop himself was there, reading out words, which were shouted around the square by the town criers, though you couldn't hear them, for the trumpets would suddenly howl, and halfway through his words, the crowd would roar.

The man turned to his neighbor and said, "It is a waste of ink and paper. Burn the lot of them and be done."

"To the roasting pan with you, *marranos*," someone cried.

I tapped the man's shoulder. "Please," I said. "I was only lost. Which way to the Bishop's house?"

The man laughed roughly. "The Bishop's right here, child," he said. "And where is it you're supposed to be?" He pointed down at my dirtied page's suit. "*Dios*," he cried, laughing to his wife. "You'd think I'd put him to the question!"

"Let him go," she whispered. "He's wearing the royal clothes. We don't know who he is."

I held perfectly still.

"Well then," he said, still laughing, "up that way. Go on, little palace-waif. And if you should meet the kings on the way, tell them, with all due respect, to have it done! These creatures will never repent. Jews cannot be other than they are."

And he patted my shoulder, and dropped me down.

Did hours pass? I don't know. I only know that at the Bishop's house, tapestries had been raised, long tables spread with silver plate and goblets of glass. Each servant I passed gave me a distant, harried look, or no look at all, and everywhere there was a clashing, whether of cymbals or roasting pans I could not tell.

"Where have you been," someone bellowed. It was the voice of the organ carrier, his eyes in their old squint of pain, his temples damp with sweat. He carried a bundle of white cloth, a rope, and a wreath, and sweat sprang out of me, too. I must have moved, because he had me firmly by the arm. "Oh no you don't," he said. "Once a day is quite enough." And he called two men to hold me there.

"Help me take off these filthy clothes," he cried. "And be quick!" And while I stood there stunned, they began to pluck and pull at me, yanking down my breeches, my shirt over my head. Still frozen, I looked down. A white robe belted round with rope. The wreath, made of small shiny leaves, tickled my ears.

"Don't have time to clean you," he growled. "Up you go." And for the second time that day I was caught and lifted into the air. "I am a musician," he mumbled. "I carry an organ, not a wretched boy. Not my duty. Not part of my—"

And I was on a platform, a rickety cart on wheels, set about with baby trees made of sugar leaves and a bark made of meat, upon which some flies had gladly settled. Beneath me there was mewling and whimpering. The organ carrier was yapping too, from down below. A vihuela floated up into my hands.

"You're Orpheus," he cried. "Get to it!"

Two small and trembling dogs came to my feet, and each dropped a little turd.

In the years to come I would see, in northern courts, such marvels as to make this pageant look like a child's game. But at the time, it was a great and fearsome thing. I sat on a little stool, which tottered as my chariot lumbered down a hall. At my feet lay the two trembling dogs, and now I saw a cat, harnessed and leashed to one of the baby trees. Three doves fluttered and banged in a cage above my head, trying to launch themselves, and sending a snow of sugar down. The vihuela felt smaller too: a paltry thing.

The dogs had been tied by lengths of rope to a small orange tree, itself set inside a barrel whose wooden sides had been plastered with leaves. Their ribs quaked, and now one lifted his leg against the barrel that held the tree, leaving a dark stain along its side. As I settled the vihuela in my arms, one dog gazed up at me, his eyes all rimmed in white. He curved his rump and dropped a second glistening turd at my feet.

The chariot had already begun to lumber through the great doors, and I couldn't leave my stool to peer around the tree. But I heard another voice, and realized I was not alone.

Just as the doors opened, I saw Inés. She made her way carefully to my side, and poked my ribs with her finger. And it's true I needed prodding. Seeing her there, I forgot what I was supposed to do.

"Play, fool," she said, smiling out at the world.

She was no taller than I. She wore, as did I, a white gown belted round with rope, and a crown woven of golden leaves, and her arms were bare. They were darker than I'd expected, as dark as mine. Her fingers were small and slim. I blushed to think of their quick, thieving ways. The way they'd fallen still under Encina's touch.

"I am Eurydice," she said flatly. "Your wife, but not for long."

"Castro," I whispered. "I saw your name today."

She said nothing, and I wasn't sure she'd heard. We rocked forward, the animals shivering beneath us. The trumpets and shawms were so loud that I couldn't hear the vihuela under my fingers. I took another glance, and saw her mouth moving, but could not hear her voice. Then the chariot jolted to a stop, and the horns fell silent. It was only us: my strings, her voice.

Her voice. I heard it now. Why had the Lord made it low and clear and fine?

I played something bright and lively, with a secret sadness no one could hear, and she knew it well. It was one of Encina's tunes. I heard beneath its rhythm another one, and the missing notes between, that only an oud could play. It was the one I still think of as "Calvi vi calvi, calvi arabi."

Prince Juan, seated on the dais, was pale, while his sister Juana bloomed with health. She turned to him, her eyes bright with loving tears, and he smiled wanly back. How long this lasted I'd never know, but for that time the animals stopped their mewling, and the last thing I noticed was the strangest of all: tears in the eyes of King Fernando. Was it the music? I don't know: he was looking at his son.

"Where," said Inés. "Where did you see our name?"

"In the plaza," I said, "on a heretic's *sanbenito*. A woman."

Inés frowned and pressed her finger to her lips. Then the cart began to move again, and the animals to cry, and when I glanced at her again, her face was so smooth and unconcerned that my old rage at her stealing my father's oud overcame me, and I thought a terrible thing. I thought, *May you get what you deserve.* Only I wanted to hurt her myself: to yank off her laurel crown, take her dark hair in one hand, wrap it around my fist, and pull with all my strength. I'd hold her down, clamp her wrists to the earth until she wept and relented, and told me who that lady was, her mother, her sister, her aunt? And what had the lady done? And I would not let her up until she answered this, and also where she had put my father's oud, in what cupboard or closet of the bishop's house. Once I had it, I'd be gone.

Gone to the Duke of Alba's, where I belonged, and would be safe.

But we were swamped by laughter, applause, and then it was over, the organ carrier standing slumped at the foot of the cart, his arms held out. "Give me the vihuela," he mumbled. "You can get down by yourself."

An even grander chariot lumbered out of the kitchen doors, full of choristers, and the organ carrier pulled me off to the side. I couldn't see Inés at all. He handed me the vihuela again. "After supper, go to the prince. Tonight you will sleep with the others in his chamber, and play him to sleep, and play him awake, and so it will be until Infanta Juana's marriage to the Habsburg is secured. Then off you'll go with her, if that's where you are needed."

Inés came out of nowhere, back in her green dress, her eyes shimmering a little too brightly, I thought. But she gave nothing away, only pulled at my arm.

"What have you been up to?" she said quietly. "Your ear is full of dirt." She licked two fingers, and before I could get away, those fingers were on my ear, cool and wet. I will not say what I felt. Only that had I still been on that cart, I would have gladly fallen beneath its wheels to have it crushed out of me.

"*Dio*," I cried.

She looked at me a long minute, and my face and hands went hot, as if I'd been dipped in snow, then dragged close to a fire.

"Say *Dios* next time," she said, her voice very low. "Say *Dios* for the three persons of God, or they will have you on the stake, too." And she was gone.

From that night forward, for three more years, it went this way: the prince prayed with his mother's confessor, and after this, he looked up at the great sword his father had hung on the wall behind his bed. Then he lay down on his stomach, face down, clutching his pillow just the way Encina used to do, as if it were a piece of cork, and would float him to safety. We played and sang for him until he slept—or seemed to sleep, for sometimes his breath was too even, and he gave a little snort here and there, as if to convince us. I had been told about this by another page; that in fact the prince slept poorly, and made these sounds to grant us permission to rest. What Anchieta said was true: if the prince followed his heart, he would have us play all night, and sing him to his death.

I only sleep well at the wrong times. That night was such a one, and in my sleep I dreamed Inés was in the room, lying very close, but that by some mistake, Juana's ruby lay against her throat. Then it seemed to be Juana herself who looked at me, but had Inés's little gap between her teeth. I pressed myself into the sheets to stop the rising ache. I remembered something Roderigo had said. "Some," he'd said, "lacking a lady, will rub themselves on any old thing."

That's when the bed above me gave a sudden creak. A stifled cry followed it, and I wilted like a leaf. I held my breath, and silence filled the room. A silence like none I'd known: the silence of shame on the high bed, and of four guards and four pages below, all pretending not to hear.

At dawn a pale gold light touched every rim of wood and edge of cloth. The prince's chamber man touched the shoulder of the oldest page, and one by one, we each arose. I searched their faces to see if anyone else had heard the cry, but their expressions were pure and very mild. We arranged ourselves in a corner, behind a screen, but we knew the prince was sitting up, his hands neatly folded, long and white against his sleeping shirt, as Doctor Soto and another physician came to his side. Then the prince bade us come out, and play where he could see, and as we did, he ate three bites of soft stewed chicken, and four of marzipan. When he swallowed, the lump in his throat rose and did not fall, and he put out his hand to wave it all away. My own throat closed; he made the act of eating look so strange, so sad.

But I am so made that my stomach will growl at the wrong times, in the deepest silence. The prince looked up, startled, and looked at us all.

"I have been thoughtless," he said. "You are all starved. Please, help yourselves to what is here."

Just once that morning, as we played, I heard Inés's voice again, and felt her cool wet fingers in my ear. "*Dios*, not *Dio*," she said, and I remembered another dream, in which I was a kitchen cat, and she a scullery maid, taking me up by the haunches to throw me out, her fingers firm beneath my fur.

Dios, I told myself, how I hate her, and all girls, with their fingers, eyes, and lips.

six

There is too much water in my story, I know. From beginning to end, too much water for a boy raised in the Vale of Granada, and all the wrong water, enough to make a commissioner feel the urge to piss a second time, and soon—the way it is, you know, when it rains all day long and you are trapped inside. And never to see the blue waters at the port of Cadiz, to which my mother and my brother surely went. And my father, where was he? What if they found each other again in a safe and southern land, and I never knew?

Well, I was pulled northward. That must be why Cadiz got caught in my childish heart as a dream of bright fish and parrots, a place where my mother steps safely onto a small ship, the one with a stern but kind captain. That rarest of all captains, one who charges his passengers only a modest fee for the journey, and who foresees that the greatest dangers lie to the west, and thus sets his course for Venice. In my dreams of that sailing I see my brother, too, standing at my mother's side along a shining wooden rail of a well-kept vessel. His big square face has already lost its sullenness, and shines with the goodness my absence has brought into his life. Later, of course, his life may become complicated again. But for a moment he is knight and protector. He offers my mother nothing but tender concern. He speaks to her solemnly: *All will be well*, he says. *I am your eldest, and will not abandon you.*

But then something startles him; he turns, as if he has seen me gazing in from my dream. And his face goes blank, as if to hide from my mother that I am watching, that I am still alive somewhere. It is a look that makes me wonder who I am, what curse I brought on myself when I hid from the blind girl. Am I alive, or are they dreaming me?

In any case, no Cadiz. I was destined for a vast gray soup plate of churning water that would, in September of the year 1496, spit me out onto that marshy place that prides itself on the bland white cauliflower and yellow-brown beer. The Low Countries, yes. Perched on this marsh were hot golden rooms, lit by so many candles that the cake on the ladies' cheeks melted as they danced.

Marshes, mud. Snow, too, but always freezing and melting. And music—soaring, complicated. Five or six voices poured into one from all directions. It made us feel very far from home, as if it meant to stuff our ears till we forgot what we knew and loved.

Of the voyage itself, what should I report? That it was Juana's wedding journey, and meant to be a joyous one? She was all of sixteen, on the cusp of that double alliance so fervently pursued by Fernando and Isabel and the Emperor Maximilian. She was to marry the emperor's son, Archduke Philippe, and Prince Juan was to marry Philippe's sister, Marguerite of Austria, thus creating a sturdy barrier against the French. Before we departed Spain in a fleet of ships, Juana was given a tiny portrait of her bridegroom. This image, and a few facts, were all she knew of him: he loved tenys, music, and the hunt.

Of Juana, what did Philippe know? Only what his French advisers said: she was Spanish, and therefore would be dark-skinned, ignorant, and a prude. Should he learn her language? By no means! Let her learn the tongues of his lands, in addition to the Latin she already had.

On the day we were to set sail from Laredo, a water cup tipped over by itself, and a trunk of wedding clothes went missing, never to be found again. Even the weather had second thoughts: just as the soldiers began to load the two great carracks and their accompanying caravels, the light dulled and the sails went slack as old bedsheets.

No matter. Let the boats be loaded, by order of the queen. By mid-morning, the royal mules were below decks, among the sheep and chickens and casks of vinegar, their own gold-trimmed velvet trappings carefully stowed in trunks, beside other trunks three layers deep in the gowns and jewels with which a sixteen-year-old with fine Latin was to win over all Europe. Isabel waited on board for two windless days, pressing little sachets of herbs into her daughter's hands: this for the marriage bed, that for female pains.

Two days. Plenty of time for a mother's secret prayers: some were requests for a good stiff breeze, and some were for no breeze at all. For what mother willingly dispatches her daughter across the sea and into the care of the Frenchman and the Fleming, neither of whom have any respect for piety? Especially if that daughter has already been declared, by royal physicians, to be sometimes "too much under the sway of Saturn," and one who "reads too much of the wrong books." Books, we will do well to remember, the queen herself loved and could not throw away, and which had nothing to do with our Lord Jesus Christ and the education of future princes. *Tirant lo blanc*, that knightly tale, is full of spicy rooftop seductions and civet-scented sheets.

I am only repeating what I heard. For we musicians were on shipboard too, below decks with the salt, may it preserve us—three *bas* musicians for quiet occasions, and a dozen horns for triumphant entries into towns. Thus we swayed in our hammocks like packed fish, laid near enough other barrels—those of vinegar and salt beef, of cod and anchovy—and a bit further along, the damp and twitching flank of mule and pig and cow and all that goes with, for all these gaseous perfumes and others to settle into our sleeves for life. Who can blame a person thus packed for closing his eyes against the sight of that gray expanse and imagining the wonders of the north? For we had heard the tales: of spun-sugar towers melting by the light of real wax candles; of a lace-trimmed gown melting too, as a gentlewoman all in pink and white offers a handkerchief to mop a young player's brow.

Rumor had it these Northern ladies favored string players over players of horns. I was too young to know why.

I will not scandalize you further, fear not. For truly, we prayed a great deal.

We prayed that Juana's slender grace and excellent Latin would dazzle all Flanders, all Europe. That they would be surprised by her auburn hair and blue-green eyes, and kneel before her, amazed and subdued. We would follow behind, to show them the dignity and clarity of our music, and make them see how wrong they were.

So I, Juan de Granada, the smell of salt cod in my nostrils, the fear of gray water in my gut, closed my eyes against the harbor sprinkled with caravels. Closed my eyes against each ship loaded with hundreds of hardy mountain men, fifteen thousand in all. All of this now draped in a silence broken only by the creak of the enormous masts, of barnyard noises issuing plaintively from the hulls, though sometimes when I closed them, I wondered in which hull lay my father's oud, one more piece of salt cod laid in, the bruise on its back left untended.

On the third day of the voyage the sails snapped and filled with a fine breeze, and Queen Isabel wept and held her daughter close, then let her go. I closed my eyes against that, too.

But listen, the daughter did not weep. Juana looked uncommonly well as she waved goodbye to her mother and the great crowd gathered for the farewell. She was at peace, for there is nothing like setting forth, the world pure promise, no taint of rot or canker or whispered gossip on a foreign tongue.

She saw herself, I think, as the heroine in a great romance, but that did not stop her mother from worrying. Behind young Juana stood the nine advisers for matters spiritual, and six for matters of state; the matron Beatriz de Talava for matters of the conjugal bed; sixteen maidens and four slaves.

Those first days of good sailing, we *bas* musicians were often called to play. I remember these occasions chiefly for someone who was not there: my old enemy Inés. She was on the vessel, I knew, but I saw her not at all. Finally I asked someone to ask someone. And the word came back: The lady Inés has no stomach for sailing, and lies below. Good, I thought, let her suffer for a change. I pictured myself rounding a corner and coming suddenly upon her. She would be wrapped in a rough cloak, little square hands fiercely clinging to some rail. I said to myself, I would treat her to a very cool silence.

But the next day a gale blew up, and everyone fell ill—all, that is, but Juana, the first mate, and the admiral.

Three nights we pitched and rolled. I remember no days; only nights. Musicians and ladies-in-waiting might be excused for seasickness, but later we heard that over half of the hardy mountain men in the other caravels knelt to puke and pray their last. The morning it was over I tottered onto the deck, and saw many ladies taking the air, but still no Inés. I felt a strange blank fear—what if she were dead? I could not work up my old simple hate; I had to find her. And I did, precisely where I'd once hoped, in a small heap of heaving wool, sometimes peeping up with a pair of dark, haunted eyes, her hair unbecomingly stuck to her tender neck. She looked like some ruined figurehead, grasping the heavy spindles and putting her head between them to spit into the swells below.

"Go away," she growled, and a flare of light leaped in me. I turned my head to hide it.

That's when we heard it: a sound like thunder cracking, a long shearing out at sea. Everyone came to the rail. The admiral looked grim, and didn't want Juana to look through his spyglass. But she wanted to look.

We all squinted out to sea: where one of the caravels had been, there was nothing but water.

Later we learned it had wrecked on a sandbank. The admiral sent word to all that many of the men were saved, picked up by other boats. That "those few" who perished died as they wished to, in service to the Crown. And that was that.

A woman wept on deck. They gathered around her, inquired if her husband or son was on that ship. "Oh, no," she cried. "It is our lady's clothes for the wedding. All of them, and jewels besides!"

Our Juana—now an archduchess-to-be—stood very still. Her face was pale and serious, her voice utterly calm. "How many are dead?" she asked again.

"You will harm yourself this way," replied the admiral. "You must trust me when I say that of all journeys of my career, this has been the least calamitous. It is, in fact, blessed, that of the two boats, it was the other our Lord saw fit to take."

"I don't care about the clothes. The men. Their families—"

She turned her face away. Toward the place where, below us, gray water lapped against the hull.

That is why she arrived at Middelburg in a simple gown, unencumbered by jewels and frippery. Not as her mother dreamed. Nor was the crowd very large. We stood once more at the rails and all searched the pier for the most decorated horse, the most decorated gentleman. But there was only a small line of well-fed gentlemen, their pink chins swathed in wilted lace while a clutch of shawms and crumhorns bleated behind. No crowds like those that clustered around town gates at home. The Flemings appear to have been dragged from comfortable beds and firesides. Doña Beatriz de Talava and the Bishop of Jaen whispered, and even we musicians knew that those whispers would bloom into carefully worded reports sent back to the Catholic Kings, only to return to Juana, months from now, in the form of further advice on when to speak, and when to keep silent, which persons to cultivate as friends, and whom to avoid. Advice it would be difficult for a young archduchess to take, on account of her bridegroom's wishes, and the wishes of those who counseled him.

We were told, that day, that Philippe had been "detained by important business," some council or other his father could not attend. But Juana kept her head high. She spoke first to us, and then, through an ambassador, to the dignitaries on shore. "After a little rest, we shall travel to meet the archduke in Ghent. To make our husband's journey that much shorter."

Applause. A great bobbing and bowing of damp lace. The Bishop of Jaen shivered, and gave four great sneezes.

"Only a chill," he said. "From the change of air."

He turned delicately aside to wipe his nose. His pale, brown-spotted hand trembled with the ague.

A moment later the bishop escorted Juana away, we knew not where. All dispersed. We—myself and the two other *bas* musicians—were taken the other way, to a smoky narrow house, where a woman pointed us to the attic, showed us the table where we would take our meals, and made signs to show us not to make our "noise" in her house.

Within the week, half of our company was ill, and rumors of distant trouble floated through: nine thousand men had been left at the coast, to repair the ships and make them ready for the voyage back to Spain with Marguerite. Funds were sent for more food and warm clothing, but it seemed it was not enough.

And it was only October, winter still a mystery to us all. Sometimes the sky was bright blue, sometimes it was rimmed with a distant line of black cloud, but each day we rose and accompanied Juana as she made yet another joyous entry into yet another town or village, she and her ladies on mules in full regalia, her head uncovered in the Spanish style, to show off the auburn lights in her hair, and alas, a slightly reddened nose and a little cough. With each new town there were more citizens at the gates, more guildsmen to lift her chair on their shoulders and sing her through the city streets. Several poems were composed in her honor, and theatricals comparing her to heroines of old: Juno, Judith, Queen Isabel herself! She was—no one could deny it—a success, and on the strength of this she asked for money and provisions to be sent to the sailors and soldiers waiting at Middelburg.

Of course, they said. It will be sent. You are not to fret.

Of the bridegroom himself, he was still and forever "on his way to her." At some point a messenger must have told him she was beauty enough to saddle up for. So he briefly shook off his advisers and made his way, all loving haste, to the harbor at Bergen op Zoom.

We might measure the time this took by the fact that her little nose was white again and her cough dispatched when at last he reached her. In the weeks she waited, I sometimes saw on her face a quaver of fear, and something shivered in me, too, though it could have come from the sour smell of Flemish homes, no matter how well-kept, infused by the smell of the disturbing vegetables the housewife put before us: this thing called cauliflower, and then another whose name I always forget, but which they stewed and pickled and still it tasted like rotting leaves.

And all this time, Inés was furious. All Spain was insulted by the archduke's delay. She told me so herself one afternoon, then made to walk away. But before she did, I said aloud that she herself looked strangely well. "The place agrees with you," I said.

She frowned. She insisted it did not.

At last, one day, Juana announced that she would like to visit the Sisters at the convent of Saint Clare. Thus we were replanted in a village even wetter and colder than the one before.

And so it happened that by the time Philippe arrived (oh, he looked like he'd been riding hard for days), it was *she* who appeared out of reach, hidden away in a cloister with the Sisters of Saint Clare. Imagine the scene: late at night in a tumult of hoofs and armor, shouts and clanging, as he and his men batter on the convent's gates, as if in one of *Tirant lo blanc*'s episodes, determined to break down the convent walls for love.

And so, on the twentieth of October 1496, everything which had been so bleak was lit by a fine autumn glow. The Sisters of Saint Clare and Juana's ladies dressed her simply, and uncovered her head. She appeared in the cobbled yard, a slender girl with red-gold hair. Picture the bright sun against purple-black cloud; the way her hair glowed.

All who were there saw the surprise on Philippe's face.

Years later, Juana would remind me of this moment. She said she felt a little spark in her breast, as real as anything, and that she found it stayed alive for a long time. I see her, in my mind's eye, holding it steady against what was to come, against the first ugly lappings of gossip, the ones that start slow but never stop building: your husband loves other women; your husband despises your Spanish ways and finds you cold. Your husband wants you locked away. You are an inconvenience to the state.

Yet many years later she would recall this moment fondly, and let all the other voices fade away. She smiled to remember how he looked, at seventeen, astonished by her. It was the first time, she said, that she saw herself gazed on so intently.

Was he handsome? I will leave that to the official scribes. Certainly he was young and fair-haired and strongly built. But there was a bit of fat still in his face, the nose a touch comical in its length—there was almost no bridge at all—so that he seemed to be peering at her with his bright blue eyes from atop a cliff. His mouth worried me—though it was said that ladies loved it. Rosy, small, and slightly lopsided; maybe they wanted to set it right. But he stood before her and gazed and gazed, and she let herself steep in its glow. Sure enough, she was gazing at his mouth: at the way it opened, just a little, at the sight of her, like that of a hungry little bird.

The lower lip was nothing he could help: the jutting Habsburg chin gave him that look. Possibly it helped establish his nickname: *Croit Conseil*, Believer of Advice. It was a look—and a habit—their eldest son, the Emperor Charles himself, would have, and Juana's grandson Philippe. Did it come from leaning forward to listen to so much counsel? Well, in any case, it would be there in all Juana's children, from the day they first clapped their hands, and sang songs in a language not her own.

But in that moment, all appeared simple. He was gazing at her steadily, with a look I had only seen once before in my life—my master Encina, before he took Inés's face in his hands. Philippe's gaze neither flickered nor turned aside to any adviser.

Then he did turn.

First to his own priest. What he said we can only guess, but I can report that the priest flushed bright pink from throat to pate, and nodded, and came hastily to Juana's side. A great jostling chaos ensued, as the priest pulled the two of them together, tugged at their hands, and bade them kneel on the small square of carpet laid down in the convent's courtyard. So they did, and so they bowed their heads. Twelve shawms and crumhorns—where did they come from?—began their great blasting, startling the poor Sisters. Our own musicians joined in—presumably their landladies had allowed no practice either, for there began a great howling of two musics colliding in the air: the Flemish all curl and lace and extra notes, and ours, so clean and austere.

We three chamber musicians stood foolishly to the side, trying not to wince. Then someone put a horn into my hands, and commanded me to play.

I blew a terrible sound; they signaled me to stop.

"All these ceremonies can wait!" cried Philippe. "We must go."

Then he turned to his bride and said something none could hear. But oh, she blushed.

The horn was still at my lip; I merely sighed into it, I swear, for I did not like the look he dropped on her.

Well, it stopped him. He glanced past his bride, and right at me, those pale blue eyes, perched atop that nose like a falcon's. And his little lopsided smile spread.

I dropped the horn to my side, and bowed my head.

When I raised it again, Juana was saying something back to him. Was it French? I only know it made a pretty stem of sound. But now it was Inés, a few feet away, who was frowning at her, as delicately as could be, as if to say, Don't give so much, so soon. Keep a little mystery.

Inés was right. Juana should have kept a little mystery. Yes, she gave herself too freely, too soon. She should have made him suffer a little for her love, there at the beginning. He should have been forced to cross an ocean to reach her, and made to wait.

seven

Philippe only looked at me because I squawked my horn. That he looked at all I cannot prove, for no royal chronicler would record such a thing. But someone saw *me* frown and cast down my gaze, and this, it seems, was reported to his Spanish bride. The next dawn, from our cold musicians' attic strewn with straw, I heard my name mangled in the housewife's nasal voice. And as Matins rang out in the freezing air, I heard another female voice say *archduchess*. And my name again, in our tongue.

There was no light at all on the steep stair, and the wall was damp and rough as any cave. Nor was it much brighter below. It was October, and the sky, which had lowered itself nearly to the mud, was a soft white shot through with the purple of a bruise. In the muddy houseyard stood a small person wrapped in two woolen cloaks, stamping her feet like a colt, her breath making a small fog of its own. My pulse tripped, but I favored Inés de Castro with a cordial bow. She, in turn, gave out her customary squint. Thus we stood a while, rooted in the muck, and into this dumb-show I dropped a remark about the sky.

"There's no purple in it," she said. "Either you're a poet or a fool."

These were her first words to me since our arrival, she who once scoured my ear with her finger, taught me to say *Dios*, and entered my dreams without permission. Her voice was hoarse from the smoky hearth fires of Bergen op Zoom.

"And you are a fool for freezing to death," I said. "Come stand by the fire."

Picture a colt, stubborn for no reason you can fathom, one you must tug to stable, to food and warmth. "Come inside," I repeated, more firmly still. "Or I will not hear what you have to say." She made a small grimace, but obeyed, and before the hearth, with its weak snaps and whispers, she pulled off her gloves, and held her bare fingertips, reddened and rough, to its glow.

She asked me stiffly if I was well, and said she was not asking because she cared, but on behalf of our Archduchess Juana, who wished to know if her chamber players had the ague like the sailors and guards and everyone else.

Inés was fifteen that year, and no taller than she'd been in Toledo, on Prince Juan's birthday, when we played Orpheus and Eurydice, accompanied by two small dogs and their terrified bowels. If she stepped any nearer, her chin would not even reach my shoulder.

"Tonight, you'll play," she said. "A lute, not your vihuela." She coughed just once into her reddened hands. I swore I saw her smile.

I asked if there was anything else, and was proud of my voice—it neither cracked nor rose.

It seemed Juana was unhappy with me. Not only had I bleated my horn, but she'd been told that I also *made a face at the archduke* as they pronounced their vows. It was—Inés paused and gave a second smiling-cough—*disrespectful* to our lady's royal person, and to that of her good husband. He had already forgiven it, but Juana was distressed.

"Please tell her I beg her pardon," I said. "Tell her, the food of this place makes me—"

Inés shook her head, and kept her gaze on the ruddy coals. I, in turn, gave my full attention to the hearth's music. It was very pure, very small.

"And tell me," I managed to say. "Is our lady happy and well?"

At this trifling question, she blushed to the neck. Was it so immodest? At last she spoke. "She is turning French. As he requires. Word will get back to her parents and they will be unhappy with her—" She faltered, shook her head.

I saw again Philippe's face at the wedding. The falcon's quick eye. The beak slightly open.

Inés brushed at her cloak as if the Flemish smoke was nestling in. "Never mind," she said. "I only wish her joy at his beauty was not so—not so—" She bent closer to the fire, so that I lost her next words. Then she stood up, and spoke very clearly. "I forgot to say— tonight you are to play the lute inside a pie." And with that, she put up her hood and moved past me, straight to the door. There she hovered, no doubt to see my great surprise.

"Doña Inés," I said, as calmly as I could. "You never said how *you* are faring in this place."

For a moment she held still, her hand on the latch. "I will be glad if I never see Spain again," she said.

"Why?" I asked. "What is there to love about this place?"

She held still a moment more—never had she lit on one branch so long. "You wouldn't understand." Then she bit her lip and squinted at me once more. "My family—we have cousins here. In Antwerp, a spice merchant and his wife and children. But I would not trouble our lady with such trivial things."

"Why not?" I said. "Would she not be glad for you?"

"In one way, she would. In another, she would not."

Another silence fell between us, more awkward than the last. But she still held there, so I took my chance. "Because of Toledo? The heretic I saw?"

She shrugged. "We are not the only Castros in that great town. No—it is because she needs her own people about her day and night. She cannot trust her husband's servants."

"Pardon me," I said. "So, will you go to visit—"

But she had already let go of the latch and turned away.

Later that morning I made my way to the luthier's house. A girl brought me through to the back, into a narrow, high-ceilinged room that smelled of fresh-sawn wood and sap. There was something impossible over my head: an oud. No—not just one, but dozens, hung like kettles waiting to be mended. On a long table lay wooden necks of all sizes, and in a corner stood lengths of wood, dark and light, thick and thin. A tall thin fellow in an apron, powdered from head to toe like a baker, motioned me in. On his table sat dishes of brown crystal and shavings. He said nothing, only pointed to a little stick.

Lignum vitae, he said, and into a saucer he sprinkled shavings, and some clear liquid from a tiny flask, and made a purple tea. He explained, through gestures and words, that this was how prisoners were set to work, to make shavings for the apothecaries—this tea could cure the whore's pox, and also make a dye for royal robes. It's in your sky, too, I wanted to say, but what words did I have? Sounds lay trapped in my throat, a single color darkening into a note, a stain spreading into a chord.

The luthier looked me up and down—I heard the word *petit*—and his gaze roved along beams and shelf. He brought down an oud and I strummed it once—but it was out of tune, or something else was wrong.

He took another down. His fingers moved along the neck between frets like those of a vihuela, but the instrument gave out a brighter, milder sound, and all I could think was how we can believe we know a thing, and not know it at all. Now the oud's back was round again, but her neck tricked out like a northern maid's, with strings of gut. I might hold her as my father had, but how differently she must be played! He would not have recognized her at all.

As the luthier took the instrument back for tuning, a gentleman entered the shop. He had clean linen at his throat and sad gray eyes. The luthier bowed, and handed him, with great care, another oud. A stool was brought for his slippered foot, and he began to play. Such was the beauty of what he played that I forgot my own sadness—or felt it met. A lightness was in it, and silence between the notes. He knew when not to play, and let the listener's ear supply the note. I learned that morning that there is more than one way to hold a lament.

The gentleman was called Pierre de la Rue—I knew nothing yet of this illustrious name. Soon I would hear him sing, a fine clear tenor, and learn that he was the *premier chansonnier* of Philippe's chapel. And a great composer, too. But that day, he said nothing of himself, only gave me seven sheets of French tablature, showed me how to read it, and suggested that I also learn to sing.

And my vihuela? It was the composer himself who wrapped it carefully in linen, and stowed it at his own house, against the day I should travel home.

So it was that in my fourteenth year, in the land of mud and cauliflower, I held in my arms an oud that was not an oud. It gave out notes, but inside those notes, others shrank to silence. Can an interval still be called hidden if you cannot, by any means, make it sound? Or is it truly gone?

The hour before the feast it rained so hard that the pastry cook stopped me before the kitchen door with a cloth. At her mute command, I stripped to shirt and breeches, removed my boots, took the cloth and made myself clean. Her helper brought me a bit of cheese and bread. My knees prickled from the cold, but not a soul looked up from the work at hand, for the good woman was angry with her butter, too. And who can blame her—what a creation she was making— a pastry big enough to house a boy. As I approached it, her helper maid, now powdered nearly white, put her trembling hand upon my arm, and made the sign of a hanging man.

I was given a pair of satin slippers. A low stool awaited me inside, and the smallest of candles. I was to be wheeled out at first dessert.

Had Inés herself devised this punishment? And could I truly be heard? I only know that after I had played a while, two hooks descended and fished for my sleeves, and in this manner I was pronged out into a great room ablaze with candles—it might have been noon—and for a moment I swore I smelled a brightness I knew from home. The clean scent of citrus, a delicate high note, pure and slightly sharp. Then it was swarmed by a din of perfume. I looked about for Inés, but the world seemed made only of powdered faces. A young lady gotten up as a shepherdess wandered by with her crook, plump in pink lace and damp under the arms, trailed by five lambs all tied together, knocking into one another, bleating miserably and popping out little oval turds. High above my head, in the musicians' gallery, Pierre de la Rue was singing, along with others, and two of my attic mates had struck up a dance tune on sackbut and cornet. The shepherdess and her flock were whisked away. I could see it would be a long night.

"There will be a good deal of shit to clean up, even after the sheep are gone," said one of my countrymen, once I attained the gallery. He didn't even whisper: there was no danger, in this place, of anyone understanding a word we said, as long as our faces kept silent.

It was after Compline, and more dancing, that Philippe rose from his chair and lifted his chin to us. I was surprised—I thought he would, as he often did, send his bride to her apartments and stay behind to dance long into the night with others. But this time he signaled to us for a basse dance, and I kept my gaze carefully on my fellow musicians, so that should he look directly at me, I would never know.

I needn't have worried. He gazed only at his bride that night, and the gossips can tell you how she shone in that glow. She was pale, yes, and it was true she had been dressed like a Frenchwoman in rosy silk, more of her throat exposed than her mother would approve. But she still wore her beloved ruby on its black ribbon round her neck, and now her hand lay proudly upon her waist.

But where was Inés all this time? Surely she should be among the ladies—and surely she wanted to see her victim lifted from his pie.

"A blessèd pair," said Pierre de la Rue. But there was the sad note again, the thing in his music, as if he looked ahead, and saw not joy, but sorrow.

That autumn and winter, as Juana's womb swelled, purple stained the sky, and mottled the throats of a thousand sailing men and more at the coast, where our ships waited to carry the archduke's sister to Spain and marriage to Prince Juan. But though the vessels were lavishly stocked, there was, it seemed, not enough money to feed the Spanish sailors and guards who waited there, and more of them starved and sickened every day. The blame was laid at Juana's feet, though she was only seventeen, and caught between her husband and her parents. Dirt clung to dirt, spreading like the cough itself. Now and again a letter made its way to her from Spain, always bearing a royal mother's advice—too little, too late—and some, we later learned, were intercepted by Philippe's men, and never seen again. Well, thank God the queen had given her daughter a little pouch of herbs. It had done half its job. She was in love with her Habsburg husband, and carrying his child. But had the herbs made the Habsburg fall in love with her? Could said herbs keep him from succumbing to the charms of others? This was harder to say. We only knew that to the Flemings and the French our lady was too Spanish, and to the Spanish she was now too French.

And Philippe. Remember his nickname: *Croit Conseil*, for it is true he believed all the advice that flowed so freely from his French counselors—and they bore a deep distrust of his father-in-law, our King Fernando. This fount of distrust never ran dry, and Philippe leaned toward it: a thirsty young tree in a French grove.

We musicians knew ourselves fortunate. We went from glittering hall to smoky room, out into that white chill and back into heat again, into rooms smelling of butter and game, black ale and pickled cabbage. I let the purple note stain my fingers, so quietly no one could possibly notice. Though once, a lady approached me with tears in her eyes and said something to Pierre de la Rue, and he kindly found someone to translate: how is it that this boy makes a tune sound dark and light at once?

I bowed my head and thanked her. I could not tell my secret: Lady, it is a color stolen from your own sky.

By November, so many Spaniards were ill that Inés stood out, one of three or four ladies still upright, though she shivered in her woolen wrappings, even at feasts. Sometimes the consort went into Juana's apartments for an hour or two: she missed the music of home. I was surprised at how often she was alone, with only one or two of her own women—and a great clutch of Flemish ladies hovering at the doors. But inside, there was peace. Her apartments smelled of lavender and sage, warm grass on a summer day. Herbs in water had been set to boil on a little hearth. She felt the cold too.

We gave her tunes from home, in a chamber richly fitted-out, but quiet as a convent cell. And from that quiet we went back out into mud and chill, and ate our cauliflower and cabbage, butter and black ale, and made our way back to public halls and galleries, grand and glittering, sharp with the voices of silver and glass and all the hearths ablaze. Everyone was damp beneath their jewels as they danced, as if it were summer at home.

By then we had moved to Antwerp-town, and Juana was even less in public. But each evening, after she was escorted away after supper, Philippe came awake like a cat after a long sleep, and called for livelier music. He was like Prince Juan in this way—he hungered for music, was skilled at playing, and could not get enough.

One night near to December we were playing for him—or rather, for Philippe and his favorites—late into the night. He played the lute awhile himself, and sang quite well, then danced with several ladies. La Rue had suggested to me that I learn to keep a careful face. I practiced this, and only watched Philippe when he was busy dancing. He was popular with all, so well-formed and fair-haired, but there was still something about his face I didn't like—the mouth too pink and small, the eyes pale sea-glass. And why was Juana so rarely at his side?

I didn't know yet, but already he was the falconer, and she the falcon. Such birds might fly free for a moment, but it takes nothing more than a raised palm, a scrap of meat on the glove, to bring them back.

One night, between dances, one of Philippe's gentlemen came to me, one of the few who had learned a little Spanish. He came to our balcony and crooked his finger. "I understand you wish to go home when Marguerite sails for Spain," he said.

I bowed and replied that, in truth, it was my duty to return to Spain and play for Prince Juan.

The gentleman laughed. "The archduke will consider your request, but you should consider where your true duty is: to stay here and get your musical education."

Philippe was busy dancing.

A wave of sickness rose in my gut. I begged the man's pardon and set down my lute, and made my way down the gallery stairs.

It was La Rue who caught my arm as I fled, and handed me a pair of sturdy boots. "Take care," he said, "or the Flemish damp will kill you."

No stars or moon—it had begun to snow—and only a faint yellow light shone from the narrow windows. I glanced back toward the dancing-rooms just as a side door opened. I stepped into shadow, sure that it was Philippe's gentleman, sent to fetch me back inside.

But it was a woman, well-wrapped and holding aloft a lantern, which tilted over the muddy path, now flecked with little flakes. I knew that gait, its swiftness, a little sudden jerk in it, like that of a small bird darting branch to branch. I was astonished enough by this, but then she walked right past me, into the woods beyond the house. Was she going to relieve herself, even though the great house had a privy? I should have turned back. I should have gone back in and picked up my borrowed lute and held it close, and clung to La Rue for all I was worth and told him all my fears. But Inés was on the move. I watched her disappear into a black and muddy lane overhung by trees. The next minute, I too was on that dark path, following the swinging light. I waited and followed, waited and followed.

I might as well have been her bird.

Time expands without measure in a dark and unknown place. I stumbled through it, one minute cursing Inés de Castro under my breath, the next fearing for her. If the local men were anything like Philippe, she was being hungrily watched. And these were their woods. How grateful Juana would be when I brought her maiden safely back. I would earn her forgiveness, then plead my case again. I wanted to be on that ship.

Her lantern was hard to follow, far ahead on that muddy path. Did thorns and brambles reach for her as they reached for me? Were there wolves? How had she gone so swiftly? We passed a house or two, then smaller cottages, far apart, each with its steeply pitched roof, its ripening smells, its animals jostling beyond low walls.

At last, her moving light met a still one: a golden sliver between two shutters. It was that light, somehow, that made me see how dark the countryside was. I stepped inside the farmyard wall, and inched closer to the house. Children's voices, a barking dog. Inés stood at the front door, her hand poised to knock. The doorway streamed gold light, and let her in. She glanced back down the path just once.

As I watched from the dark, a woman stepped outside, pulling her shawl close, and called out, "Who's there?" in our tongue, and waited a long minute, though she did not step beyond the stream of light. At last she crossed herself, very broadly, as if on a platform before a crowd, and went back inside.

I waited a long time there. I was cold, but couldn't bring myself to knock and frighten them all. And what was Inés thinking, taking such a chance? How was it I could scowl at the ground and be chastised for offending Philippe, and at the same time, she could wander in the dangerous night without rebuke? How was this not as "disrespectful to our lady's person" as my scowl?

I had a good many words at the ready.

And yet I was the one outside in the cold, forever peering in.

A family was gathered around a table: there stood a great clay pot, and some bread. The woman ladled something into bowls, but I noticed that very little steam arose, though it was a cold night. After she was done, she went to the hearth, and brought from its dying embers a spill, and lit a tiny oil lamp. The table went quiet, and the mother looked up at the window—again, as if she'd heard a sound. Then a young man came to the window and pulled the wooden shutters tightly to.

I saw nothing more after that, but I listened. I listened as I had done in the abandoned garden at Toledo, though this time, of course, I stayed standing. The earth was heavy and black; no sound of river or voice could bubble up from below. Then I heard, as faintly as if it came from town, a husky female voice, rising in a song whose lilt I knew. A prayer, a Sabbath *piyyut*, one my mother had sung on Friday nights. A melody I never thought to hear again.

A cold wind moved against my face. I smelled cow dung, wet grass, the faint salt-tang of a nearby marsh. Snow pattered on the leaves and on my own chilled face, cold slime soaking through my clothes. I confess my stomach was no longer sickened, but empty. Ravenous for whatever was in that stewpot.

I didn't need to see to know that Inés's eyes would be closed as she sang, her fingertips aglow with lamplight. And the voice—faintly though I heard it, I cannot deny it was sweetly rough, huskier than the night of the Orpheus cart. Something crumpled in my chest, a bit of useless paper in an empty hall.

I waited for her in the dark; I did not knock at the heretics' door.

You understand why: to protect Juana's reputation from taint. And to get myself onto that ship going home.

At last the meal was over, the murmuring and laughter done. Inés stood long in the doorway—and I heard the young man's voice twining with hers, and my heart gave a wretched squeeze.

I did not follow her right away. I told myself she had her lantern, and could fend for herself. I waited until her light was nearly too small to follow.

Under La Rue's good boots and above my head there hung a blanketing dark. The branches dripped and sank low. Inés's lantern swung ahead, never stopping, never turning, until it reached the house where Juana and her ladies stayed, and was swallowed by the torchlight there.

I myself went dutifully back into the dancing-rooms, though I was sure that Philippe's man would come and whisper some small French phrase in my ear, then laugh to see me confused. But it seemed Philippe had gone to bed, and only a few of his men remained, half-asleep on benches, still in their finest clothes. I was surprised to see two young women nearby, unchaperoned, their shoulders bare and agleam under the last lights. They beckoned me over, and with a

great deal of fuss, pointed to my lute, and themselves, and I understood they wanted a music lesson—well, to pretend they did.

I saw I had no choice, and offered each my arm, and an escort
home. This seemed to satisfy. They giggled and slipped and hung on
each other and me, and in loud voices said things in their tongue as
if they wanted all the world to hear. My ears burned, and I was right
to worry: as we entered the smaller lane, the shutters of the first window came together with a sharp clap. This only made the girls laugh
harder. As I left them at a fine house, one gave me a crude kiss, right
on the lips, and nearly collapsed in giggles. "*À demain*," the other said,
in a hushed voice.

A little phrase, but it stuck in my ear, even when I was alone again
in the dark lane. And when I reached the dancing-rooms again, La
Rue was still there, having a pipe, his eyes half-closed. I pulled off the
borrowed boots and handed them over, crusted with mud.

He gestured I should keep them—if I needed them once, I might
need them again. I thanked him in my paltry French, and he glanced
at me as if he would speak. Then he sighed, and shook his head, and
looked thoughtfully at his pipe.

There was still a little red glow in the hearth when I got back to
my lodging, so I drew a stool close. The *piyyut* sung in the cottage
would not leave my ears; around it went. My two countrymen came
down the attic stairs; they said they could not sleep. We traded stories, and spoke of lemons and olives and the bread we missed—and
the wrong taste of the water here—until the housewife came down in
her shawl, and pressed her hands together in a pleading way.

But just as we stood up, one of my fellows gave out one last tune:
a wonderful old bawdy thing from home—and this, at last, drove the
old *piyyut* out of my ears. It drove out the husky voice that had sung
it, too. But it couldn't drive out my fear that Philippe would see me
educated before I left. Nor could it vanquish the harmonies the spice
merchant's son sang so easily with Inés.

I am sorry to disappoint: no one, male or female, educated me in
Flanders, and I congratulated myself that I could slip between great
dangers and not get caught. The predator's eye might briefly catch,
but could not hold; the eye went on, seeking easier prey. How else
to explain why none of Philippe's servants came for me, to take me
to his master's bed for a quick fondle, or why the two yellow-haired

maids did not tug me into an alley and give me a lesson in Northern music then and there.

But for all that I went unmolested, the image of Philippe on his wedding day would not leave me. I saw his small lopsided mouth, his falcon's eye. I was sure he wanted me tested and tamed. The fear must have been in my face, for once, after we had played for a private supper for Juana alone, she held me back a moment.

"You know the archduke is no longer angry with you. In fact, he thinks you very gifted, and we wish you to stay here with us when the ships go back."

The cold sea itself might have run in my veins then. I bowed.

"But what?" she said, frowning.

"Prince Juan needs his musicians for his wedding."

"That may well be," she said. "But we both know there is something else. My husband thinks you are afraid of him—he has no idea why." Her lip trembled, but she did not ask me if it was true, and I only bowed. At last she said, "I will ask if you may go."

I knelt and thanked her. When I raised my eyes, there were tears in hers.

By February, half our sailors were dead, and five thousand others gravely ill—and such are the mysteries of the world that Juana was blamed for the calamity. The truth—and everyone at court knew it— was that neither her parents nor her husband gave her the funds to assist them. Oh, there was plenty enough to convey Marguerite and her great entourage and carriages full of goods to the port. And the fleet, however thinned its ranks of sailors, made ready to sail. I still had not been told whether I would be allowed to leave. Our consort played for Juana or her husband every day. Sometimes I played vihuela alone, and once or twice, accompanied Inés, who sang for our lady alone.

She was alone a great deal in those days. Very naturally, of course, due to her confinement. Sometimes she was persuaded to dine in state, for all to see, and on these occasions Philippe looked on her with convincing warmth. She was, after all, going to give birth in spring—God willing she would have a son.

Two nights before the fleet was set to sail, I still had not heard whether I should pack my things. But near the supper's end, I was told to approach the dais. It was Juana who spoke first. She said, very simply, "We are sending you back to Spain. You were only on loan from the prince."

I remember looking at Inés, who stood nearby, wondering if she'd persuaded Juana to let me go, and whether it was to keep me safe from the falcon, or because she was tired of my foolish remarks and my face that could not hide its weather.

"I thought this would please you," Juana said. "You've missed home so." Then she paused. "Are you worried about the voyage itself?"

"Not at all," I said.

"Your fingers will be happier in Spain," she said, with a trembling smile.

Then Philippe leaned over and whispered something in her ear, which she gave to me in Spanish. "The archduke would rather keep you here," she said. "And so would I." Her own eyes were brimming now. "But this is a promise I must keep."

Philippe lifted his eyes heavenward. "Ah, to the Angel?" I heard him say, in a cool and mocking tone. For a moment Juana's eyes flashed: he had insulted her brother, her mother. But Philippe only smiled and said something in French directly to me, something I couldn't understand. She bade me lean forward before she would speak, and her voice was so low I could barely catch the words. "The archduke says you must return to us soon, and when you do, we will give some light to your music. It is twelve times too dark."

I gave a courteous bow, and as I did, she said, very low, "The darkness gives it all its beauty."

"What did you just say to him?" Philippe said.

She took his hand in hers. "Only, my love, that I could not agree more."

I wanted nothing more than to watch his face then, to see if he believed her, but at that moment, out of the corner of my eye, I caught a little movement.

It was Inés, slipping out a side door. Juana's gaze followed her out. But the most astonishing thing was that Juana did not seem surprised at all.

I wanted so badly to follow, but Philippe was on his feet, calling for music. He wanted a *pavane* of La Rue's. He would dance with his wife.

It was the music La Rue had played for me in the luthier's shop, and as Philippe took Juana's hand and helped her to her feet, his face went still and sad and fine. The piece worked on him as it had worked on me. So full of melancholy, yet giving light and air.

They danced, and we saw nothing but perfect devotion from him, and adoration from her. I saw why Inés was worried: Juana gazed in unmasked wonder at this figure from her books and girlish dreams. That wonder was dangerously mixed with pride. And why not? She had accomplished everything her parents asked of her, and wasn't her womb good and round?

There was applause as the husband led the wife, with pomp, to the door of her apartments, bade her goodnight for all to see, then went away to his own.

There is something about a great hall after the significant persons have gone to their beds. A great emptiness steals in. Every mask has been discarded, every decoration has wilted or melted, as if it knows it is no longer needed. Kitchen maids flutter in to take up the plate and cloth, and men follow with great rush-brooms, and rags to mop up all the melted things: of wax and sugar, of sculpted butter and ice. Here is a scatter of roasted bones and the last ruined stem of grapes, a crust of bread and a small hunk of marbled cheese. Stories are hidden in these things, but they lie trapped, enchanted.

I made my way to the door through which Inés had slipped. I could not imagine what I would say. I told myself I would be content to glimpse her in that window, to see her safely back through the dangerous wood. She need never know she had been followed.

As I slipped out the door, a female voice called my name—it was one of the two young women from the earlier night. One was very anxious, her lace damp, and her bare throat all ashine. This time, she stammered a little Spanish—*lesson, lute.*

But why did this girl look so afraid? From the other room I heard music rising like one of their towers of spun sugar, so delicate it seems to be leaning dangerously—at any moment it might fall apart. She glanced longingly back, as if she wanted nothing more than to be back in that room, dancing with the others.

I thought of Encina's pure simple tunes—could I teach her one of those, and be done? Then I took a deep breath, and said, "Another time. One of my lady's people has gone missing, and I must fetch her back before she is hurt."

The girl went pale, as if I'd struck her down. "Here," I said. "I leave you this as my pledge." I thrust my lute into her arms and stumbled toward the door.

It is a little thing to step forward; be it a step into clear air, or a step into the forest leading to a house. When I look back, I think of the cliffs of the Tagus, from which I once thought to simply step like a bird into air. One step that crackles the forest leaves, one step that leads you closer to the person you should not love.

I took a lantern and followed the path past the town houses to the countryside. It seemed less far this time.

I have heard it said there are two kinds of men. One will sit patiently with grief in the cold dawn, and ask nothing. The other yearns for the hearth fire and new bread, and will do any weak thing to get it. But what if there is a third kind—one who likes to stand in the dark and look into a stranger's warm, lit house? If, in looking, my eye rested longest on a certain young woman, forgive me. I see her still. I see the little gap between her two front teeth as she forgot to worry, and let herself smile.

Did I make some sound out there? I only know she came to the door and stood in her wrappings on the threshold. "I know you're there," she said in the firm voice she used for misbehaving creatures of any kind, maybe even Juana, if she had to wake her melancholy mistress out of a long, sad, daylight sleep. But I could be stubborn, too. I could make Inés sway against the doorframe and wait for me.

"Enough, Fool," she growled. She stepped closer. "Come in out of the cold, before you die like all the rest." I bowed my head to hide my happiness, and stepped into view.

And that is how I came to enter the house of the Castros of Antwerp.

That night, the children's eyes were wide; the mother tried to fold the youngest child into her skirts. But Inés told them not to fear me, and the littlest daughter came forward, finger still in her mouth, tugging me to the hearth. The mother gave me a seat, a cup of something warm—there was a bright spice in it I thought I knew.

"Cinnamon," she said. "Inés brought it to us herself from home.

What do you think? Will the Flemish want it?" The good woman laughed, and didn't wait for an answer.

The tablecloth, it's true, had been freshly laundered on a Thursday. The silver candlesticks had been polished that day too. The father and his grown son wore the fringed shawl and the little cap. The mother covered her head with a bit of white lace, and moved her hands, then held them to her eyes. She sang. Call it a *piyyut* if you like. I only know that when she opened her eyes again, they shone with all the light she'd gathered in.

That night I heard what Inés's voice could do. I wanted to hold her there, singing. *Dios*, she'd said so long ago. And wiped my dirty ear as if she knew it had lain in the dirt of Toledo and listened for the lost songs of its Jews.

But the prayer was over. "Are you hungry?" said the mother, and Inés herself passed me the braided loaf, as kindly and simply as if she were one more daughter of this house, and I myself a stranger in need of welcome. A warm meal, kind faces, nothing more.

But the truth is, it took all my strength to look directly at Inés that night, and to smile at the young man of the house, to whom, I was sure, she had long since been promised. I was afraid of myself, of what my face would tell her.

I forgot to say that I had noticed, as I stepped inside, a faint scent of spice in the air—no doubt coming from the merchant's storerooms within his house. It was a deep and surprising scent, full of exotic notes, and it filled the house that night, as if some cask or door had been opened wide to let it in. I recognized some things: cassia-cinnamon and cardamom, saffron and grains-of-Paradise, but there were other things, too, whose names I never learned. I only know that many years later, in a country house not far from here, I smelled it once again.

That precise dark chord like no other, haunted by everything lost. I cannot explain. But the feeling cannot be unbound from that night in Antwerp, the warmth in the spice merchant's house, the cold trees waiting just beyond.

But not yet. For now the mother ladled out a hearty stew, of chickpeas and meat, and as I took a bite, I must have closed my eyes. When I opened them, they were all smiling.

"His stomach misses home," said Inés.

"Well," said the mother, "there is much to miss. But some of it we carry with us."

It was too much for me—my mother's words, the family's warmth. "Forgive me," I said, "I will be back," and I rushed out into the cold, and breathed and breathed.

At length I gathered myself and went back in. There was a vihuela in that house, long since brought from their old home, and they put it in my arms. The table was cleared for music. How long I played I can't remember now. I played the old simple tunes everyone knew, and when I played Encina's songs, I watched Inés. But she was already aglow; I could not tell if she changed. Once in a while I wondered if we should stop—if there was a danger, even this far north, in singing such songs, but then the other danger flowed over me in waves, of Philippe's pale blue eyes, watching women, watching us all. May this night go on forever, I prayed to myself. And for a time it seemed my wish had been granted. For after the singing everyone wanted to dance. Nobody cared that a stern rabbi, watching, might have said, to dance and sing, especially on a holy day, is wrong. Never forget the suffering of our ancestors. Never forget how we were sent out to weep on the riverbank. It may be the pious way. But we answered silence with song—the oldest holiness we have.

That night, Inés let me walk with her in the dark, and we did so in peace, in shared solitude, with neither word nor touch. A silence strangely thronged.

At the door of the great house, I gave her goodnight and said nothing more, and she bowed her head by way of thanks. My lute stood against the wall where I'd last seen the pale girl. She had given up waiting. I felt a pang of guilt, and took it up.

When I got to my lodging place there was a letter bearing the Habsburg seal and stamp, and my official orders: I was to be in the lane the next afternoon, to go with a few others to Bergen op Zoom and board the *Julienne*.

And so I had my wish, to go home, with some others, on the ship bearing Marguerite to Prince Juan, his mother's *Angel* and Spain's great hope. I thought I would feel relief, but I felt as if I was being sent away, too timid to stand the rigors of the north.

Inés, of course, was not timid. She embraced the future. I remembered her remark: *I will be glad if I never see Spain again.* She must have said it to Juana, too—Juana, who seemed to be permitting her friend a secret freedom. I remembered them as young girls in Granada, putting their heads together and murmuring as they rode to the Nasrid gates. Who knows what secrets passed between them. They had long been friends.

There were no farewells. In the morning I returned the lute to the instrument maker, and he gave me back my vihuela. She was well-wrapped in soft cloth, and ready to sail home. Of my father's oud, I still knew nothing. For all I knew, it was hanging, stripped of its strings, about to become something else. But its old bruise would still be visible, if you knew where to look.

I came out into the house-yard in the afternoon. There it was again: the whitened sky with the little purple in it, just as on that other morning. Everything was the same, except that Inés was not in the yard. But she might as well have been, for still I saw her, as in a dream, the little boots stamping, her breath warm and white in the autumn air. I saw her toss her head, and take herself away. She was a good walker, and soon out of view.

eight

A girl in two cloaks and wooden shoes walks between dripping trees. She takes off one cloak, then the next, and hands both to the spice dealer's son. You may picture me on the ship bearing Marguerite to Spain, but Inés de Castro is all I am given to see. Inés, standing at the table, lighting her cousins' candles, and bringing her hands to her eyes as if to hold the two lights close. She sings an old song to welcome the Sabbath in. I am safely steeped in shadow, but when someone opens a door, light and her voice stream out, and it is my ear that does the catching—my ear, that barbed thing that always keeps what it should throw away.

Everyone knows that the simplest, most homely gesture may hide the Devil. Am I not to be praised for walking away from Inés, from the family scene at the spice dealer's house, even from Juana, whose eyes also filled when she heard a ballad from home?

Why, then, did the old guilt stir awake again: the blind girl of Granada putting out her hands, my quick step out of reach? Never mind, I told myself, you are nearly fifteen and taller than all girls, and you have done nothing wrong. And if you ever see Inés again, she will be a plump Flemish housewife with the smell of cabbage on her hands and in the warm creases of her neck.

I was proud of the hard stone of my solitude. Yet it kept looking out from its hiding place at a girl breathing freely, singing forbidden tunes in a country not her own.

I will not look back, or cling to the old. That is a habit of my ancestors. Is it not a blessèd act to scrub ourselves clean of these moldy ways which hunt us through the centuries? I have spent half a century at it, and scrubbed myself raw.

I must hold to my story, wherever it goes.

And so, once again, I give you a fleet of ships, each vessel groaning under her special burden of jewel and sword, casks of vinegar, wine, and dried fish, of hoof, hide, and feather, and the mountains of dung produced by animal fear. A French carriage rocks on its thin wheels below—the first Spain would ever see. And if you look into the admiral's quarters, you might see that we carried ill-fortune itself, in the shape of a seventeen-year-old Habsburg beauty.

Three nights out: we are playing for the lovely Marguerite. Between tunes, a pause, in which we hear nothing. No creak of rocking masts, no lowing of beasts, no splash of wave on hull. The hush holds us all amazed, until Marguerite lifts her hand in delicate command: *continue.*

Gentlemen, it suits us to call women delicate, until one day we learn otherwise. No doubt the good commissioner knows this, having escorted his share of females to the burning-place. But that evening, Marguerite stood up—so did we all—and together we watched at portholes, as one by one the stars were swallowed whole. The first great swell tilted us up and sideways, then dropped us deep. Then the low howl, the first plashing drops. The Admiral cordially invited her to stay below, and she just as cordially refused. All that night, and the next day, she would brace herself at the rail, just as Juana had on the journey north, praying her beads and wiping the Admiral's brow with her napkin for *bon courage.*

A riddle: how was Juana blamed for a thousand sailors' deaths on land, yet Marguerite drew only praise, though our ship nearly wrecked? I have no answer, and still it clouds my mind. Some things do not want us to see how they are done. Like the fate that swept over the Castro family, or the fate that kept me solitary and out of harm's way. For here is a mystery. The Holy Office tells us that heresy dwells in blood and bone; that if, on a Friday night a hundred years ago, a great-great-grandmother changed her blouse and swept her yard and lit her lamp, and served a chickpea stew, we must watch the great-great-granddaughter very close, and all her cousins, too.

Why, then, did no one watch me? Why did no one care that every

August my fingers stiffened, and would not play? That a little prayer-tune lay trapped in my ear, and I could not force it out?

At any rate, Princess Marguerite was beloved. The sailors called her *la sirenuca*—they thought her presence saved our lives. As for me, I staggered to the nest of rope Inés had found, and kept my black thoughts to myself. A few great trunks were tossed overboard that day, to lighten our load. And also a mule, its gray fur stiff with salt, its thin legs kicking, its voice and eyes no help to it at all. It took four men to hoist it over, but the sea found it easy to digest. But don't you find that it is the smallest, least important objects that float up to betray us, to show us how afraid we are? I saw, that day, on a dark gray swell flecked with dirty foam and slyly rising, some object bobbing. I looked closer: it was a lady's slipper, all by itself. Had a trunk opened below the waves and sent it up, just as I looked out? It had no back, and would leave a woman's tender heel exposed. It was this, somehow, and not the grand heaving of the ship, that made my stomach rise.

But never mind that. Thank God the gilded carriage was saved.

One day a bit of seaweed floated past. A boy went up the mast and gave a happy shout. In time there were bushes and trees, stone houses and a pier. All looked very much like rescue, and all rejoiced. Yet in my ears the welcome was puny and out of tune: a clattering of ugly old shoes, the people all in black and winter-starved.

I was ill, that was all. Nothing and no one looked like home.

If Marguerite, *la sirenuca*, missed her northern home, she gave no sign. As she stepped onto land, she straightened the shoulders of her velvet cape, and the crowd gave out a triumphant cheer. "Venus herself," proclaimed the gossip Peter Martyr. Without him, we must ask, what would history know?

The Angel, unlike Philippe, was on time to meet his bride, and though it was a cold day in early spring, he was dressed for love. Did his mother choose the short mulberry cape, its clasps so neatly closed? His hands trembled only a little as he greeted his bride. I am sorry that I notice these things; they are of no significance. The truth is, I was afraid to close my eyes, for when I did, I saw again the dark gray swell, foam-flecked and sinister, playing with the slipper. I managed to stay upright until the happy couple was out of view, then heaved my last hard biscuit into the brush and sank to the icy ground.

Water on my face, some noxious stinking herb waved under my nose: was it yet another baptism for Juan de Granada, the excessively blessed? And who had lowered himself to this task? The Basque composer—ever closer to the prince—Juan de Anchieta, his skin more yellow than I remembered, his reddened eyes ringed with fragile, drooping skin. It was he who helped me to my feet and put a fresh shirt into my hands. Then he leaned close to my right ear—the one he'd boxed five years before, and that sometimes still sang a high sweet note. "The prince is ill. No one else will say it. Nor will you repeat it."

"Will they delay the wedding till he is well again?" I asked.

"No," he said, and sighed. "No—they may well move it up."

March, a season of mud and cold and needling rain. The kings had run out of gold and it was Lenten-time besides, but all must celebrate. The ban on bright clothes was lifted, but in the countryside, people seemed not to know, or care: they stood in fields and gullies in their worn dark clothes to watch the gilded carriage pass. At Burgos, Queen Isabel had borrowed back her pawned crown, and wore it for the day, greeting Marguerite with trumpets and choir. Throughout the land every hamlet and village exhausted its coffers in the joyous exercise of jousts, and it was said that as far south as Granada, our sovereign lady had ordered all remaining *juderías* razed for tournament fields to honor the prince. A good thing, the people said, otherwise you had to pass those empty houses every day.

Never mind that the Angel himself was pale and thin; that his little cough sometimes brought up a spot of blood. The anticipation of love, it was said, had dimmed his appetite. And Anchieta was right: it was Prince Juan himself who, in early April, announced that the nuptials would take place sooner than originally planned. The court gossips were delighted: Marguerite was all one could hope for in a bride; of course the prince wished, as they put it, "to get more quickly to the desired embraces."

I could not rid myself of the swaying-sickness. It played in my blood as the Angel weakened: a black disfigured tune to his plaintive verse. Still Anchieta assigned me to play, with a few others, on the prince's wedding night, behind an arras. The order had not come from the queen, but Prince Juan himself, and we understood: we were to fill the silence, or hide the love sounds—whichever it would be.

Thank God those two were not noisy at it, because the instruments we played that night were all of quiet voice. How small the vihuela felt in my arms; I swear she wanted cradling. I heard the darkness of her timbre, as if she'd drunk from an older, deeper well than her cousin to the north. A well of whose depths she was forbidden to speak.

That night, my ear caught one faint cry. You might imagine it was Marguerite I heard, the virgin's tearing-pain. But it was not. I knew that little cry, having heard it at Toledo, in its muffled, lonely form. Though it held, now, a measure of relief, still it held its thimble-full of shame and the sound of terrible surprise—as if the prince had stumbled, and nearly fallen, into his own deep well, and caught a glimpse of all that lay ahead.

The lovers celebrated spring and summer in the towns of Castile. The air warmed, fanned, it seemed, by the strenuous couplings of the bridal pair. It is impossible to count how often our consort was summoned, and arranged itself behind a screen or door. By August our calluses were firm as stones, and we had learned a hundred variations on a few old tunes.

Everyone, it seemed, was a composer that summer. By August even I had written a tune, and the prince, in his love-stupor, had ordered a scribe to set it down. It was a clumsy thing, of no consequence, and tilted sad, for like my father, and his father before him, I am always sad in August—and it held too much of Antwerp's bruised white sky. But the prince was weak from so much love, and liked everything. Poor Angel, the *desired embraces* wore down the clasps of his mulberry cloak and its velvet lining besides. He looked, mornings, like a man trying to rise from some sea-wreck of his own. We heard that Doctor Soto had even taken Queen Isabel aside and begged her to speak to her son: the act was being undertaken too often; it might soften the marrow of his bones. The royal lovers should spend a little time apart.

The queen was offended by the doctor's suggestion.

Let no man tear asunder what God has joined together.

No doubt she was waiting for happy news. Juana had produced it quickly enough in Flanders, and might produce yet more. But it was only her brother who mattered; Prince Juan, the hope of all Spain.

Behind arras and door I shivered as I played. I was a very sieve for food. I gave thanks to the Father, the Son, and the Holy Spirit that Inés de Castro was not there to raise her eyebrows, and measure, with her cool fingertips, my bony wrist and hollow cheek.

No one sees an omen in an ailing musician. No: the only shadow recognized in those jubilant months was a jouster killed by an errant spear. The courtier Peter Martyr, in later years, said the knight's death *did* strike him as a fearful sign. But nothing was said at the time, and when Spain learned, in September, that Marguerite was at last with child, the celebrations grew wilder still.

Juan and Marguerite arrived at Salamanca late in the month, to a chorus so young and vast—singing from every balcony and square and decorated platform—that the prince, holding back tears, bade his own trumpets cease.

It would never be heard again, that joyous lifting of young voices. So much bright dreaming.

Salamanca—that city where my master Encina grew up and studied, where his family still lived. Where you might, at all times of day and night, hear laughter, cheerful argument, or singing, floating up from fine archways, echoing in canyons of well-carved stone. Its freedom astonished me, though Anchieta, ever one to dampen hope, said it was not the place it had once been. He surprised me then: in a quiet voice, he remarked that a great scholar he knew had found a notice nailed to his chamber door, and the place itself emptied, swept and clean. The scholar's blood was discovered to be less pure than at first supposed. How had it happened, after thirty years of teaching and study, medals, honors, acclaim for his Christian works? Someone wanted him gone, and now he was, in exile or prison no one knew, and a younger professor of purer blood was in his chambers now.

And here stood Anchieta, holding back tears. The man who based a great mass on a little ditty about the departure of the Jews. What did he really think?

A little fear struck me then: I knew Encina's older brother was a Professor of Music there—one Diego de Fermoselle, was he by chance the scholar? And somewhere in town, Encina's father, also by this name Fermoselle, stitched leather for shoes, that ancient Hebrew trade. I thought of Encina himself, his quickness with a flame and paper. Surely he was safe, under the protection of the Duke of Alba, at whose house he worked, and besides, had he not changed his name long ago? Did this not firmly show where his loyalties lay?

I wanted nothing more—and dreaded nothing more—than to meet my old master in the street. I knew how it would go: Encina would coolly nod and move past. And after that, I would be doomed to see him everywhere, and be unable to speak.

That night we played a feast in a university hall, in a musicians' gallery very hard to reach—so much so that I wondered how the guests could hear us at all. We were very near the end, tuning up one last time, when I heard a voice at my ear, and felt a hand on my shoulder.

"Young Master Bones, is that you? Still so thin?"

I held the comforting drone in my ears, and held very still, my palm springing sweat on the vihuela's neck. But there he stood. His face was flushed, a heaviness beneath his eyes, but they were still brilliant hazel, with the dreamer's shadows beneath. I opened my mouth to speak, but he stopped me with a hand on my sleeve. "Forget all that. You were a child, a pawn in their game."

"Pawn," I repeated. "Whose game—"

"A charming innocence," he said, then brightened his voice. "Can you be missed for a night or two from the prince's side-cupboard? Come to my family's house tonight. Let my mother fatten you up."

I was afraid to look up and show my joy.

He smiled—or something near to smiling. "Remind me never to tell you a secret," he said. "Your face shows all."

Then one of the players cried, "*Tan Buen Ganadico*," and Encina gave a bow, and another musician lifted his gaze heavenward. I remembered my mother. *There are times to shine your light, and times to hide it.*

But we played the tune, and I marveled afresh, for in it lay nestled traces of the song we'd heard together that glowing night in el Albaicín, before everything went wrong: "*Calvi vi calvi, calvi arabi.*" *In my heart is the heart of an Arab.* Traces only, and with a new, bouncy rhythm that belied its place of birth. It took me a moment to realize that Encina had left us, and was down below in the hall, moving sleekly from scholar to courtier, speaking with utmost seriousness to one, and laughing with another. What had happened? His stillness was gone, and some of the solemn beauty of his face, too.

Encina came back to the gallery as we were packing up, but would not speak till we were in the street and alone.

"The Low Countries did you no favors," he said at last. "I meant what I said. You are too thin."

"And you?" I asked. "The Duke of Alba treats you well?"

"They love nothing more than music there—except for mummery," he said. "His people can eat four ecologues for breakfast. And at Christmastide, three for supper and three after Compline. But you will not hear me complain." He lowered his voice. "Listen to me. The choirmaster at the cathedral here has fallen ill. He is not expected to recover, and everyone knows I am the right man to take his place." He glanced across the street at the university's walls. "Everyone knows it," he repeated. "But someone is against me. I have an enemy, I don't know who it is. A word from the prince would settle it. And you are very near him now. At his chamber door."

His mouth held a bitter curve.

"I am well outside the chamber," I said. "But Anchieta—"

Encina waved his hand. "Anchieta will not look at me, let alone speak with me just now. Who knows but that he is the one holding me back. Never mind. We will discuss it later. Now tell me about the great Pierre de la Rue—and that other fellow—by the name of Agricola. Are they really as good as they say?" He cupped his jaw as if he had a painful tooth.

"I don't know Agricola," I said. "Monsieur de la Rue is very fine. But no one comes near what you do."

Encina laughed—but his voice carried a hard, false edge. "I asked for that. Now play me something of your own—you have, I suppose, composed a tune or two?"

"Here in the street?"

He clapped me on the back. "Yes, here. No one will mind."

So I leaned against a wall, and tuned, and played him the simple thing, the one the prince had liked.

From down the street came a shout, a scatter of applause. But a house window over our heads slammed shut.

"An old professor's judgment, no doubt," said Encina. "But not so bad. I can hear what it lacks, and that is a good sign. Have you had a woman yet? Did you taste the salty skin of little Inés?"

A sudden swarm around my ears—of bees, of dirt—I couldn't

breathe to speak. He caught me fast by the arm. "What's this? Is our prodigy sick with love?"

"Not that," I said, but my breath would not come. "I was ill on the boat."

"Well, well. But what about Inés?"

"Nothing. She thrives in the north."

There was a beat, a pause, a gathering at his brow.

"Thrives how?"

"There is nothing to say," I said. "She has some cousins there— they deal in spices. They are kind to her. That is all."

"Kind to her, that is all," said Encina. "How many in the family, and is there a son to whom she has been promised since birth?"

I shrugged, but couldn't fool him. He patted me on the back. "I'm sure it's for the best," he said, and raised his hand as if it held a cup of wine. "May the loss of Inés be the gain of Spanish music, for now you will feel moved to write your own *chanson de regret*, in the manner of your new mentor, this famous *Pierre of the Street*. And look, here is home already."

How his wit had changed—it flashed as it had before, but had gone black and sharp as steel. Yet he was the one whose voice I knew, and knew me best. And he wanted me to see his home.

I'm sure it's for the best. A cold little phrase. Was there anyone else so swift at learning, who gave so little news himself?

We stood before an open door. The smell of baking bread, a dream of warmth. A woman beckoned us forward, and once more I let myself step in.

Certain little sounds, early in the morning, can carry you back to your first lost place. A mother singing, the tapping of a spoon on the side of a bowl, this is the music of kitchens. In a room under the eaves at the Fermoselles', I kept my eyes closed and listened, and tried to shake the blackened edge away. *Dio*—pardon—*Dios*: here I am a child again, in a white room far to the south. A little window. A square of palest blue. Snow on the way—

No snow. But a peaceful quiet in the streets below: the students of Salamanca still abed. Encina had told me that the students, having caroused all night, would sleep till afternoon, then rise to celebrate their prince again. As I lay there listening to the mother singing down below, and a child's voice piping up with questions, a brown-haired boy in a servant's smock appeared at the door. He had hazel eyes and a finely pointed chin, and brought me a bowl of steaming soup with practiced grace. It was a clear gold broth, fragrant and bejeweled with fat. I let myself drift—just for a moment—in the pleasure of being served by a person my own age. Then I sat up straight, and thanked the boy, and told him he could go.

He did not move. He sat down on the bed and fixed his eyes on me—how to describe that gaze? Bright, amused, but searching, too, as if he were preparing to make a sketch. "I am Pedro de Fermoselle," he said. "My brother wanted us to meet."

I held the bowl close, and hoped its steam would hide my rising flush.

"Please tell your mother thank you," I said. "And I humbly beg your pardon."

"You are pardoned," he said warmly. But there was a little catch in his voice he couldn't hide.

I saw I'd made another error. Why did I not beg his pardon first, and thank the mother after?

He went on, still in the kindest voice: "Alas, our servant is ill, and there is no one to wash your clothes. But I have something that might fit you. There—in that cupboard." And then he was gone.

It cost me something to go down those stairs. My face still burned, for I had usurped a bed, called a brother *servant*, and was now dressed in his own clothes. Oh, to never be seen again. But there was no sign of Pedro below. In fact, all men and boys were gone; only the mother was left in the house, very busy at her bread. By her side, in her own white cap, stood a girl of seven or eight. It was she whose voice I'd heard asking questions—and she was busy too, making tiny people from a piece of dough. The mother's face was so kind, so full of questions itself, that I had to look away. The child saved us both. She tugged at my hand, and took me to see her special kitchen corner, and all her little treasures. But as we walked, she snatched another tiny piece of dough, and without her mother's permission, threw it onto the hearth coals. I closed my eyes, but it was too late: I saw my mother at our own hearth, breaking off a bit of dough and handing it to me to toss into the fire: "A little gift to God," she'd say. "Don't forget."

The child's mother put her hand to her own cheek, as if the girl had struck her a blow. She took her little daughter by the wrist, and put her in her corner. The small mouth trembled, a great tear fell.

I begged her not to be afraid. "She meant nothing by it," I said. "And no one saw."

She bit her lip and her eyes brimmed up. "I am a pious Christian lady, but still I cannot rest."

Encina himself was gone all morning, and when he returned, he too seemed worried, and paced before the hearth. I thanked him for all the kindness, and the bed, but thought I should leave to spare his mother the extra work. "With your servant gone and all—"

"Stay here with us another day or two," he said. "The prince is very ill, there is no music. Even Marguerite must keep away from him. The only person he will see is Deza."

Diego Deza was the prince's tutor and confessor then, not yet the inquisitor general I would meet in years to come. Encina's voice sliced sharp when he said that name, and with it he cut open some old wound in himself. "The Duke of Alba is good to me," he said. "But these past few years I should have been with the prince. I have done nothing others have not done, and my music and my teaching pleased him best of all—he once told me so. Someone wants my place."

Then he glanced my way. "I meant to ask, before," he began. "That night at Granada, the night you saw me with Inés. Did you tell anyone about it? Did anyone see us besides yourself?"

I shook my head.

"But there is something," he said. "Something you're not saying." He waited, and again it worked on me. I told him what the guard had said, how he called Inés *the little Jew's harp.* Encina frowned again, and held very still. "Why did you never tell me this before?"

That was easy enough to answer. "You never spoke to me again," I said.

I remember how quickly he smoothed the furrow away, and softened the muscles around his mouth. It took no time at all, and yet, when I recall it, the moment seems to last forever.

"Never mind," he said. "He was only a guard." He gave a brief, pained smile. "My mother likes you. Stay a while. And as I said, there will be no music until the prince is well."

"But Pedro doesn't like me," I said. "I offended him."

He sighed. "Nonsense," he said. "He is just loyal to his family, and wary of strangers. Give him time. Stay tonight at least." Then he seemed to hesitate. "You might take care of what you say to him. He has just been made a courier for the Salamanca Tribunal, and is under oath to report everything he hears and sees to the Holy Office."

I thanked him for the warning. But it felt—for reasons I could not explain—as if he'd offered it too late.

That night at the evening meal I met the rest of the family—all but the great music professor, Diego de Fermoselle. There were three more young boys and the father, a cobbler by trade and a gentle, brooding sort who looked wearily upon his lively tribe. And I saw now that Pedro's smock was not that of a house servant at all. He told me that he helped his father, and his brother the professor, too, delivering manuscripts and documents, leather, needles and awls. He did not mention his work for the Tribunal, and I wondered if his parents knew. Master Diego himself was spoken of in hushed and reverent tones. The little girl sat at my side and it's true, the child's delight in my company made her mother glow.

And Pedro—I saw the warmth, the loyalty, his patience with the younger boys. That measuring glance was leveled only at me, and I foresaw I couldn't stay beneath this roof for long. So when the mother asked me, very kindly, if so much travel wore me down, I saw my chance. I said I was used to it, and that in fact, I would be leaving again soon.

"A shame," said Pedro, leaning forward. "And what is next for you?"

"Portugal," I replied. For Anchieta had long since told me how it would be: when the prince recovered, the court would travel to see the young widow Isabel marry King Manoel.

What had I said wrong? A look passed between the parents. "We knew people—not well," said the father. "They went there with hope when they could not stay here." His wife shook her head as if to stop him speaking. "Never mind all that. But if King Manoel forces them to leave Portugal, where will they go?"

"Antwerp," said Encina, his voice very light. "A good place, Juanico, a safe place, isn't that right?"

I felt the quiet, the eyes of all upon me. Pedro's eyes, especially, so bright and curious.

"I suppose," I said. "Some find it so."

"Brother, who is there that we know?" said Pedro. "In Antwerp, I mean."

"The Castro girl, Inés," said Encina, his voice betraying no feeling at all. "A good thing, too. That family has a history of trouble, going back—"

The mother rose from the table, and the father, too.

"Let them live their lives," she said, and the meal was done.

Pedro bowed his head, and put his napkin to his lips. But he wasn't done. Afterwards, by the fire with a cup of wine, he was friendlier still. "Weren't you just at Antwerp?" he asked, looking at me, and then at Encina. "I was struck by your phrase, *some find it so*."

"I only meant I didn't care for it there, myself."

"But these Castros," Pedro went on. "This merchant's family— is it spice, or wine, well, it doesn't matter—do they seem comfortable there? I wonder, is it wise for one of Juana's ladies to spend so much time with them? That is, if something were to come out about another Castro, say, in Toledo, who has confessed to Judaizing and been condemned, might not this connection taint the court—and the Crown itself? The scandal—" He stopped abruptly, and put his hand to his brow in a great show of concern.

He was too quick for me. How easily I'd paved the way for his suggestion: that danger might lie coiled in a simple house so far away. But why did Pedro de Fermoselle care so much about the Castros? Why so much interest in Inés—did he know more about his brother's early wild days than he let on? There was no time to think it through: Pedro looked at me gently, and finished his wine, as if some anxious beast had, for the time, been fed. "I have upset you," he said. "I only ask because the Castros of Toledo have, as my brother said, a long history of trouble. One was burned in effigy some years ago, and a friend of mine saw her *sanbenito* himself, hanging in a Toledo church. For her own good, if nothing else, your Doña Inés should either stay away from her Antwerp cousins, or never return to Spain."

Neither Encina nor I said a word. Then Pedro spoke again, "With your permission, I will pass along what you have said to the Tribunal here at Salamanca. There is nothing at all to fear. Inés will never come here, and your gesture, so freely given, will keep your reputation safe—and hers."

"But what gesture did I make?" I cried. "And how does it protect her?"

His smile settled like a small black worm beneath my ribs. "You worry far too much," he said. "My only concern is that the Castros of Antwerp are too kind to her, too welcoming. There is nothing at all to this. I am sorry to have pained you so."

And Encina? All this time, he gazed into the hearth coals, saying nothing at all, and now I understood too well. What could he safely say?

"And who is to warn her to stay out of Spain?" I asked. "She goes where her lady Juana goes."

Pedro smiled again, but with a little sadness about his eyes and mouth. "If she is pious, she has nothing to fear. If she has gone astray, you should be glad to help her back to the fold."

The room went deadly still, and then he sighed and shrugged, and bade us both goodnight. A moment later Encina said he too was tired, and longed for bed.

In the morning, I met the Professor of Music, the great Diego. We were all in the room when he came to the door, a solemn personage in scholar's robe and cap, and several others with him. Was it seeing him surrounded that made his mother go pale with fear? I could not imagine how they lived: the whole family must be pious and do everything exactly right, not only at church, but here at home. The Tribunal lived inside their home.

Diego, it seemed, had come with other news. Anchieta had asked him to help spread the word among men of letters and music: Prince Juan was now in his last hours. He had already said his farewells to Marguerite, and Deza was hearing his final confession. A messenger had been sent to the kings, and Fernando was even now riding from Alcala de Henares to be at his son's side. Great care was being taken to keep the news from Isabel. The bishops and Fernando agreed: she was not, herself, well enough to travel. But if she knew her Angel was dying, there would be no stopping her.

There was no music in the house of Fermoselle that night. Nor any talk of Antwerp or Portugal or the troubled Castros of Toledo.

The next day, the whole family went to early Mass, and I went with them, and did everything they did, for they were perfect Christians, having practiced so carefully all their lives. The moment we came home, Encina slipped away, and his mother told me he was writing music for the prince's obsequies. He was not alone: almost every composer in Spain was doing the same thing. The chapelmaster of the Salamanca cathedral, Francisco de Torre, himself unwell and soon to be replaced, was composing a great requiem.

A messenger came, and told me to return to Prince Juan's lodging. The consort was not to play, only wait outside in case he woke and asked for music.

When I told Encina this, he stopped his work. He told me to wait, and while I did, he wrote something out. He sealed the paper, and told me to give it to the prince. I shook my head but he pressed it to my hand. "If you go in," he said. "And if he is awake. Just leave it there."

Ambition—like a pox or worm—had eaten his wits.

The streets were very quiet, but not with sleep: students were everywhere, weeping and rumpled and smelling of sour wine. I went to the fine house where the other *bas* musicians stood, their instruments all wrapped or tucked away.

At length Doctor Soto came out, and bade us step inside the gates, and deeper still, beneath an arched passage. Wait here, he said, by this door. He himself said he thought there should be no music at all. But the prince had awakened, and begged for it.

I felt the paper in my pocket, and when no one was looking, I let it fall to the ground. I squeezed my hands together to stop their trembling. I had done what he asked—*just leave it there.*

Encina was waiting for me when I returned.

"You don't have it any more. To whom did you give it?"

"No one you know," I said. "But I left it there."

"Well, I thank you." He sighed. And then he said, "He is going to die in Deza's arms."

"And so he should," I said.

"There was a time," said Encina, "when I thought such an honor would be mine."

The hairs on my arms stood up. Where was the old Encina—and where was I?

He shook his head as if to shake the fever away. He told me he had work to do—his music would be needed soon enough.

In my dreams that night the little slipper rose and fell on its sly gray swell. It fell plaintively into every little watery trough. It seemed to be singing—a halting, broken lament. A shoe singing—I shook myself awake. But it was just a little night-bird, calling out from its tree.

"All Spain Is Sad," composed by Juan del Encina on the occasion of the prince's death, is a miracle of heartbreak and beauty. I fear my portrait of him has put you off. Forget the man, but let his music carry you to the depths he was not at liberty to show in life. It is a miracle, too, that the song was not lost, for there was a great sea of elegies and funeral masses and works of every kind. The days that followed would overflow with astonishing works—Juan de Anchieta's *Libera me, Domine*, and a Requiem mass by Francisco de la Torre. Too many to name.

And in the end, another man got the vacant post, the one Encina wanted so badly. But it was Encina's haunting lament that caught the nation's ear, and has stayed with us since. He is long dead now, but I have heard people far out in the country hum the tune, though most have lost the words, and the name of the man who wrote it.

Marguerite was so veiled and swathed that no one saw her face. But she kept her hand on her swollen waist, for all to see, that we might keep a little hope.

That was good. Because Salamanca's light was out.

And here is something strange: with the death of the prince, my swaying-sickness disappeared, and my appetite returned. But is it really so odd? For three days I had been away from the court, away from the prince's sick-chamber, and from the bitter scent no perfume can mask. I had spent those days fed and nourished by a lady with a gift for broth—and a love of music, too. Sometimes, even now, I see myself in another life, standing by her cooking hearth, and Encina— Encina as I knew him first—stands there, too. No Pedro anywhere in sight. I am telling Encina and his mother about the northern lands, about the cauliflower and cabbage, the butter and the brown ale, about the Castro family, gathered around a table just like theirs, and in this dream of ease there is nothing to fear in the telling. There is no devil's work in the light, in the hands covering the eyes. In the throwing of a piece of dough into the flames, in anything they say or do, and no consequence at all.

A family scene and nothing more. Think of your own. Of silver candlesticks and wine and light on children's faces. Why should it matter how many candles are lit, and when they are blown out, or what words are spoken over them?

I spent one last night at the home of the Fermoselles. I gave the mother my warmest thanks and great regrets, and ruffled the little girl's silky hair. Pedro came forth and wished me well, and the child ran away, then back, and brought me a doll made out of dough. The doll had been baked and glazed to a perfect golden brown. One arm was outstretched, and a tiny finger pointed away. I took the figure in my hands, and asked the little girl to point the way I should go. She smiled and shook her head and said I shouldn't go at all.

I begged leave to go to bed, but Encina asked me to come to his chamber. He said he had a parting gift. Once there, he ducked under the eaves and took up his vihuela.

"Remember that little tune you showed me in the street? I have given it words, and four voices." He played it, and I heard the difference—the play, the lightness, the movement, whereas in mine, each chord lay unadorned, barely speaking to its neighbor.

And now there were words, too. A sad story of ruined love. It goes like this: *I am sorry to tell you, Carillo, that the daughter of Mino-Mingus has married a youth of the town . . .*

He seemed very pleased with it, and looked at me as if I should be pleased too.

"It is greatly improved," I said. "And the words are amusing."

He cocked his head. "I left out the deceptive cadence—that's yours."

My blood was on fire, but I turned away. I was determined to keep my thoughts to myself, for once. I even wondered if he was testing me, knowing the lesson very hard. He taught me all too well. I did not tell him his message to the prince lay soaked in water on a dirty street. I did not tell him what else I had done that very day: that I had mimicked his own lost courtliness, and asked Anchieta if I might be of use to Queen Isabel, after the wedding journey to Portugal. I had reminded Anchieta that if the queen went to Granada, I could be of use, not only as a musician, but as a translator.

Now I bowed again to Encina, and made of my face a smooth hard mask.

"I'm sure you are right about the deceptive cadence—I use it too much. Goodnight."

"Listen," he said. "We may never meet again. But let me give you some advice. The only cure for Inés is a different Inés. It will improve your playing, too."

I could not make my mouth speak. A funny croak came out, and nothing more.

In three months' time, Queen Isabel would see her country briefly blessed. Young Isabel would marry King Manoel of Portugal, and find herself with child. And as a wedding present to his bride, Manoel promised to expel the Portuguese Jews—they might go where they would, to Venice or to an island full of snakes—but if you please, they could not stay in his realms.

The blessing of young Isabel's womb was to prove itself cruel. The young widow-bride, that girl in black beside a clear blue pool, would die giving birth to her son Miguel, and Marguerite's own babe—a little girl—would die in the womb. But the queen in her grief would not give up. Fernando was already in Granada, and she was determined to join him there. Wagons were repaired, musicians and servants assembled. The organ carrier shouldered his burden once again, and swore for all to hear. The infant Miguel traveled south in his grandmother's arms, and the queen's own youngest, Catalina, rode at her side. And that's how I found myself swept south again, my mother's house key still in my pocket, a useless charm. I had the feeling I had made the wish myself, in some dark dream I could not recall.

But not yet. It was still October when I left the house of Fermoselle.

As I did outside the house in Antwerp, I watched, but did not make myself known. It was Friday evening, but I saw no secret Sabbath rites. Only, at the highest window of that home, a troubled man at work, his head lowered as he wrote. I see him still. His words open on the page like seeds bursting open in a fire. Inferior melodies come his way, and are lifted by surprise, colored by sudden depths. The man himself might be a flawed and bitter vessel, but beauty is born from his pen, and will show itself to be the thing that lasts.

It is October, and a little rain, fine as needles, has begun. I see him, and I see his mother, too. Still awake, moving through her house, late at night, a mother cannot stop neatening, straightening, making everything look right. I hear her humming to herself—though she keeps it very low. Tell me if it catches in your ear. Such sweetness. Go on and sing it back to me. Then try to send it packing.

nine

Granada had not a single Castro in it, then or now. In fact, our young scribe here might rest his hand, and the commissioner visit the privies, while I recount what happened in the south. It occurs to me to mention, dear commissioner, that on your way there, you will pass the palace wine cellars. Later, I promise a full tour of their wonders—we have some fine rare things down there. Our cellars are legendary, in fact: they were excavated and expanded by order of our sovereign lady's eldest son. Emperor Charles himself, yes. We were all astonished when he gave the order to extend the caves—not here, where we sit, but on the Street of the Kitchens just nearby. It is a mystery, truly, for he has never loved Tordesillas. He was always anxious and melancholy when he came to see his mother. It was—by his own command—so very quiet here. But he felt obliged to visit her, and his standards in all things, from keeping his mother in hand, to the drinking of good wine, were very exacting. Alas, he has the gout now—and cannot drink as he likes.

But never mind that. Now that his mother has died, he will not come here much. If at all. You must take a bottle when you leave. Take two.

But about Granada. As I said, she matters not at all. Write nothing down. She is only a street gone quiet in the noonday sun, and water singing over stone. Blithe child, that July of our return she acted like she'd never been conquered at all, only briefly mishandled, then soothed back into her tender skin by a mother's hand. Imagine a conqueror's distress, awakened at dawn by the scent of jasmine and the call to prayer in el Albaicín. It could not be. After all the

Catholic Kings had suffered—a son and daughter dead, their greatest hope a sickly, fretful babe—still the Moorish women went about in robe and veil, murmuring the wrong things on the wrong days, and the men carried daggers in their belts. Our city: ever her sensual, wrong-headed self, with the exception of a little emptiness in the Jewish quarter.

Our city—I misspeak. Nor does it mean anything that I still carried, on my person, a little key to a door in that emptiness. Remember, I am the fool who saw purple in the sky. And everyone knows you cannot put a color into music.

Nor was the quiet real. One night a bailiff went into el Albaicín to make an arrest, and was stabbed in the street, his body hidden by the people there. The Moors had armed themselves, and no one could get in or out. It took Bishop Talavera three days to reach their leaders and bring some calm—I know, for I went along one day, wearing a special translator's badge, to ease the speech between them. He was a good and generous man, and trusted by the Moors, and this was, I believe, the last time words were used in the art of persuasion. The kings were, by then, under Bishop Cisneros' sway, and by his lights, Talavera's methods were too soft, too slow. It was only a matter of time before Talavera himself was accused of having impure blood. Soon enough, he was himself under arrest. Later, these charges would fall down, but not until the purpose was served: no more Talavera to reason with the Moors.

The kings were done with reasoning.

I was sixteen that year, and full of sinful dreams. I sowed them only in my mind of course, and confined them to the exotic Albaicín, to a certain courtyard vined with delicate horns of white, a dark-eyed singer veiled and dancing at its heart. Inés, it's true, got in my way from time to time: a stubborn girl with a steady gaze I could not meet. But I learned how to give her a Flemish apron and heavy shoes, and to repeat like a spell Encina's words: *The only cure for Inés is a different Inés. It will improve your playing, too.*

All such dreams were short, made shorter still by the anxious Basque, Juan de Anchieta. If our instruments needed repair, or our bodies physic, he said, we must find our help within the fortress walls—and as he said it, his lips seemed to twitch with something he could not say. I took him to mean that another kind of relief could be found there as well, late at night in some far lane or corner of the gardens—if, that is, a player was ever free to roam. It seems to me we were forever readying ourselves to play, or playing, or resting so we might play again. In between, we knelt and prayed and took the Sacrament and learned to love the Only Son of God.

And then we played again.

A new young vihuelist was with us that July, so freshly baptized he still wore a crust of oil and chrism on his brow. A brilliant, quiet Granadan Moor; blind from birth, and not yet twelve. He was put in my charge, and was no trouble at all: he learned very swiftly how things were done, in chapel and at court—far more swiftly than I. One morning not long after his arrival, Anchieta called us both to his side. At the queen's command, he said, we were to go to a certain corridor, and find there a large trunk. He told us where to find it— he said it was larger than all the others—and bade us bring out "the Moorish peasant clothes and the lute you find in there." He said this very quick and low, as if the words themselves might be a sin.

"Lute?" I asked.

"A Moorish lute," he said. "The old outmoded kind. You two will perform a little scene to please our lady, to make her smile." With a wave of his hand, we were dismissed.

It was the very trunk—big enough, I swear, to fit a man—where, six years before, I'd cried *bywlh*, *'ud*, and Encina had been forced to drag me away. I had never seen it unlatched, but now its lock was gone. Together we lifted the heavy lid. It was full of bright old clothes and caps, velvet capes and masks—and my young friend, who could not bear bad smells, reared back from the musty cloud. I was nearly shaking as I plunged and dove, like any pirate who has, at last, drawn near the thing he dreamed. My hands rooted and dug, and felt about, until I reached smooth wood and strings, and heard a muffled, plaintive twang.

Gentlemen, I lifted out my father's oud. She was badly out of tune, her strings in ruin, and when I held her in the window light, I saw her back, and the little wound—it was neither crack nor dent, but an old crust of dirt.

I held her close, then took her to the man who mended all our instruments. At first he refused, but then I explained it was by Anchieta's order, to entertain the queen, and warily, he relented. What

I hadn't expected was that I myself would falter. That afternoon, as I held the oud under Anchieta's bland but watchful eye, my fingers stiffened and refused to move. I pretended I could not remember how the thing was played, and handed her to my Morisco friend. So in the Nasrid gardens, under a silken shade, he and I wore the clothes of Moorish country boys—yokels, you might say—and together we mocked the music of our conquered home. For all that, his fingers moved like lightning on the strings, and I felt a kind of joyous pain. I have forgotten much, but will always remember his fingers moving on the strings, how they knew, like water over stones, exactly where to slide or stay.

Queen Isabel smiled, and all the courtiers followed suit. She was soothed, and the playing might have gone on till Vespers, if little Miguel had not begun to whimper and fret. The queen raised her hand to call it done, and Anchieta bade me take "the old thing" away, and put it back where it had lain.

I did as I was asked. But now I knew her hiding place.

Autumn came, and Fernando went to the mountains to witness a great event: the baptism of the village of Lanjaron, or what remained of it: a hundred women, children, and old men in one afternoon. There was not a moment to lose: while the chrism dried to a crust on their foreheads, his soldiers came and slaughtered them all.

Thus they went to heaven as Christians, and taught a lesson as they went.

Lessons the other mountain villages could not seem to learn. For if Granada simmered, the Alpujarras boiled and rebelled. The queen went, for safety's sake, to Seville, and we all lumbered there with her, even the organ carrier, his face ever longer, his spine a tortured curve. In Seville I passed my sixteenth year, and my seventeenth, too. And still I had not found the cure for Inés.

Then it was July again, and we returned to Granada. Many among us had fever at night, as did the queen herself. Her face was pale and swollen, nor could she sit astride a horse, for the blood would pool in her legs. The child Miguel wailed, or he was too quiet. He could not sleep, or he slept too much, and we had no more mummeries or plays. Then, one summer night—the child was nearly two—the palace quiet was broken by a grandmother's cry.

The hope of all Spain had died in Queen Isabel's arms.

He was laid to rest in the new cathedral, while the workmen hammered just beyond. The obsequies went on for days. The queen wore black and fasted; she prayed and haunted the rims of the Nasrids' pools. Her youngest, Catalina, stayed very near: she was bound for England soon, and the queen began to fret about the future, as well she ought. She still loved music, but the sounds of plucked strings made her pale. She told Anchieta to let his chamber players rest. For now, she said, we will have only voices, and only in church. She bade him write new work.

He went to his writing table, and though he felt unwell, he wrote, that autumn, some beautiful things. And while he did, our little flock, like any in a darkened pen, began to press our noses through the slats, and look for the unlocked gate.

I meant to say before: musicians and chapel singers slept as we always had, in whatever alcove or passage would hold us, most of us on pallets, our masters on beds. Anchieta had his high and curtained place, and I had a pallet on the floor nearby, the blind Morisco player at my side. I was still a light sleeper, and Anchieta still a deep and melodious one. I was awake a good many hours each night, lying beneath those fine blue ceilings, beneath the Quran's words, written over and over: *There is no conqueror but God.* It was on one of those endless nights that the idea came to me—a mad idea, as you'll see. To take the oud from her trunk, and hide her somewhere else, until such time as I could visit el Albaicín as Encina had once done.

So it was that one night, as Anchieta's night-song rumbled peacefully away, that I rose and woke the young Morisco. I took his arm, and stole a rush-light from the wall. I had made no real plan—it was all a kind of dream to me. But I knew where to begin, and soon we stood in the corridor, kneeling before the great trunk that held the costumes and my father's oud.

The torch sputtered, and gave out little light, but I thought I knew exactly where I'd put her back, and plunged my hands into the tangled nest of old clothes. And though I was careful, it seemed that every curve of wood or silk or tambor's skin wanted to slip its bonds and sing my name. At last the Morisco laid his hand firmly on my arm, and whispered, in our native tongue, "Here, let me try." From darkness into darkness he dropped his delicate hands. Without a single sound he rose her up, as if he knew precisely where she lay. But something else was wrong. He gave out a little cry, quiet as a catch in his breath. I made him stop, and hold out his hand, and in the weakened rush-light I saw his thumb: a sliver of wood from the ancient trunk was lodged in its plump tip, on his plucking, strumming hand.

In the morning, I brought him to the barber, who frowned and lanced it and wrapped it well. "You should have come before," he said. "The infection has already set in."

Of the oud: I wrapped her in a cloth, and then a sack, and slipped her, that night, beneath Anchieta's bed.

The night after the final obsequies for Miguel, Anchieta gave everyone "a night of rest." We were, of course, to remain within the fortress walls. But beneath my cloak I had put on my translator's badge, and once he was asleep—and the young Morisco, too, though he tossed a little on his mat—I slipped away under a rising moon, along pool and fountain, into the gardens of the Generalife. I came to the last watchman with his rush-light burning. I showed him the badge, and he gave me a wink, and I remembered what Encina had said: *This is the guard I know.*

Beyond the walls, I floated free, like water released from stone. Only one small night-bird sounded the alarm. I must have passed the place where I had fallen from the tree, where Inés had whispered my name in my ear and told me to keep it to myself.

I took the moonlit slope at a trot. I was ever the child I had been. On my back, my father's oud. And in my pocket, my mother's key.

There were two or three great houses left, and one of these bore lights. These, I guessed, had been emptied out and given to nobles and merchants owed favors by the kings. I came to a turning, and it opened to a field bestrewn with fallen flags. No houses, no doors, no Ana's for bread or the vegetable stall with its scattering of onion skins on market days. Of silks and spices in baskets, nothing. A guard passed by, tilting his lantern to see my badge. He pointed to the field and crossed himself most piously. "They made this field to honor the prince," he said. And so it was: they had flattened thirty homes for a young man who had crumbled to bits.

The synagogue now a church. And in the lane just below, a house for the poor and sick, and before it a plaza, and yet another field. A dry hot wind blew across it now, and drove up dust.

I went into the church where, as a child, I sat with my father and prodded him awake. And I prayed again, and well you may believe it, to the correct God this time. The key lay heavy in my pocket. I knew I should throw it away.

But a moment later, I fingered it again. I stood in my street and closed my eyes. Imagined the street still a street, the door still a door. In my heart I went closer still, and felt around the lintel till I dreamed a little bump: my mother's *mezuzah*. If my lips moved, it was without sound, and without my will, and if I put my key inside a lock, it was only in a dream that it still fit, still opened to a familiar room, a tiny cooking hearth, four cushions plumped against a wall. Only in a dream do I take another step, and then one more, and as I go each room unfolds herself to me, until I am in the courtyard, beneath the fig, making water under the rustle of summer leaves.

In real life I was still in the rubble of the old street, and voices rose, not far away. I opened my eyes, and firmly closed my lips. The house, my hand, the key. I was suddenly very tired—otherwise I cannot explain why I walked further down instead of up. Down past a cluster of empty stalls where once a thousand stood, stalls for silk and spices and fruits, for shoes and jackets and lace. Down, the wrong way to go. For all these streets led to the Darro, and to the little bridge, and beyond it, the rebellious enclave of el Albaicín.

I crossed the little bridge and followed the river up the other side. A sweet white curve—the smallest of lanes—such things have always drawn me. Ghost from that other hill, I made my way in, and began the climb.

A bright and simmering quiet: I knew it now for what it hid. Not a soul was visible in that first steep street. Nothing but the pale clink of forks, and hushed voices speaking a language I hadn't heard for seven years. What were they talking about? Fernando, and the baptized souls of Lanjeron?

Or just how good the cooking was.

A trickle of men began to make its way past me, headed downhill. I kept winding upward until the houses stood far apart, and then I saw the first hole in the rock, whitewashed, too. A woman sat outside it on a smooth stone, sorting out beans and watching. She glanced up and wrinkled her brow at me, then went back to her sorting.

The lane up the hillside wound higher still, until all was scrub and rock and spiny plants I hadn't seen before. One last insect sang his fading song, and over it, from the hills above—from inside the rock itself—I swore I heard strumming, voices, festive shouts. I remembered how I'd thought I heard murmurs in Toledo's springs, and shook the dream away. But at another cave, another old woman glanced up from her work, and gave me the faintest smile. It was all I needed: "Music?" I said, in the tongue I thought we shared, and showed her my oud. She looked puzzled, but lifted her chin just once, and so I went in.

It was not the courtyard of my dreams, with its vines and stars, but a smoky, low-ceilinged room, yet one thing was the same: musicians ranged against the wall, tuning, chatting, waiting to begin. The room—I remember it well—seemed otherwise full of grandmothers in black, with brightly colored shawls. I thought, this is the curse you brought on yourself: you seek a dark-eyed singer veiled in white, and you are sent a grandmother who has lost all of her teeth. And what a smell was there—of garlic and goat and human sweat—and wine soaked into the straw at our feet. Women came through with baskets of bread and fruit, but I could not eat; between the smell and my anxious hopes, I was a ruined thing. But the oud was my badge of entry now. They smiled and pinched me and showed me what teeth they still had, or the holes where they used to be, and a place was made for me at the end of the musicians' bench. My fingers fumbled at first, but not for long, and the men nodded and seemed not sorry to have me there. We played some time, and the grandmothers danced and sang—and some mothers and girls as well. But no one cast an eye my way.

And then I felt a tiny shift, as if I had somehow stayed too long, or some other business was about to begin. I stood and bowed to all, and began to make my way back out the front, when there was some jostling and chatter. Then I was tugged back in. One of the old women pointed me to a low, dim passage in the rock, so low I had to crouch as I made my way back—and further back. "Where—" I began, but she pressed her finger to her lips and pushed me further still.

You want to know what waited for me ahead, but first let me tell you what lay behind. For the moment I was out of that room, the music and the singing changed; I understood what I had felt was true: they didn't want me there. I remembered, dimly, how something like this had happened with Encina, too. How a man had come and said, "It is best if you go now." As then, the music seemed to change, to take on some deeper life, and the musicians had stopped their playing: everyone sang, and only hand-claps kept the beat. If I hadn't known they were all in that one small room, I would have thought a great procession had come up the hill, for the way it rang out, and seemed to carry a marching beat. It might have been a ballad once, but like a little river swollen by a season's rain, it had grown, in almost no time at all, to a torrent.

They wanted me out—but not out by the front. I saw this now. The old woman had left me in a low back passage, and from here I felt my way further back, until I found myself in an even smaller room. An oil lamp was all that gave it light, and it was too small for chair or pallet or anywhere to stand upright.

It took a moment to see I was not alone.

A young girl, very frightened, was tucked into a corner of the place. Small and dreadfully thin and wearing a long white shift, her arms covered only by a shawl. I pardoned myself and edged a little away, and set down my oud. In time, she ventured out, and then—impossible—laid a hand upon my sleeve.

"You paid?" she said.

I shook my head. "No—no—not that. Trying to get out."

She cocked her head like a bird—I wasn't sure she understood. And in the other room, the passion of the song took yet another turn. One voice emerged—a man's—and it was as if a heart had found its voice, and showed, with open throat, how much it ached. My ear went there; I could not keep it in this room. This room where I knew I should not be.

"Here, lie," she said, taking my hand to her chest and tugging me toward a heap of faded silks I hadn't seen before.

Did the music reach a sudden pitch, or did I cry out myself, in my fear of what might happen next? I sat down, and she put forth her little hand, like a kitten's paw, and laid it where a man should rise.

Well, nothing did.

She looked at me, surprised.

I shook my head and put her hand aside. "Eunuch," I said. "I have no—" and the child looked at me as if I were her brother, her friend. She grasped my hand and held it to her chest again, and more amazing still, she crawled into my lap and began to rock. And if you may believe me, she began to hum, and put two fingers in her mouth, and I thought, the child is going to fall asleep. In some other life, I thought, how I would love to cradle a child of my own like this, and lean against an ordinary wall and rest. I held her awhile, until my arms went nearly numb. I lifted her away from my lap, and looked at her eyes in the wretched light. They were dull, exhausted, blank as stones. Now I understood: she had been told to keep me there, out of sight, as long as she could.

There was a rattling of the doorway beads, and a grandmother stood frowning, beckoning me out with haste. The music had stopped, and I heard sounds of jostling and rushing about. *Go,* said the grandmother, and urged me through another passage, narrow and low, until we stood together on a path cut into the hill. She pointed toward the ravine between the hills, and gave me another small push.

So much for my dream of a dark-eyed singer dancing in her veils. I had received, instead, an hour among grandmothers and little girls, all in their bright shawls, the smell of spice and earth. Once more I stumbled out from a home, falling forward with my father's oud.

From the path I could see the Alhambra on its hill, the moon fully risen now. I began to pick my way down into the ravine, and some hours later, from its depths, I looked back up to see the first flames of a fire set that night in el Albaicín. By Christian guards, or by the people themselves, to keep their new masters out?

I never knew.

Master Anchieta's advice was right, of course. I need not have left the fortress to find the relief I sought. I came back in the way I left, and within three steps of the winking guard, I found I was not alone. A woman linked her arm tightly through one of mine. A big man stood just beyond, where I could not see his face: a cloaked and hooded figure in the dark. *Seventeen maravedis, lad*—and this I gave—and with a swiftness I have never known before or since, I found myself pressed against a fortress wall, unlaced below and bare as a tender babe. I was caressed and handled in places high and low until I thought to weep—or burst apart.

And then I was no eunuch, sirs. It was over and done.

A whistle and a throaty laugh. "Well, well, this one's circumcised. What's your name, young man?"

I was lucky that night. Somewhere in the distance, shouts and cries began. "Not again," sighed the woman, straightening her skirts and shoving me away. "There's trouble across the way."

I was treated to another kind of silence now. The kind when walls themselves go mute. You didn't know they speak? They do. Except for those days—which I pray you learn to hear—when even they, in all their innocence, feel overwhelmed by shame.

I put the oud away, deep in the trunk, and walked quietly to my sleeping place. In the first gray light I saw: the high bed empty, bedclothes strewn about. The pallet empty too—empty of my Moorish friend. I remembered his hot red thumb, the tossing sleep. My heart began to thrum.

He was not at Matins, nor at Prime. And when I asked where he had gone, Anchieta looked worn and grave. "And where were *you?*" he said. Then he shook his head. "No matter now. There was nothing to be done. The infection was severe. He will live, but he will never play. He is gone from court."

Long lithe fingers, such speed and surprise and all he might have done. The great vihuelists yet to come: Narváez, Milan, the great blind Ludovico himself, whose inward dreams took flights no human fingers could truly follow. And where did *this* young Ludovico vanish to, with his ruined thumb? What became of him? Here was yet another thing I would never know.

I am thinking of intervals again. It strikes me now: any small gesture might carry tenderness, and inside that, the shadow of the future itself. What do I mean, you ask? But surely you can guess. Have you ever dreamed a pretty path, a place you used to know and love, and the people too, who sang and baked and tried to live their lives in peace? You dream of going, you touch it—barely—in your sleep and feel the sunlight on your face. Stay here, stay here—and you tighten your fingers round its slender neck, and as you do, it goes awry, becomes a frightened child, a smiling mouth of rotted teeth, a hole in the earth where one day, a cellar will stand. Don't look down, for you might be lowered to places far worse, and harder to believe.

Why is it that some people walk like dreamers to the darkest place? Some might dream of scented chambers draped with silks, where love will revive and make us whole. Others see a table spread with pure white linen, silver, bread and wine, in whose candle glow we close our eyes to hold the light inside. Why must sweetness curdle, or awaken someone else's fear and hate? One twist of the rope. Two twists. It is good and tight—are you still not ready yet to tell us what you know?

I meant nothing—no. I never meant to go so dark.

It took Queen Isabel's household a few more months to leave Granada. First she had to send Catalina to England to marry Arthur, another frail, ill-fated prince. Her majesty's legs were too swollen, her fever too high, to accompany this daughter to the ships. And so we waited. There was no hurry: Juana and Philippe were very slow to make their own journey back to Spain. It seemed Philippe had been told by an old wise woman that he was destined to die by water. Therefore they must travel overland, and linger at Blois at Christmastide, for all to see. There was so much on Queen Isabel's mind that it mattered not at all what we packed for the journey north. I never troubled her about the oud, nor Anchieta either: I simply went back to the trunk and fetched it out, along with a few Moorish costumes to go along. I took these to the organ carrier and his men, and lied with great ease: these things, said I, are to be brought to Toledo "for mummeries and things to entertain the Burgundians at court."

I received no squint or trouble at all, only the sigh of the organ carrier, a man well-acquainted with elaborate and foolish requests.

It was not until spring of 1502 that we stood at the gates of Toledo to welcome the Burgundians in proper style. Three hundred Flemings were in their train, some with trumpet, shawm, and pipe—and *bas* musicians too, waiting with their vielles and lutes to play in chambers at quieter times. These lutes, I should say, were hastily put in their cases. The Catholic Kings preferred the vihuela to the lute. Was it because the lute looked so much like its ancestor, *al 'ud*?

Well, whatever the reason, the Burgundians were about to be given music lessons, and taught how to properly say their prayers and dress and eat.

And if, in Toledo's swollen crowd there was one small and frowning female face, I confess I searched and found it, then quickly looked away. I steadied my heart to a firmer beat, and cooled my face into a somber mask. I was a man of experience now, and Inés de Castro must be very, very far behind.

But why was she wearing a gown and hood of deepest black? Had she married the spice merchant's son after all, and was she already his widow?

I refused to think of what she might have suffered—the death of a husband very young. No, I was seventeen, and could think only of the fact that she had lain abed in sweet-smelling linen sheets, the scent of cinnamon in her lover's hair.

No rough bark, no fortress walls for her. No haste or shame or mocking laughter.

She was so strangely fleet. I could not seem to catch her.

ten

If I were a piece of music, instead of one who plays, you would hear what I am afraid to say. My variations are sometimes light and thin as northern lace, other times too dark and slow for dancing. But always, beneath, a tune whose notes yearn to bend.

No. A bright surface is just that, and nothing more. There is no mystery in the way certain notes cling firmly to their places on the staff.

Nor was there any mystery about Toledo the year I saw Inés again, and yet I felt uneasy there. It had been over a hundred years since the city's two *juderías* had been purified by a righteous mob, and since Inés's great-grandmother, like so many others, had buried her silver candlesticks and sent her children to the old synagogue to kneel before a baptismal font. Still, the new residents complained of disturbing sounds in cellars and caves, especially beneath the palace where long ago the prosperous Jew Samuel ha-Levi, adviser to kings, lived and gazed out on the synagogue he'd built.

That palace now belonged to the Marquis of Villena. Everyone knew that the Pacheco family might be scratched for old Jewish blood if the need arose. But this was unlikely to happen. The Marquis was a cousin of King Fernando himself. So Queen Isabel, perhaps to show how unafraid she was of Jewish ghosts, courageously planted her daughter Juana and her Burgundian there, along with both their households.

I only bring it up because I am slow-witted, and can't make out how one noble family rises, while another finds itself forever kneeling at the abyss.

And also to say how strange it was to find myself back in the garden where, some seven years before, I had pressed my ear to the ground and thought I heard the murmur of Hebrew chant.

It was quiet now.

Old gray cistern, little pear tree. Abandoned between owners, why should you keep singing?

No more poetry, Inés would say. And she would be right, for it is July again, and here is her fool, reprising his role as Orpheus-in-a-garden that rolls on wheels. Again I am robed and sandaled, laurel-crowned, cradling a vihuela in my arms. Are these the same small dogs as before, shivering and shitting at my feet? The same white doves fluttering and shitting in their cage? One thing is new: this time Eurydice stands so close behind my stool that when our "chariot" lurches forward, her knee sometimes presses against my spine: I feel it even now, so small and insisting. At any rate, you know the tale: she is following me out of Hades' realm, and if I look back, I'll lose her forever. No danger of my looking back: if she saw my face, she'd know I was keeping a secret from her. Her bright eye, always searching.

I forgot to mention: widow though she was, they had veiled her all in white to play my bride. I'd gotten a look as they helped her up: still slender, dark-haired, small. She had not grown plump on Flemish butter as I'd hoped.

"It is good you are seated," she said. "Or else a breeze would send you flying."

"I was sturdy enough for the women of Granada," I heard myself say.

Or did I simply squeak like a cornered mouse? For she made no reply, and here came Philippe, already calling himself Prince of Castile, to inspect our little scene. He was in full feather, all black silk and martin, trailed by a noisy train of Burgundians, but bearing on his pretty face a faded rash of spots. The gossips had long since given out the news: how he'd been stricken by the measles just outside the town, and the triumphant entry had been delayed. Still, he'd played it like a hand of cards: Fernando was forced to visit him in some country house, and pay his respects.

Now Philippe said something to his nearest man, who gave it to me in turn. "*Monseigneur* says your playing has improved. He hopes your education did not cost the kings too much."

I bowed, and lowered my eyes until the party had moved on.

Inés leaned down. "Education?" Her knee pressed against a knob of my back—I felt it like a brand, and prayed the booming noise in the Villenas' great hall would drown us both, or at least hide my clumsy playing.

She tried again: "I, for one, hope your teacher *was* well-paid, so you're less afraid of ladies when the prince decides to drag you north."

I bent swiftly to the strings. I had good reason. Who could tune in all that noise? It hardly mattered: the Burgundian procession took up all light and air. And so, while she could, Inés told me of her fears: how *Monseigneur* only paid for Juana's expenses once a male heir was born; how he made his wife tell him everything her parents said, then shared this with his French advisers. "In return," she said, "he tells the gossips—and her parents' own ambassadors—that she is fragile, ill, unfit, and they, of course, send it further out. She is 'too much under the sway of Saturn,'" and here Inés gave out the faintest growl.

"Who would not be, if raised to rule then treated thus?" she said. "Tell me, would her husband be so brave in bearing young? How is she unfit?" And then she said, "*I* think she was born under a planet not yet named."

She might have said it of herself, of her great-grandmother and all women in between. And of women I have since met. For what planet is it that does not shelter a bright and passionate voice, but raises high its own four winds, and bids them gust each way at once?

Then she told me how neither Fernando nor his son-in-law had learned the other's tongue. Only Juana could interpret and translate, and this good work, without which nothing could be done—including those arrangements excluding her—would barely be noted in the official report. Well, let it be noted here.

"And here at home?" said Inés, pausing for breath. "Is there any gossip, any news?"

I held up my hand: we were drawing close to the dais. If I told her what Encina's brother had said, and warned her to be careful, what would it stir up, and how far might the panic spread? So I shook my head, and kept my eye on Princess Juana—would I see signs of her famous melancholy as she knelt before her parents and kissed their hands? It's true she was thin, but her face and gestures were graceful, calm. It was the queen who worried me: the chilly gaze, the tight mouth. I saw what Inés meant: this royal daughter might write poetry and compose, Latinize, perform an elegant dance. She might be brave at sea, marry a northern nation, produce a litter of healthy heirs, and interpret for men who wanted her out of the way. Yet somehow this mother pursed her lips, and this father's eyes, though swimming bright, held something back.

Clearly they wished it was their Angel who performed before them now. The Angel, who might croak out the tenor line for a motet and receive thunderous applause. Somehow it was not enough that Juana should do whatever they asked, and stay alive in the doing of it.

At last I took a chance. "And you?" I murmured. "Did I see you in widow's clothes?"

"I was promised to the spice dealer's son," she said. "Since we were children. Then winter came."

Something kicked in my chest, and I saw Encina pressing her against the Alhambra's walls at night, her hood flung back, her chin upraised.

She didn't wait for me to gather my wits. "I fear for our princess," she said. "*Monseigneur* has a way of getting what he wants."

I nodded. And like a dreamer helpless in his dream, I heard my words fall down a well: "But Doña Inés, is there anyone to worry about you?"

She leaned in close. "You are kind," she said, in the lightest voice. "But why should anyone be concerned for me?"

"No reason," I said. "Only that the Castros of Toledo have a history, and all must know of your return—"

"What do you know of our history?" she said, her voice very low. "And who is 'all'"?

For an endless moment we rocked along.

"Tell me what you've heard," she said. "And from whom. Be quick. Or I will—"

"Nothing, no one," I said. "I only meant your great-grandmother, and the lady I saw at the *auto de fé*. I don't know anything else."

"Liar," she said. And then, "Keep playing!" For it seems I had stopped. We had reached the dais, its canopy of cloth-of-gold. The prince came up, and knelt at Juana's side.

A scene of royal harmony, of youthful health and light and readiness to lead. I played. Inés sang.

Later we learned that Prince Philippe, warmed by our music, paid a visit that night to the chamber of his "fragile, unfit" wife, and got her once again with child.

That summer, at every ceremony, mass or dance, I learned where Inés would likely stand or sit, in what pew or clutch of ladies, and at what table. I had, from the musicians' perch in the Villena house, a good view, and the luxury of appearing occupied if anyone glanced up. Inés was always where she ought to be, and still favoring green—did she *want* to stand out? Yet no one pointed her out, or whisked her away, nor was I called to testify, under oath, about what I had seen and heard in Antwerp. I began to think that Pedro de Fermoselle had simply been testing me, to demonstrate to his brother how weak-witted I was, and not to be trusted.

Or no one, at the moment, cared. There was such a frenzy about that summer and fall, a constant need to celebrate. Juana let it be known she had dreamed of a boy, and her mother swiftly added a prophecy: this one will be raised in Spain, and learn to speak our native tongue. In the meantime, the kings tried to keep their son-in-law from leaving—for he hated the heat, he hated the food, there was nothing to do. Again and again the royal coffers were filled and emptied to keep him entertained. Every Spanish heretic worth saving seemed to have a little casket packed with heirloom jewels, or gold and silver coin saved up for years, and more than one Flemish singer thus found himself suddenly in possession of a fine old house—if, that is, he was willing to put up with the last faint stench of eggplant in the walls. For all that, Philippe's musicians grumbled as we had done up north: olive oil and salted fish, and everyone in somber, scratchy wool. Pierre de la Rue was with us now, as was the composer Encina had mentioned, Alexandre Agricola. I still shudder to think how vain I was, how bold in Agricola's presence. I went so far as to work out some of his songs for vihuela. He patted me on the back, indulged me, invited me to play them at suppers. He declared the vihuela a fine instrument, and called her "the melancholy cousin of the lute."

In August my fingers stiffened as they always did, and my tunes turned sad, and I slept too much or not at all. At night I lay awake, picturing Pedro's little smile, how even now he might be seated beside an inquisitor, making notes about Inés in a great ledger. I remembered my own words that night in the house of the Fermoselles, how I'd stupidly cried out, "What gesture did I make? And how does it protect her?"

It had felt so right and brave in the moment, then revealed itself, in the quiet of night, as what it truly was: a deadly foolish thing. Yet would it have been any better had I *not* cried out? Wouldn't he have taken my silence as permission?

Well, either way, Pedro was going to take it. The deceptive cadence, in this case, belonged to him—he had left me in mid-air, caught in a musical phrase I didn't dare resolve.

One morning, early in August, there was to be an *auto-de-fé* in the plaza Zocodovar; I reasoned that if Inés had more relatives awaiting trial, they might be paraded that day, and forced to hear their punishments read out. I kept my eye on her that morning at Matins, and sure enough, just after, I saw her speaking with Juana, then curtseying deep and moving away. I caught La Rue as he emerged from the choir, and asked if he would speak to Master Anchieta on my behalf, and tell him I was unwell.

He gave me his old sad smile. "Again to the chase?" he said. "The same young woman as before?"

"The same," I said, "but it isn't love." And I followed Inés out.

She didn't have far to go. The Villena palace lies just at the edge of Toledo's oldest *juderia*, and a few steps further on, she paused to read a notice nailed to a fine house door. She went into the old narrow lane where stalls and small shops once thrived: sellers of salt and spices and leather goods, of dried fruits and swords and silk. Some were boarded up for good; others belonged to Christian merchants now. And did I dream her pockets began to sag a little as she went in and out? Last of all, she slipped into the church of Santa Maria la Blanca, and crossed herself at the font, and knelt before the Virgin, then stood up and looked up to the old balcony, as if the ghost of her great-grandmother sat there still, itching to give her good advice.

Nor did she linger there. Within minutes she was walking up the steep hill toward the plaza, joining a noisy, growing crowd as I had done those years before. And as before, the distant thunder of drums rushed through my veins. The balconies and arches of the plaza were even more filled than before, and there were more criers stationed about, ready to shout themselves hoarse. Papers were posted on every door, proclaiming the Edicts of Faith, in case anyone needed to be refreshed. Now that the decree against the Moors had come down, the list of heretical acts was twice as long: the clean blouse on a Friday afternoon, the sweeping of the stoop, and why is the fire cold come Saturday? The failure to eat pork! So many things to watch for in one's neighbors, business partners, servants, employers—whom have I forgotten?

After the sermon, the people were blessed. And then a brief hush fell, only to be followed by waves of jeering shouts as the first penitent emerged from the church doors, and another followed, until, once more, a snaking yellow line of dejected forms, some very tidy and clean, others with their legs smeared dark, came shuffling past. There was one line for men, and another for women, with sometimes a child or two in tow. If they wept, you couldn't hear for the trumpets and drums, the crowd, the criers and the chants of vendors selling sweets. One by one the condemned knelt before the bishop and his men to hear their sentences. After each arose, a little clutch of well-wishes surged up to encourage them before soldiers pulled them away.

I watched Inés, and saw her lurch a little—three times in all—as three women stepped up to the scaffolding and knelt at the bishop's table.

Behind me a man made a sound of disgust in his throat. "Shake a *converso* tree," he said, "and at least one branch will yield a bit of rotten fruit."

"Tell me," I said to him. "Where do they keep the prisoners?"

"In too comfortable a place, from what I hear," he said. "Sometimes they say their old prayers in there, and trim their beards on Friday afternoons. And we pay for it. I say leave them in a hole to rot."

Inés had slipped through the crowd, where women should not be. She was nearly to the front, and I must have begged pardon a thousand times, to keep her within view. I was just in time to see her lift her left foot ever so slightly in the air—a little dance step, nothing more, that would lead a dreamer off a cliff.

I caught her in my arms, and found myself strong enough to hold her there. "Beg pardon," I said, in a clear voice for those nearby to hear. "I saw you were about to faint."

She held unnaturally still in my arms, and why, I don't know, this frightened me more than if she had struggled like some maddened bird. Then I felt her go limp. "The crowd," she murmured. "Can you take me home?" And arm in arm we went, like brother and sister, or cousins long betrothed.

But as soon as we were out of the plaza, she wrenched her arm away, and turned toward me, her eyes bright with tears. "Why did you hold me back?" she said.

"What is it you're trying to do?"

"Repent," she cried. "Are you that big a fool?"

"I'm sure I am," I said. "It would be so much better for you to sleep in prison tonight. But your lady needs you—and what would this do to her?"

She said nothing more, but turned and ran downhill toward the Villenas' palace. This time I did not give chase—did I always have to?

But my action helped my dreams not at all. Still I saw the ledger, her name in Pedro's hand, and my name on the list of witnesses, a list sure to reach Toledo, where it belonged. In the midst of my worrying, one bright, sour note broke through: *when the prince decides to drag you north.*

I took a day or two to weigh my possible fates, and went to my friend La Rue, who was in charge of all the singers, and had the prince's confidence besides. He didn't understand why I wanted to leave, to go back north again. "All because the young lady rejects you?" he said.

"*Pas d'amour,*" I said in my dreadful, halting French. "*J'aime ta musique.*"

He laughed. "No more French, please," he said. "Or I will tell him it is about love."

Dust and summer heat, a mother-in-law's demands—and the sudden, suspicious death of his closest adviser—all things conspired to worry Philippe. He could not wait a moment more, or he feared he too would be dead from poison. By autumn we were at Saragossa. Juana was herself at the mercy of low sullen cramps and her mother's distress over Philippe, and no doubt aware of her husband's country ramblings, disguised as a Turk—it was a joke at market fairs: *Look, here comes the prince, to joust and court a local lass.* Well, who can blame him, so hemmed in by his mother-in-law's rules—or was it by his growing fear of his father-in-law, who was forever handing him a cup, and hovering near to watch him drink?

One day, after yet another audience with Queen Isabel, Philippe could stand it no longer, and informed his wife he was leaving Spain; he could not wait for the child to be born. She begged him to stay, and he said he regretted it, but he must go *now*, and she could follow once the child was born. Juana, it was said, gave full vent to her rage—is it any wonder—and her husband had never seen her so, and was very shocked, and told everyone.

He always told everyone.

But now I had my wish: the list of musicians to travel north was published, and I found myself on it.

You are wondering about the oud—did I manage to bring it along this time? I did, though later I would find myself wishing I had left it behind. I asked La Rue to speak to our new prince on my behalf, to call the oud "a delightful curiosity from his future realms," a sort of "spoil or prize." It worked: Philippe loved everything exotic, and had gone himself in "Moorish garb" to various fairs and jousts. I was given leave to pack my father's oud neatly among a few old peasant pantaloons and cloaks.

It would be two years before I saw it again. I would ask both the organ carrier and La Rue—others, too—but no one seemed to know or care where the old instrument had gone.

Inés did not ask me to stay, or even say goodbye. I thought it likely she would never speak to me again at all. But just before we left, a young boy brought me a small parcel and a message from her. The note was brief: *Please carry this packet to the Castros of Antwerp, with my loving regards.*

I looked inside the parcel before we set out. There was nothing heretical inside. It held three small linen pouches, each containing a handful of dried seeds or pods. They left, in my palm, the faintest scent of my lost home, too pale to satisfy. Was it a kind of joke on me—she had to know I would open the pouch, if not out of curiosity than out of cowardice. A taunt in it, too, for having opened it, would I deliver it, or throw it out along the way?

She could not have made me feel more foolish, or shown me more of myself. Timid smuggler, reluctant spy, I was somehow in her service, no matter what I did.

Philippe was determined to take the overland route, through France—remember, he believed he would die by water—but for all that, he grew very ill in that country he so adored, and nearly succumbed. Who is to say it wouldn't have been a better thing? I don't say it. But someone must have, for among the Burgundians rumors of poison swirled—by which enemy this time heaven only knows. By spring Philippe had recovered enough to travel north again, and word had reached him of the birth of a son. If the child's name, Fernando, bothered our *Monseigneur*, he kept it to himself. By the time we reached the palace at Brussels, he had regained his appetite. He was young. He was grateful for the food and drink he knew, the dear old woods for hunting, the best music for dancing. A hot bath. The finest sheets for after. Who would not fall into them with a pretty maid? Is it not a prince's privilege? Everyone knows it is.

At Brussels we were not lodged in attics, but in a fine house near where Philippe stayed, so we could be called to play at any hour. For if music had been the only food the Angel could stomach, it was drink to Philippe, and the more trouble stirred on his borders, the greater his thirst. Our chamber consort played while he dressed, and while he ate, and before the hunt and beside the tenys court, and of course for the dancing. He danced most with one young woman, famous for her braids of bright gold hair. He dined with her, too, where everyone could see. Nobody minded. Even the children—being raised by their beloved Aunt Marguerite—liked her very well; little Charles, almost three, showed her how fiercely he could pedal his little cart.

The composers were kept busy too: La Rue and Agricola and others wrote new pieces every week, for every occasion. I still love some of these songs, the voices winding and weaving till there is no room in your mind for all that you miss. I went so far as to scratch them out on paper as they might be played on lute or vihuela, and gave them out at evenings, with a singer or two, and with endings whose cadences were not deceptive at all.

That was a quiet, untroubled year for me. Philippe was very occupied, between his pleasures and the trouble at his kingdom's borders. But the end came sooner than I thought: he had not, it seems, forgotten his Spanish wife and the great realms she might bring him if all went well. I know, because I found myself called, now and then, to compose a letter in Spanish to Juana from Philippe, for immediate dispatch—and pen it myself, too.

Now that the child is born and healthy, you must leave Spain, and join me here! Your place is here, with me.

It was hard to imagine how he would balance her return with the golden-haired lady we saw so often at his side. But it was easy enough to picture Juana receiving these letters, her long fingers holding the sheets, already dreaming of escape, the embrace of her handsome knight. *Tirant lo blanc.*

Easy enough, too, to picture Inés at Juana's side, singing with her, reading with her, listening to everything she had to say, and listening, too, to her deepening silences. From messengers we learned the queen was at Segovia, and keeping her daughter close. Isabel was in ill health, and the messenger said, in no uncertain terms, that her daughter was greatly to blame. I had trouble paying attention, I admit: I heard Segovia, and felt only relief. Not Salamanca. Not Toledo. Perhaps Inés was safe.

I admit something else: I had not gone to Antwerp yet, to the cousins. I told myself it was because he kept us so busy, but it was not very far, and I could have gone. It was October that woke me. One night I dreamed of my mother, and a little lemon tree we had, and woke to a pale blue sky. My blood felt alive and aching. It was a strange thing—as if some stupor was lifted. I went to the prince myself—so bold—and asked for two days' leave. He gave his permission with surprising speed, and even said I should take a good horse. Then he smiled, and I knew what he hoped: that I would have a night of sin in the thriving district of that town, and come home refreshed—and shall we say, better educated.

I love the road. I mean the journey itself, neither the leaving nor the arriving. Only between two known points on a map am I fully master of myself, invisible in the sweetness of dusk beneath a line of poplars, the steep thatched roofs of that landscape giving way, here and there, to a fine one made of glazed tiles. Seven years had passed since I'd been here, and there were times I didn't recognize the road: then it had been muddy, rutted, and overhung with great trees, a path through woods. Now, the nearer I came to town, the more it was lined with houses, taverns, shops, and stalls. Wagons lumbered along-side the docks of the great Scheldt, piled high with sacks of grain and cloth, with barrels of herring and salt, and something new—there was one wagon, piled high with cloth sacks, that made me sneeze as I passed, and another, with a bright sparkling scent. Well, I thought, poor Inés's seeds and pods will make a paltry gift.

The Castro house looked different too—the old hearth-room was a shopfront now, with shelves of spices to the ceiling, and in barrels, too. Two young men rushed past me, shouting, as a wagon stopped at the door, and an aproned girl stood behind the counter. Were these the Castro children, all grown? The father of the family looked at me kindly, but I could see he was harried, and didn't remember me.

"Wait here," he said. He opened a trap door to a cellar, and went below.

When he returned, his wife came out from a back room, very richly dressed, and full of watchful dignity. I bowed and said my name, and she, too, frowned and wondered who I was. I said I came with greetings from their cousin Inés, and that I was, myself, deeply sorry about the loss of their son. A look passed between them then, and a long moment, and then the father took my arm, and bade me follow him into their home.

Once inside, I said how fondly I remembered the evening I had spent in their company here. I would not stay; I had brought a little token from their cousin Inés.

A brief light came into the mother's face, and the father took me once again by the arm, and we went up a flight of stairs, and another still, until we came to a room with a table, a hearth, and a window well where a small gray cat sat among pots of herbs, watching every-thing that passed. The atmosphere was strange; I find it hard to describe: On the one hand it was a family scene of such warmth and ease as I had not seen in years. On the other, they acted as if I were a constable, come to peer under the tablecloth and into the bookcase.

I handed the little parcel to the father.

"No note," said the father, with a smile, and the mother shook her head, and said, "Of course not, it's from Inés." Then she emptied each pouch, and held its contents in her palm, and inhaled, before putting the seeds back, and carrying the pouches to the window-well. I asked what she was growing.

"Lavender, mint, and cumin," she said. "Come back next year at this same time, and you will see a little lemon tree."

Gentlemen, I confess I never did. But I saw it anyway, in my mind: the dark waxy leaves of home. The bright scent of hillsides far to the south.

"I would invite you to stay," the father said. "But we are expecting a great shipment of pepper tomorrow, and all will be busy. It shouldn't be, but it is."

I asked him what he meant.

"Isn't that why you came," he said. "For the Great Fast?"

"Tell me," I said. "I don't know."

"We used to go barefoot, and keep the fast, and beg each other's pardon, and that of God. But we are Christians now, as you see, and there will be none of that." Then he looked at me. "Don't you think it's strange you should come today, of all days in the year?"

I said I truly didn't know what day it was. I said—my face growing hot—that I had dreamed of my mother, and felt moved to come.

They were both very quiet for a long time. Then the mother said, "Do you know where she is now?"

"Venice, I hope," I said. "And my brother, too."

"Then," she said softly, "the chances are she is safe."

After a while, I tried again to speak. "I used to sit by my father in synagogue, and listen to his stomach growl."

That's when the father smiled, and put his hand on my head, just for a moment. He did not let it drift down in the old way, but it was kindly meant. "Maybe some part of you still knows," he said. Then he shook his head.

I stayed to supper, and they used some of the spices from home, and at dinner, the father asked me about Inés. Was she attending church regularly, and staying away from those who would wish her harm? We worry about her, they said. She was always a careless, headstrong child. Her mother was that way too.

"Her mother," I asked.

"We don't know where she is," said the woman. "If she were free, we would surely know."

I murmured something about Toledo, and the Castro women in the prisoners' line.

"Don't tell us anything more," the mother said. "No names. But when Inés comes back, make sure she visits us. And perhaps she can stay."

News from home that year was as scarce as the food I craved. Bits reached us like flotsam on the river Scheldt: little Fernando thrived, his grandmother, the great Isabel, sang to him in Spanish. Of his mother, Princess Juana, we heard only a little, none of it good. She had recovered well from the child's birth, but was very low in spirits, and sometimes ate nothing at all. She and the queen could not live in harmony, so they lived apart. The queen, very ill, remained at Segovia, and the princess was biding her time in the fortress called La Mota, near Medina del Campo, waiting for her parents to permit her to travel north. She knew herself detained, and was growing restless.

Then we heard that one of Philippe's letters, written in my own hand, had reached her. She would have read it the way a dreamer reads, and moved forward without thinking, seeing herself as one of the great queens of old, escaping captivity on horseback, by night, with only a few provisions. What did she have but tales of brave women her own mother had told her, or given her to read in the old romances?

No one had ever told her they weren't true stories. Or that if they were, they had darker endings than she had been allowed to hear.

This letter, it seems, gave her such hope that she gathered her small household and ordered wagons readied, everything packed. She was stopped at the fortress gates by her mother's guards. It was November, and very cold, yet she refused to go back inside the fortress, and waited by the portcullis, abandoned by all. "Like an African lioness," said the messenger who told us the tale.

I couldn't help but think there was someone by her side as she stood there, shivering. Someone who went back inside and fetched a blanket, and said to her, Look, my lady, here is a little fruit shed, let us take shelter here, and we will send word to your mother, and it will all come right. And I could hear Juana reply: Will you stay with me, no matter what? Whether we go by sea or land?

I will stay with you, says the faithful Inés.

And in my dream, they travel north that very night, and when they arrive, I escort Inés to her cousins' house and together we stand before the lemon tree and admire how it has grown, in so short a time, to be so sturdy, and bear such bright fruit.

It would, in fact, be three months before Juana was allowed to sail for the Low Countries, and during that time, more dark rumors would spring up. One: that her childish resistance of her mother's wishes was hastening that great lady's death. And another: of a princess still determined to escape her castle-prison and make her way to her handsome prince.

Locura, the legend of her great passion for her husband. Where do these things begin? In the countryside, where people have time to spin tales? Or at court, where it suits those in power to shape a tale? Well, they are doomed to compete, and never harmonize.

Who knows what story of her own poor Juana might have told, had anyone asked?

I was there when her ship arrived at Blankenberghe, and Philippe came on time to meet his wife. There was no lack of pomp and fanfare. Such a pretty scene. He stands on the pier as she disembarks, and her children—Leonor and Charles and small Maria—wait with their attendants on the shore. Philippe takes Juana's hand as he did on their wedding day, once more the knight in her beloved books. She looks up at him, and I watch Inés, who closes her eyes, ever so faintly, against the dangerous open joy that shines in her mistress's face.

All rejoiced. And for two full weeks, there was no sign of trouble at all: no down-curve of petulance that so often lingered about his mouth after an unrewarding hunt, or a tenys match postponed for some business of state. Nor was the golden-haired mistress anywhere to be seen. He looked—for those two weeks—as he had when he first arrived at Brussels. We could see that he was glad to see his wife again. Did he find her lovely again, made more precious by her long absence? And oh, she was very slender, her eyes quite large in her thin face. Did he feel, briefly, some urge to protect her? Or was he just thinking ahead, considering how he would get her in hand while they waited for Queen Isabel, already ill, to breathe her last?

There was much he didn't know, that none of us knew. How, that November, on her deathbed, Queen Isabel would add a codicil to her will: if Juana were not present in Spain, or in some other way unable to rule, King Fernando would be regent of Castile in her stead.

Fernando. Not Philippe.

As I said, it was something he didn't yet know. So, that day, we all watched the falconer raise his arm and call his bird. We heard her little bells jingle, such a plaintive sound, as he lured her from her mother's branch. *Here, my love*—and he held out his well-gloved hand, *look what I have for you.* And she had been well-trained.

And Inés? She stood well back, surrounded by *morisco* slave girls all in white, and apart from that brief closing of her eyes, she gave no hint of all she had seen, all she feared. Her eyes didn't have their usual brightness; but I told myself it was just fatigue from the voyage. She, for her part, did not look at me at all.

Everyone has their version of what happened next—how Juana discovered her husband's golden-haired mistress, and ordered her tresses cut, and how Philippe shouted at his wife where others could see and hear. Soon enough the tale was everywhere. You would have thought we had the plague, and in a way, we did: when our princes are ill, the whole realm takes to its bed. There is a song from that time, by the Fleming we called Urrede, so long had he lived in Spain: *Nunca fué pena mayor*, about the long and gloomy life of a lover betrayed. We played it sometimes, for it was beloved in Spain and far beyond. La Rue once used it in a Mass—a secret musical gift to Juana, our sad royal listener. Death itself would be less a torment, sings the lover.

Music at such times is small consolation. She woke each morning to find another of her country-women gone, and a stranger in that woman's place, waiting to serve her but unable to understand a word she said. Doors were locked from without, and her letters home went mysteriously astray. The news of her mother's death took far too long to reach her, though once it did, she found a way to mourn. Let me explain. One night she called me in for music. The room was draped in black, and many candles lit, as if a catafalque might stand in its midst. The Flemish guards, the Flemish ladies, all nodded solemnly as I came in. Juana was already at her clavichord, and Inés stood at her side. And before that tribunal of Flemish guards, I accompanied them as they sang Queen Isabel's favorite tunes, with subtle turns of melody and mood. Then Juana and Inés looked at one another, and Juana said, "And now we will sing a tune the vihuelist doesn't know, and he will learn it on the spot. It is one from long ago, sung to us by a long-lost nursery maid, Doña Teresa de Castro. We have missed it more than we can say."

And Inés and Juana began to sing, and my heart to squeeze, for I knew the song all too well—it was that old lullaby I told you about before—"Nani, Nani." I suppose it was safe enough to sing in the north. The Flemings did not know who loved it best—Christian, Jew, or Moor.

But what matters most is the solace the music brought our broken royal bird. It carried her back to childhood, to memories of Inés's mother, who, I could see, had played no small part in Juana's early life. Inés's voice was beginning to crack a little—from the Flanders smoke, from all her night-walking, from remembering the mother she'd lost—for what offense she never knew.

But Inés did not weep.

"You should stay indoors, and wrap your throat," said Juana. "You are ruining an excellent voice."

Inés smiled, and then, her eyes very bright, she said, "I'm not like you. I have made no babies at all, but if I don't walk, I will look like a mother of five." She laughed her rough laugh, and my blood jolted against my will.

I still remember how it went that night: Inés's voice against the clavichord, against my own slow-strummed chords. When at last I said goodnight and went to bed, it took some time to find my way to sleep. When I did, it was Inés I saw, wandering the dark woods of Flanders in her white gown, smudged now with the dirt of the woods, and calling back for help. In that dream, I neither stepped to the side, nor held myself back. In that dream, I was a different kind of man. I went to her. I picked up the hem of her gown, to keep it from the mud, and she did not flinch or run.

I have a reason to tell you all this, and it is not to shock you with tales of sin. But there is a little something more along those lines: I fear that night of music inspired our sovereign lady to make a notorious mistake. For one night, soon after, I was sent again to the luthier's house. He was busy, but I didn't care: I could spend my whole life there, looking up at those sweet and undone lutes, still without their frets. One of them was the size of my father's oud, and so like it that it took my breath away.

"Look what we have here," said the luthier. "It is quite a marvel."

He wiped his hands on his apron, and gazed down at the oud, lying there before us both.

"Is it real?" I asked.

He laughed. "It will be," he said, "if you can remember how to tune it."

I held it, and turned it over, and saw the little dark smudge on its back.

"I can fix that," he said. "Shall I?"

"No thank you," I said, my palms gone damp. "But how did it come to be here?"

The luthier shrugged. "The organ carrier brought it to me, some time ago. It was in a box of costumes the prince brought north."

I made to take the oud with me.

"Ah no," he said. Then with mock solemnity, "It belongs to the Crown. It will be waiting for you tonight."

After the evening meal I was sent to the queen's apartments. The Flemish women stood guard as ever. But something was afoot. They lifted their eyes to the ceiling as they sent me in.

The smell was the first thing—have you ever smelled civet? Some men love it; others it makes gag. I have heard it is good for colic. I am afraid I don't do well with it at all.

Many candles had been lit, and a small lamp covered with a red veil so it glowed. Bright cloth had been draped from high corners, and pillows thrown on the floor. Juana's four slaves were draped in silk—or so I thought, until I got closer and saw that these robes were nothing more than bedclothes artfully arranged. The girls lay disported like ladies in a seraglio—how could this be?

Still more impossible: Juana herself lay back against the pillows in her softest robes, her hair unbound.

Inés was the one who beckoned me in. I was, I saw, the only musician in the room, and the only male.

It was Inés who handed me my father's oud.

"You are to play it in the old Moorish way," she said.

"It isn't that simple," I said. "I cannot just—"

She smiled sadly. "You have to," she whispered. "She thinks this will win her husband back."

So I took my seat among the slaves. "It should be played with a plectrum," I mumbled, to no one in particular. And though my palms had sprung sweat again, I gripped the neck. The fingers of my right hand began to move, and looking down, I thought I saw my father's hands.

Did Juana hope that Philippe would be moved by the sinuous voice of an oud? Or by those tones believed by the church to cause irresistible desire to run in the veins—did Juana know this from her girlhood reading? Was such hope still in her, that such sounds might work a miracle of seduction in a disdainful man?

We all heard the tread of boots along the passage. We heard his voice rushing along, speaking to some councilor about matters of state.

Juana was flushed to the throat.

"Play," she commanded, and I swear it was not her voice at all, but that of an invented ancestor, the queen in *Tirant lo blanc,* who had ordered her best sheets sprinkled with civet, and whose lover was so desperate to reach her that he broke a hole in the roof of her bed-chamber.

Alas, there was a makeshift quality to our little scene: old bed-linens stitched to make a Moorish tent. The pillows all the wrong kind. The smell of cat—

The slaves rearranged themselves; it was hard to hold the pose.

And now the lover stood at the threshold, and put his hand to his mouth and nose.

"*Mon amour,*" she said, and gave him a girlish smile.

Well, it's true he was provoked. We saw his throat and face flush as bright as hers. But it was not with lust he burned. His face showed a darker weather now—pursed lips, little shakes of the head, every-thing to indicate disgust, and the depth of this latest affront.

Then he came to where I sat, his lower lip atremble. He looked almost frightened, and it did not take a knowledge of French to know that he wanted me to stop.

Then he was gone.

Juana did not move. She lay very still in her languid pose.

"Play the Urrede tune," she said to me. "The famous one, about faithless love."

eleven

One minute I am holding my father's oud, the next that oud has vanished, and Juana's fragile *tableau d'amour* has entered history as a madwoman's lewd mistake. It was Inés herself who lifted the oud from my arms—*Trust me*, she said, *I will see it safely stowed.* It was Inés who ordered the little encampment dismantled, sent the slaves to their sleeping place, and helped her lady to bed. Two Flemish guards observed it all. I learned this the next day, when Anchieta and I came back to see if Juana wanted music. The chamber door was bolted now, and those same guards stood by, very stiff and worn. As was Inés, pacing the passage in yesterday's gown. A chair stood by the door, but she would not sit; back and forth she went, like someone awaiting news of a birth.

We were allowed in, but under a condition: Philippe—who demanded we call him *His Majesty* now—required that we report everything his wife said and did, and turn over any letters she put into our hands. Especially letters to her father.

His wife. Her father. Not *her majesty*, or *the king*. Philippe was shaping the story his way. And did I catch the faintest twitch of despair around Anchieta's somber mouth? My old hatred almost slipped when I considered all that Anchieta had seen and stored away to keep himself alive, at court, and making music. *Hey Jews, pack up your things!* Was he in disguise himself, on guard lest someone accuse him of carrying a drop of the wrong blood in his veins? Perhaps, in his way, he'd been trying to teach Encina how to survive at court—Encina, who burned too hot and bright to listen.

Well, I was listening.

But Inés—Inés, in the passage, could not keep her own mask from slipping. All her movements, from the lifting of a handkerchief to her eye to the adjustment of her headcloth, which needed no attention, read unnaturally small and neat. She was composing a blurry tune—but not blurry enough.

"Her Majesty is tired now," I said to all when we came out. What I didn't say was that there were three Flemish serving women in the room the whole time, watching her every move. Nor did I say that the new queen of Castile, in her royal prison, mimicked precisely Inés's small moves: the lifted handkerchief, the headcloth shifted without real effect. The same sensation had overcome me as I watched: there was a secret language here, but I was untutored, and Anchieta too well-schooled. One thing was clear: by her silence, by the way she kept her eyes down as we played, I knew she felt betrayed. Who was I but one more servant who had seen her shamed? Had she lain awake all night, learning to see her world anew?

Now she saw: nearly every servant, down to her own musicians, had been swept into her husband's camp while she was far away in Spain. She was alone, and being watched.

That morning, I worked out something else: that all this time, Philippe's eye had not been trained on me at all—or rather, his eye wasn't the thing I should have feared. No—it was Juana's open heart, such an easy mark. He had easily picked off her allies one by one, and closed every door. Who could possibly object? He was, after all, protecting his wife from humiliating herself, the court, and a great nation.

Had I appeared to put myself in his camp when I asked to go north?

Safely stowed, my father's oud—but where? Inés would not say, and every day it was harder to ask. I didn't see her for several days, and began to think she'd been dismissed, and gone for good to Antwerp. But no one knew. A silence tightened all around Juana: to be kind to her would be to fall under suspicion. She did, just once, try to slip me a letter to send off to her father, but I pretended to be busy with a broken string. Anchieta took it with a bow, and gave it straight to Philippe's guards.

Better I had taken it, and dropped it down a well.

The silence lasted into the new year, and I saw Inés once again among the court women making ready to sail for Spain. It was January and when the sea went ominously flat and quiet, I knew what it meant. Soon a little wind would commence, then grow, until the waves heaved us sideways to the sky.

A question: Philippe thought he would die at sea. Hadn't an old woman told him he would die by water? And hadn't his father-in-law, who smiled and held out cups of wine that tasted strange, insisted he return to Spain by boat? With all due respect, if Philippe understood all this, why didn't he fling himself bravely overboard as a gift, and save us all?

The answer is simple: in the event that he survived, he was prepared, this time, to stay in Spain and rule all its lands—fathers-in-law be damned. To this end, the fleet was prepared, along with cooks and servants, two thousand German pike men, and a great many advisers and knights. Let us not forget a swarm of French and Flemish noble ladies, though these last had to be smuggled aboard other ships, lest *Monsigneur's* unpredictable wife fly into a rage and toss them overboard herself.

Of singers and musicians we had a fair number—though there were more who begged to stay behind. We had two chroniclers, of course, to keep a record of every Mass attended, every meal and joyous entry into towns, and what finery and jewels the royal couple wore. Whether they wrote down all the occasions on which we played, I do not know. I suspect they were not interested in music. I only know that they were devoted to Philippe, and that their words must proclaim his grace, his beauty, his devotion to his people and to God.

The first evening, all was still well, and there was music all about the ship, and the feeling of starting anew. We played so late that even Inés felt free enough to thank us. I asked her if she would wait nearby a moment more. I said I wished to speak to her about the queen.

But it was Inés herself I wanted to know about. And so, as the ship rocked lightly under a net of stars, I asked her how she was— and how she'd lasted so long at court. Not sent away by controlling Philippe, nor by Juana herself in a spate of jealous fear.

"*He* doesn't like his women dark," she said in a cheerful voice. "His eye never lights on me." Then she caught her breath. "I wish I could have stayed behind."

"Your cousins are wealthy now," I said. "They would have taken you in."

She sighed. "I don't think so. Their house is already too full."

I thought she merely meant the usual bustle of the merchant business. "As you've said yourself," she went on, "our lady needs me now. There's almost no one left who knows her. Who loves her."

"Did you at least visit? Did you ask if you could stay?"

She gave me, for my trouble, the merest shrug.

"Do you remember," I said, "when you told me you wouldn't be sorry if you never saw Spain again?"

I couldn't see her face, but her voice was strangely warm. "And who are you, my own private inquisitor?"

"And who are you," I replied. "A person who refuses to see the way things are?"

Two sailors walked by, and I knew that in a moment she'd whisk herself away. "Do you know," she said brightly, "not long ago I saw your little lemon tree. It's almost two feet high. But they should move it; there isn't enough light where they keep it now."

Of how Philippe nearly fulfilled his death prophecy, I am sure you can read in his chroniclers' accounts of the great storm. There, too, you can read about his courage; how, barefoot, in shirt and breeches, he knelt on deck and humbled himself before company and crew, and begged our forgiveness, and how, while the storm raged, Juana sat with him, cradled in his loving arms. Oh, it was a portrait of marital harmony to make you forget what you knew. But earlier that morning, I had staggered past a very different tableau. The poop-cabin door had swung open, and a low moaning caught my ear, so I stopped and peered inside. The cabin was lit by a few small swinging lamps, enough to show the seawater sloshing back and forth. Then I heard faint clankings, a leathery creak. A vest of silver mail floated past—a tiny raft of stars—and was swallowed by the dark.

I remember thinking, apropos of nothing, that an oud weighs very little. If she was here on board, she might be tossed overboard and make landfall by herself, though she'd be warped near to death.

Then the lamps revealed what we might call, with all due respect, Philippe's own *tableau d'amour*. It was composed of four Flemish knights on bended knee before a great leather casing big enough to hold a full-grown man and keep him afloat on the sea for days, alive or dead. And in fact it *did* hold a man: one who gave out little choking sobs of fear. In the swinging light, I glimpsed some writing on the back of the case.

Here is Philippe, King of Castile.

Then the ship pitched, and I went down on one knee myself, just beneath a *prie-dieu*, its dampened votives flickering beneath the porcelain head of some sainted lady—I never knew which one. Among the votives lay a scattering of golden coins, but what I remember is how the lady's eyes looked alive in the flickering light. Her lips were curved in a faint smile, as if she were about to speak.

Then another light hovered at the cabin door, and Queen Juana stood there all alone and carrying a lamp. She was richly gowned and seemed to be wearing every gold chain and gleaming jewel she owned. She towered above us in her tall chopines.

Only one of Philippe's knights managed to raise his head and speak.

"Will Madame make a generous offering to save our ship and king?"

She rummaged in the pocket of her gown, and brought out a single copper coin. In two strides she was across the cabin's tiny sea.

She lay the coin among the ducats and looked down at her husband in his leather case. "I am sure we will be safe, for I have never yet heard of a king drowned at sea."

It wasn't Juana's last show of wit—far from it. In England, where we took refuge and waited for the fleet to be repaired, everyone saw her quiet strength. Even King Henry took note. Surely he'd heard the rumors of her "malady," but he also knew how and why a tale is spun. He praised her elegance and called her sane. In all his praise of her we caught the hint of what he could not say: that perhaps it was her husband—with his obvious hunger for power and constant play—who might not last.

We were three months in that green place. Long enough for Philippe to forget how small he looked in a quaking leather case.

Juana came to Windsor only for a little time, to see her sister Catalina, who was Arthur's widow now. Inés was at her side, her face rosy from the cold. She thrived in northern climes, I don't know why. I only longed for warmth and light myself, for a southern, silky air.

It wasn't easy to catch her alone. Since that night on shipboard, she shrank from me, having, as she told me now, said too much.

I was the same fool I'd been before. Sometimes we don't know what is growing in us. But it—the growing fear—knows well enough what it is, and out it comes.

"Please stay in England," I said. "Find a way."

"You are always trying to get rid of me," she said, smiling. Then her eyes seemed to widen. "Or have you been trying to tell me something all this time?"

I tried to tell her what I knew, but I began too slowly, and too far back. It is ever a fault in my storytelling—and Inés's smile made it worse. "Some years ago, I happened to stay at Juan del Encina's family home," I stammered. "The Fermoselles of Salamanca. When Prince Juan was still alive. I met the whole family, and stayed there some days, and Encina asked about you."

"And?" Her smile was gone, and she was pale.

"Nothing. Only—he has a younger brother, Pedro, who watches everyone, everything. He kept asking questions—"

"And you told him what?" she said.

"Only that the people in Antwerp were very kind."

"Kind," she said. "That can't be all. You must have said more. Why did he ask you about me, and what more did you say?"

"Nothing at all," I said. "And I'm sure it doesn't matter. It was years ago—and in Salamanca."

"Very true," she said. "So why are you telling me only now? Wouldn't the danger have passed by now?"

I bowed my head. "I'm sorry to have worried you," I said.

"Don't be sorry," she said, more softly now. Her eyes were brimming as she turned away. It was the first time I'd seen her close to tears.

There is a kind of French song—a "regret" *chanson*—that I learned to play in Philippe's court. The poet would rather die, but he, or she, is fated to live on, with a memory that refuses to dim—sometimes

the beloved is the betrayer, sometimes the betrayed. It doesn't matter which: it's the long years that matter, the body kept alive to sing
of something no one wants to hear. Is the history of our obscure Inés
as worthy of song as the legend of an unfortunate queen? Consider: if
I were dead, and singing to you from beyond the stars, who is to say
which tale would give off the greater glow?

Gentlemen, I will not choose. Let us remember them both.

In April we sailed again for Spain, and of that voyage I have nothing to report—no storm, thank God, no wreck. There is one thing,
perhaps. A trifle, a curiosity, a small failure of duty that might interest our young scribe.

One night I found I couldn't sleep, and took myself above deck for
a bit of fresh night air. In the faint lantern light nearby, I swore I saw
a fellow leaning overboard. How odd that he is ill, I thought, with
the sea so calm. Then I saw him move his arms as if he was letting
something go, and swore, as I watched, that from his hands fell the
whitest of doves, several of them, fluttering, cascading, then one by
one, swallowed by the sea. Well, it was very dark, or I had gone mad.
I waited till he slipped away, then took myself to the railing where
he'd stood. I was in time to see the last fragments disappear. Not
doves at all, as our scribe might already have guessed.

Not doves, but paper. Fine paper, a chronicler's pages, some whole,
some torn.

As I said, the story matters not at all. But I thought it curious.
Something, after all, had been deemed unfit for history's eyes. We
will never know, gentlemen, what it was.

Not long after, we landed at La Coruña's port. But no father stood
with open arms to greet his daughter—now our queen—and listen
to her fears, to tell her what to do. Oh, he had advisers there, and an
envoy by the name of Luis Ferrer, a dour fellow who kept to himself
and said very little, but was always nearby. Fernando was playing a
longer game, with a greater command of the board than his daughter—let alone his son-in-law—could ever grasp. Meanwhile there
were trumpets, banners, local grandees at the ready with fine words,
feasts, and the first faint inklings of demands.

Long after we had disembarked and were on the road, I witnessed
a little marvel worth reporting here: an old woman who stepped out

from the crowd after Philippe's horse had passed. She looked after him, this Galician grandmother all in black, then remarked, in her native tongue, "Mark my words, this king will see more of Spain dead than alive."

On we traveled into summer, the dust rising in the roads. Fernando's absence played Philippe as the wind plays a harp. The strain showed beneath his eyes, though Fernando's envoys did their best to keep him entertained: come watch this bullfight, or try the reed-spear joust. All this he did, but seemed to glance about him more than not. And the more he busied himself, the more Juana withdrew. Still she waited for her father, for his instruction and advice. By then she was waiting for something else, too. Inés told me. Her Majesty had all the signs: the tenderness and swelling of the breasts, the taste of copper on her tongue. Juana was twenty-six years old, and this child would be her sixth.

In June, while she stayed quietly at Burgos, her husband and her father found a way to meet at last. In secret, of course, without telling her. The game between these men grew ever more complex, but one thing was clear: it left the wife and daughter—I doubt they ever called her queen—completely to the side. By the time the court came to stay at the Count of Benavente's house, she had found out about their meeting. She understood they'd signed a treaty to keep her from ruling, on account of her "maladies and passions." There were more machinations here than I can stomach or repeat. What matters is that she knew, and responded in the only way she could.

Once upon a time, I want to say. Once upon a time there was a queen, an exile in her own land, who loved poetry and music and the color red, and bore five healthy heirs before she was twenty-six—and now had another on the way. Such a person must be locked away, for her own health and the health of the nation.

As in all such stories, a great park surrounds the house where the queen is kept, a park bordered by a forest of ancient oaks. The queen has seen this wood before, riding with her intimate, one Doña Inés. The two like to ride along the border of those massy trees, and peer into the fragrant dark, so like the woods in the tales of that beloved old romance, *Tirant lo blanc*.

It is the Count of Benavente himself who takes the two ladies riding that warm day in late June. And it is Juana who, by the count's own judgment, seems quite sane and charming as she asks him if he hears a strange rustling in the woods. Even Inés, riding at her lady's side, doesn't know the plan: that Juana is looking for a clearing in the woods, a path through which to make an escape—though to where, or to what end, it will never be clear.

So Juana rides, and beside her, Inés, that little bird perched gingerly on a big horse. The count, by then, is irritated by the summer heat, by a woman's excitement over a little rustling in the bushes. Furthermore, he needs to take a piss.

He dismounts his horse—it is only for one minute, nothing more—but by the time he looks up, the two women have vanished into a wall of woods.

Imagine those woods, so dark and still on a summer afternoon, only the sound of horses' hoofs on acorn and dry leaf. They are very good riders, these two. How can they not feel, in those woods, an interval of heedless joy? Forget men and their secret meetings, the treaties and their plans to lock you up, the ploys and counter-ploys that will follow in their wake. Juana shakes all that away, but surely the anger still lives in her body, travels straight through to her heels, which seem to kick the horse's flanks with a sudden furious life of their own.

What is poor Inés to do? She must follow where her lady goes.

It was ever thus: a queen spurs her horse to gallop toward a dream of freedom; her favorite is the one who hears the hoofs and horns of guards behind. It is her favorite whose eye discovers a wisp of smoke, a thatched roof ahead: cottage or farmhouse though it be, it is the only shelter on the horizon. Quickly she points it out to her mistress, whose face has gone a little pale. *Ride toward that house*, says Inés. *We'll have a drink of water, and make our way back.*

It so happens that at this house, a working woman—a pastry cook by trade—stirs a pot of stew over quiet embers. She still has to sweep and lay the good white cloth. This woman glances up at a sudden sound; the impossible is already in her doorway. It has taken the shape of two young women in elegant riding clothes—too fine to be mistaken.

She falls to her knees as she should. She is prepared to kneel there for the rest of her life if they ask her to. The sweeping, the stirring, the laying of the clean tablecloth—all have been wiped in one stroke from her mind. What's in that mind now? How do I hide the candlesticks and Kiddush cup, the fine embroidered blouse I've just put on? How do I warn my husband before he comes inside? And our daughter, always alight with questions as she steps into a room—Mother, who are these ladies? Why are they dressed like that? Have they come for the Sabbath meal?

It is hard to say whose luck is worse: the unfortunate Judaizers into whose lives these two noble ladies have burst, or the ill-starred Inés, with her talent for finding the only heretics for miles around. Was it her own buried yearning that brought them to light?

At the cottage door, the queen has regained her sense of privilege, of the great drama of the moment. She says to Inés, "I will stay here till my father comes himself to set things right."

If I was cursed by my own habit of falling just to the side of danger, of life itself, Inés was cursed by its perfect opposite—the habit of falling straight into its arms. Just the week before, the Edicts of Faith had been pronounced in Benavente's church, and the populace invited to keep a sharp eye out: this is how you recognize a secret Jew or Moor. The cottage stood a mile from the town, and the family lived modestly, without servants. The pastry cook had a young apprentice, but she had sent him home just moments before. He was not to return till Monday.

Inés told me all this later: the look—more than pure surprise—on the woman's face when she opened her door. The mingling scents of cumin, cinnamon, and clove that rose above the smell of onions and cooking meat. That was the way Inés's own grandmother, so long ago, had secretly made the Sabbath stew.

Juana seemed to smell it too, and Inés held her breath—what would the queen say?

But Juana said nothing at all. She begged the woman's pardon with simple grace, then turned to Inés. "I will stay in the bake house, out of their way, and a simple meal will do. Ask them to treat me as they would their dearest friends. It won't be long before my father comes."

Her face gave nothing away: innocent, selfish, or perfectly masking all she knew?

Or might guess. For instance, that the Count of Benavente had followed her just far enough to see where she stopped, then returned to report her flight. That it was Philippe, and not her father, who would soon be on his way.

And where was I all this time? Where I ought to be, of course, at tableside or tenys court, playing when required, silent when required. Philippe's face, when he was told his wife had slipped away from their host and taken refuge in "a farmwoman's humble home," is nothing I wish to recall. A civil, public face, of course: a lifted chin, a small, cold smile. Still, a flurry of orders ensued. He would go to her himself, with gentlemen and musicians and archers and plenty of the German soldiers too. The company would surround the house till she saw reason and came out.

He called for a priest and singers to ride ahead, to calm her temper and smooth the way. Mysteriously, no priest was free to go, nor any singers. But my hand was in the air, and in an hour I was riding toward those woods.

It was Inés who came to the bake house door. She treated me coolly; I didn't yet know why. I thought it was her anger with me, over the business of the Fermoselles.

"How little he knows his wife," she said, "if he thinks sending *you* will make her submit. And by the way, the 'farmwoman' is a pastry cook. They got that wrong, too."

I asked how long the queen planned to stay. And if a little music might bring her peace.

Inés shrugged. A silence fell. Then she said, "There is something you should know before you step inside."

I waited.

"Can I trust you?"

I swore she could.

"These people have not given up the laws of Moses," she whispered. "They are every minute fearing for their lives. And now she is on top of them."

"I don't think she will notice," I said. "I think, in some way, they are safer with her here."

She looked at me a long time. "Orpheus," she said, "could make the animals follow him, but could he comfort an unhappy queen?"

"Let me try."

I took a chair and my vihuela into the bake house, its ovens quiet in the afternoon heat, its great table scrubbed and clean. There was only one other chair, and a simple cot, but the queen said she was happy there, and needed nothing else. She sat near a window, looking out on a yellow summer field. She had nothing to read or stitch, but her hands lay calmly in her lap.

I asked what she would like to hear.

"Nothing at the moment," she replied. "But since you are here, do this for me. Go to the kitchen yard. Find out what it is that smells so sweet."

It catches at me still—just how much Juana might have known. For when I went to the yard, it was Inés I found, stirring something in a pot over the last embers of that Friday afternoon. That small figure, with its back to me. Always with its back to me.

The scent of lemon rose on the air, and sunlight fell on her bare arms, on smooth dark hairs I knew I shouldn't see. The back of a neck with a faint rim of dirt. She turned, one small boot showing from beneath her skirts.

"What are you cooking?" I croaked. "The queen wants to know."

"Lemon marzipan," she said. "I'm taking a lesson from the cook. Come and see."

The embers were warm at my knees, and her arm went round and round, her fingers curved on the long-handled spoon. The golden stuff pulled away from the sides of the pot. "Almost done," she said, with the pride of a small child. "Go and tell the queen."

Her husky voice sank into my ears.

"What will you give me in return," I heard myself say.

She finished her turn; she never dropped her spoon. I might have dreamed that kiss, but her lips were real and summer-dry. I thanked both the single God and the one who came in threes, and took myself away.

That night I played vihuela for family and queen, and Inés sang her mother's favorite songs, and I observed her only from the side, and only when she looked straight ahead, and still I was made of ashes, hot and cool. After the little girl was put to bed, we sang "There is a Tower at the Sea" at the queen's request, and she sang with us on the third verse,

If the sea were milk
I would become a fisherman
And fish for my sorrows
With little words of love

But her voice began to tremble and it was just as well that she fell silent on the last verse; it is as unseemly as it is tender. Inés, however, sang it with no trouble at all.

Give me your hand, dove
So that I might climb to your nest
You're unlucky to sleep alone
I'll come to sleep with you.

And after that, the queen went off to the curtained portion of the bake house. The singing went on a little longer, but more quietly.

The family offered me a kitchen corner to myself, but I preferred to sleep outside; because of that last verse, I thought I'd never sleep again. It didn't help to think I still heard singing after the parents and their child had all gone to bed. How long it was till the song shaped itself into a dream, I'll never know. Only that I felt, warm against my belly, a shape that fit, a pair of soft dry lips against my throat, and hands to guide me where I should go. A warmth bloomed in me, and a hand clapped itself smartly on my mouth, and I thought, with a kind of wild joy, that I was now ready to meet my death.

But I didn't die. It was that night that Inés de Castro told me her little trick. "If you ever need to disappear," she said, "think of something that brings you peace." And I said "You," and she, as ever, corrected me. "No, before me." Maybe it was witchcraft, for as she spoke, I sank into a depth of slumber I hadn't known for years. I was a child again, warm under three robes, beneath a window square of blue.

A barking dog, a rooster in the dark. A sudden emptiness in my arms and that husky voice once more in my ear: "Pretend you're still asleep. Wait to tell her till the time is right." I remember thinking, "Tell her what?" then waking suddenly to summer light.

A house with a child in it, on a late June morning, should be bright with sound. Not silent as this one was, silent except for the rough scratch of a quill, dipped and tapped against its thick glass well. A man's voice called out a litany of household words: one large cooking pot, one frying pan, four wooden spoons and five silver forks. On it went. I stood outside and watched as two men went from cupboard to shelf, opening everything from one end to the other and writing down what was there. One, I later learned, was the Recorder of Confiscations. The other was the Scrivener of Sequestrations. What would they do when they came to inspect the bake house? Two wooden chairs. One narrow cot. One escaped queen. I thought I'd better get there first and warn her.

Juana sat exactly where she had the day before, gazing out at the yellow fields. Behind her, on a row of shelves, lay wooden trays of tiny, perfectly dusted yellow globes, and I wondered if the two men would count them each by each, and include the ones they sampled themselves. Sweet miracles, each one rolled with care by small swift hands—where were those hands now?

The queen still hadn't moved, but she lifted one hand and pointed out to the horizon, where something sharp and silver caught the light.

"Thank you for the music last night," she said. "Especially the last tune. I thought Inés had forgotten it, but she remembered all the verses. *Give me your hand, dove, so that I might climb to your nest.*" She let a delicate silence drop. Then she went mildly on. "She must have gone to her bed very late. I never heard her at all. Tell her to come to me now."

"I believe she went somewhere with the family," I said. "But I'm sure she'll be back soon."

She fell silent again. "What do you mean?" she said. "Where would they go so early on a Saturday?"

"I don't know," I said carefully. "But there are two officials in the cottage, making an inventory of the family's goods."

She rose up from the chair so abruptly that I took a step back. "What are you telling me?" she said. "And what does Doña Inés have to do with this?"

There was a knock on the door, and we looked out once more. The bake house was surrounded by soldiers, banners, gentlemen, horses—as if some jousting field had suddenly sprung up where we were—and the voice at the bake house door belonged to her husband.

Oh, it was very soft and kind, and I swear to you I saw her face brighten again with hope. Hope of what, I could not grasp. That his voice would, from now on, be this soft with her?

So her husband stepped in, and her musician stepped out. Half the village was in the road by then.

The Recorder and the Scrivener, those stalwarts of the Holy Office, suffered most that day: their access to the bake house was delayed, and due to the royal nature of the persons within, they were forced to wait. Theirs is a thankless job, especially when a heretic's store of goods amounts to so little.

It would be another day and night till the queen was fully persuaded to emerge. She came out on her husband's arm, her expression as serene as if she were making Joyous Entry into some great town. By afternoon, the cottage, from a distance, would look as it always did. Only if you rode up close would you see the notice now nailed to the door, stamped at the top with the insignia all Spain had come to dread: an olive branch on one side, a sword on the other, and a knotted wooden crucifix between.

twelve

The smallest melody can change a life. Let us lay down the little phrase: the pastry cook's apprentice, sent home early on a Friday afternoon, is still in the road when two women ride up, dismount, and knock on the cottage door. He watches for a moment before going on his way, and once home, he tells his mother what he saw: two ladies in fine cloaks and hoods, and the pastry cook on bended knee. His mother tells her neighbor, and by sundown all of Benavente knows that the Queen of Castile has taken up residence in Catalina Sanchez's bake house. A perfect distance, on a warm summer night, to take an evening stroll.

You know the way strands of hair and dust and dirt will gather in one corner, drawn together until they make a shape that blows where it likes? That's how gossip moves, a polyphony of dust. "Why was Catalina's house chosen, and not our own, which has more rooms?" "I know what you mean—and I hate to say it, but more than once Catalina overcharged me for a pie." A third voice enters: "It's really no surprise, it's always like that with them—you know who I mean—those who don't know how to cross themselves, who stumble over the simplest prayers, and hold their noses at the smell of pork. And come to think of it, I've seen that Catalina rinsing lamb in salt water—five or six rinsings before she says it's clean enough. And every bit of fat cut away, oh yes, and the vein as well. My boy once saw her do that. What a way to ruin meat!"

From here, it only takes one person, strolling by, to sniff the Friday air for the smell of frying fish, and catch instead a hint of stewing beef with chickpeas, cumin, cinnamon and clove. Step closer, and it's possible you'll hear—if only faintly—a certain old cadence, or six notes in a row that should not be, or three people answering the call of one, again and again.

"There's something not quite right about it, but I've heard it before."

Well, and what happens if you don't report, on Sunday, everything you've seen, heard and smelled on a Friday night? One of your neighbors will, and he'll take it straight to the visiting inquisitor from the Tribunal at Valladolid, on his inspection rounds this month. "Ask Maria," his wife will say. "She's known the family for years. Her son is an apprentice there. You mean to say she hasn't already come to tell you what he knows? I'm very surprised. That's very strange."

And now we have a sturdy shape, a lasting tune.

Later, the queen would feel she was to blame. She never said it, but I saw the set of her mouth, the worry. It was part of her deepening quiet.

But by then she was caught in a tightening net herself. Her husband was forever squinting at the horizon, where, in his dreams, a fortified castle might appear—old or new he didn't care, as long as it had high walls and was convenient to a town. So she, in turn, spent those hot summer days astride a mule, in public view, in regal Spanish dress for all to see. One evening we were passing near Coceges, and she saw her husband signal his men to take another road—a road that led, she knew, to an old castle not far off. Tell me, was it really *madness* to stop her mule and lie upon the ground till he turned the men and horses back? Her husband begged her to remount, for appearance's sake, and this she did. But she stayed on its back beyond the town till break of day. He could not move her forward. Nor could he jail her in broad daylight.

Three months would pass this way. The shining joy of the bakehouse night was gone. She was still allowed the solace of music, but we never played without Philippe's servants in the room. Watching her, watching us.

Three months. And still no sign or news of Inés de Castro.

By early September, the court had stopped at Burgos, at the palace held by the Constable of Castile. Juana was, by then, beginning to show. One evening, she sat at the clavichord and we had a drum, two vielles and my vihuela. "There is a Tower at the Sea," she said in a bright, clear voice. "Does anyone else recall the tune?" She put her fingers to the keys and began to hum. I waited for her to play it through. I asked her to repeat a phrase or two. She had it all by heart, as I knew she would.

But before the group could take it up, she broke off playing and turned to me. In the same clear voice she said, "What do we know of dear Master Agricola, who wrote such intricate things, and fell so ill? Did we lose him at Benavente, or did he come with us as far as Valladolid? I never heard—is he under good care, so far from home?"

Benavente. Valladolid. Just enough weight on those two names. Surely she knew he'd died in August at Valladolid—of fever or plague no one was sure. No, she was trying to tell me something else. I'd always thought she couldn't dissemble. But what if beneath that sad and open face, she was keeping something to herself? A little mystery, after all. Agricola seemed a clue: she'd always loved his musical tricks: the way he'd carry a phrase just a beat beyond the usual stopping place. Or make a line of notes rise up when the listener thought it would go down.

She was creating a language only I could hear, and in it, giving me a task.

Find Inés.

But how was I to do this? For her husband had a secret language too: the next morning, he required *all* her servants—musicians, too— at his side. It seemed a celebration was being arranged for him. It might go on three days, and he needed everyone present at the grand events. All but his wife, who must rest and guard her fragile health for the sake of the child.

Feasts, excursions to local fairs, jousting and tenys. Music at courtside and siesta, procession and dance. He rode and paraded for all Spain to see, writing Juana out of the story with every trumpet, every shawm, every Burgundian banner raised.

But soon even his own musicians began to complain of aching fingers and wrists, of dizziness in the heat of day, and not enough sleep at night. All this misery led, during one siesta, to talk of the plague, which led, in turn, to talk of Agricola's death the month before. I took my chance. Between two tunes, I asked Philippe's interpreter to tell him that if it were wanted, I would gladly ride to Valladolid and make sure that everything had been done to honor the Flemish master so far from home.

Philippe looked surprised and touched; I'd found a secret spring. I saw his brow contract as he worked it out: Spain must feel the splendor, the superiority, of all he'd brought to our backward land. "His Majesty will think it over," said the interpreter. I bowed. Philippe was the kind of person who never really thought things over. It was now a matter of time, or rather, of a well-timed reprise, lightly buried at just the right turn.

I was learning how to wait.

By the sixteenth of September, exhaustion had set in. But there was no stopping Philippe. We began the day with a local reed-spear joust, followed by an hour of tenys, though there were few observers left. Even the banquet tables stood forlorn, old fruit and cheese lit on by the last besotted flies. But Philippe continued, full of life. Racket still in hand, he turned to the constable and said he looked forward to the next day's hunt. The constable looked appalled; it seems he was worn down too.

But a serving man was promptly dispatched. For of course the party must set out before dawn the next day.

There were, to my recollection, no women at the festive grounds that afternoon. Maybe the flinging of sweat drops had driven them away. It was very warm. A few Flemings were still upright; there was no Spaniard but myself nearby—I was showing myself most loyal. *His Majesty* swung his racket, ready to show all Spain how to properly cock the wrist, if only we had the wit to watch. His own men wiped their necks and feigned interest.

He cast his eye around, and called for water. But there was no water boy in sight.

That's when his eye fell on me.

Why was I standing by the abandoned banquet table, nearest the pitcher and the cup?

Because I was a skinny wretch and always hungry.

Why was there no water boy?

That is harder to say. As hard as it is to say what urgent business kept Fernando so far away. Unfriendly. Disapproving. But he could always say he'd kept his ambassadors there, including the one I mentioned before, Luis Ferrer.

This kept Fernando pure and blameless should something go amiss.

In any case, no water boy. It was wrongly quiet, as it had been when we arrived by ship at La Coruña. No Fernando waiting to greet their majesties, with whom he was supposed to rule. No sight of him at all: only the scent of an old fox waiting somewhere out of view.

"Water," shouted Philippe. "Juanico, you there."

His cup lay close to my hand. Brim-full already, as if the water boy had thoughtfully done his duty before running off. In the cup floated the usual specks. The surface looked oily, as if, after a bite of meat, someone had taken a sip.

I looked down at it and shook my head. *Monseigneur* was ever one to catch the off-note, every bit of fluff or fleck or mote on fork or plate. It is a royal trait. Our poor Prince Juan had it too, though he always seemed sorry for noticing the flaw. He lived amazed by his younger sister Juana, who bore so well the natural way of things. Dirt and blood and cruelty and rot.

With Philippe, this delicacy came out in a different key: horror at the imperfect dish—and outrage at those who served it.

But in this case, he saw me hesitate. Of course he must give a manly laugh.

I shook my head again, said something in our own tongue about finding the water boy, and a clean cup, though I knew he couldn't understand a word. That's when he frowned at me, all impatience at my cautious ways.

He drank it down, legs planted wide in a sportsman's stance.

A bird piped in the woods nearby: one, two, three pipes. It made me notice his mouth—so small and round, set in that jutting jaw. He always put me in mind of a fish. Now something tugged on that mouth, an invisible hook, set just on one side.

He called for his interpreter now. "Tell the others we'll play a little more," he said. Then, as if it had occurred to him suddenly, he turned my way and said, "Is the queen feeling well today?"

"She is," I said. The hook had caught, and I gave it a second tug. "She is glad the consort has pleased you these last few days. But if you are worried about our good Agricola, may he rest in peace, remember my offer to go to Valladolid, and see what needs doing."

A stricken look came over his face. "He is no longer with us? And not with us in Burgos?"

I was surprised by this lapse of memory, but simply bowed my head. For a long moment neither the interpreter nor I dared set him straight. Then at last I said, "You remember—he died at Valladolid. We spoke of the plague?"

As the interpreter gave it to him, his skin, so rosy the moment before, went the color of damp clay, and he seemed suddenly beset, as if a cloud of tiny flies had descended on his face. He managed a hasty nod. "Stables, a purse. Back within the week," he mumbled. Just as he began to wave me away, he turned abruptly on his heel, as if Fernando himself stood just behind, demanding his attention now.

There was no one there. The interpreter gave me the faintest look of fear.

But I was free to go.

Why is there always a dark wood where Inés is concerned? As I rode away from Burgos, my vihuela in its leather case, the little bird piped again, three short notes, and I pictured Philippe riding this same way at tomorrow's dawn to begin his hunt—would he hear it too? Would it please him, or prey on his uneasy mind?

I confess I made a little wish.

Benavente, the queen had said. Then *Valladolid*. She wanted me to start at the beginning, at the pastry cook's house itself, though she surely knew Inés had been taken to Valladolid, to the secret prisons there. I didn't want to go to Benavente; it would add two days. Besides, a closed-up house is a thing I don't much like. It calls up other houses once open and welcoming, now locked, or mowed down altogether so that an emptiness lies on the ground. When the priests speak of the hell that awaits us if we don't repent, it is *this* I think awaits us, not flame and heat.

At day's end I saw in the gloaming two white squares floating free in the dim blue air—two papers now nailed to the cottage door. There had only been one when I left. I approached and saw: the cottage and bake house had been emptied out and put up for sale. A quiet had infected everything. The house stood in its field, alone and exposed for all to see.

I slept that night in the bake house yard, under the same tree as before, and woke the next morning to the bells at Benavente's church. It was a market day, but I went first to Mass, and let myself be seen. I had another reason, too: all along the nave, on either side, hung the yellow tunics of disgrace. They fluttered in the autumn breeze, making it hard to see what names were written on their backs. Nor could I stare: I was the only stranger in the church, and you know how vigilant the pious are. It is their duty to keep an eye on us all.

After church, I went to the market street, and it was there, among the vegetables, that two old women looked me over with great interest—one more small onion to check for spots.

I begged their pardon and asked if they knew the family of Judaizers that had been taken away.

"The stink of eggplant in that house was enough to make you faint," said one, running her gaze up and down my cloak, catching at the royal badge. "Why did the queen go there, of all places?" She and her friend exchanged a look. "Is it true she is again with child? Has her Flemish husband locked her away?"

I found I couldn't speak. A sickness flooded me, as if I had drunk a whole pitcher of that oily water. But at last I got it out: how one of the queen's ladies had disappeared that day.

Now they eyed the vihuela case strapped to my back. The talkative one put her hand to her breast—serious or mocking I could not tell. "What a romance," she said. "And you have been sent to find her?"

"If it seems I should," I said.

"Well," she said, "if she was in the house with those people, she's gone to Valladolid. But tell us, are the stories true? About the queen being not-quite-right in the head?"

"These are tales," I said. "She has all her wits." And before she could go on, I said, "Tell me, is there a women's prison here?"

I was treated to a shrug, a narrowing of the eye. "They send them on to town, which is just as well. Where would they keep such people here but in our church?" Both women crossed themselves. Then they looked at each other, and again at me. "You should tell the queen how fortunate she is. Likely they've discovered a heretic hiding under her own roof." Then she shrugged again. "Anyway, our sovereign lady has other worries now."

I thought she must mean the child on the way.

But the woman leaned closer and tugged my sleeve. "It's plague or poison," she said. "He's on the point of death."

"Pardon?" I said. "Of whom do you speak?"

"Where have you been?" she said. "The whole world knows. The queen will be a widow before the week is out."

And they went back to sorting onions.

Gossip. It might be true or it might not. But as I rode away, I felt the hair rise on my arms. A cup of water, my little wish. But I also thought I would not be missed a few more days.

Another day's ride brought me to Valladolid, where, just two months before, the queen had entered with such grave pomp, all in black on a white horse, the standard of Castile held high before her, against her husband's will. I saw her again in her black French hood. It had hidden from view her trusting eyes, the hope in her face. Whereas I—my face exposed for all to see—felt no hope at all. Raw, scraped, a man of stone sent to enter a tomb of stone.

What made me ride past the Tribunal building, the place I knew she wanted me to go? Cowardice—or my growing sense of a foolish errand? I rode right past it, like a man asleep, and in that trance I took myself to a workshop I'd visited once with Agricola before he fell ill. It belonged to the best vihuela maker in Valladolid, a *morisco* of extraordinary skill—of such talent shaping wood to sing that he had not yet been stripped of his livelihood and made to take up some menial's work. He was too valuable, too rare. His vihuelas went to all the best gentlemen of court and town. He had been inside all their homes and the homes of their friends.

It didn't feel like luck, exactly—more like doom—when he welcomed me in, and set me down to wait while he finished one last thing: he was, it seemed, finishing an instrument for the Bishop Diego Deza. It so happened that the inquisitor general was visiting Valladolid for a few days, staying in the Tribunal's private apartments. He had come for some important business of course, but also for a portrait sitting and the new vihuela. My host laughed ruefully and said he would gladly give the honor of delivery to someone else.

Diego Deza—Prince Juan's last tutor. The man in whose arms the prince died—that role Encina had felt was rightfully his. Of course

Deza wouldn't remember me—I'd been only a boy, and one of an ensemble endlessly waiting at the prince's chamber door.

But it was better than nothing. I asked the vihuela maker if I could be of help. He gave me a puzzled smile. I suggested it might please Deza to see a former musician of his beloved prince. In the end we agreed: we would go together to the entrance, and I would go inside on his behalf.

What I didn't know was how my own heart would change its beat as I walked up those stairs. At first, there was nothing to it, nothing at all. But gradually, the steps began to suggest different tones, depending on the feet of the walker: in fine leather boots or the thinnest soles, held together only by a small strap. And for those of us in between, in workaday or traveling shoes, the cold stone creeps more slowly up the legs, its work to merely thin the muscle of hope until the legs feel almost too weak to carry the witness—or the petitioner—a step further.

A guard waited at the top, as one always does, if for nothing else than to remind you that an ordinary mortal can't come in. But if it happens that you're accompanied by the best vihuela maker of Valladolid, and wearing a blue musician's cloak with the royal badge in view, and if you've been so long at court that you've finally learned how to look supremely bored, as if sent on an absurd mission by people who do nothing but send people on absurd missions—well then, you might get through.

I stood beside my kind friend, this gifted man with the dark hair and deep brown eyes of someone who, by virtue of someone's envy of his talent, could tomorrow find himself missing from the world, tucked away in this very building, or somewhere even harder to find. As we stood there before the guard, I confess I nearly laughed: it struck me that we both hid, in our best breeches, our circumcised cocks equally wilted by fear.

It was entirely possible that the guard did too.

The instrument maker gave his name, then showed forth the vihuela in its fine case. Then he introduced me, saying something too kind about my playing, and my long service at court. I showed them my vihuela, too. And as he had instructed, I said nothing myself, and aimed my gaze slightly past the guard's right shoulder, as if setting my sights on some spot inside the entrance. I murmured my thanks in the purest of monotones. This too is a form of vanishing.

Still it seemed like magic when the guard inclined his head and stepped aside.

Soon enough I'd learn that miracles, in this time and place, will only go so far. But I was twenty-two years old, and still felt a thrill at the sudden turning of a key in a lock. Yet another door opened, and the first guard spoke to another, and it was explained that the vihuela had arrived, and here to bring it was the legendary virtuoso, Juan of Granada, known as Juanico, twelve years in the employ of the Catholic Kings. I flushed to hear it, and my palms went damp.

But here was another door, and another, until I stood in a chamber warmed by tapestries and three great silver candelabra, by books on every wall. High windows gave no view, but let the evening light and air stream in. A table and chair sat at the center, and someone sat there, very still, in a long white robe and short black cloak. Gray hair curled out from beneath his velvet hat. He didn't move as I walked in, but held unnaturally still—was this Deza or a statue of the man? More books were stacked on the table beside him, some open, some titled on their sides. Then a voice behind me said, "You're standing in my light," and I turned to see a small, angry man at an easel.

I tried to step backward, out of the room, but the archbishop gave the smallest of smiles, and let his palm fall away from the arm of the chair.

"So this is the fabled vihuelist from Granada," he said.

I murmured something about our lost beloved prince, about days gone by. It was enough: Deza's eyes seemed to shimmer and fill.

The painter gave out the faintest sigh, and laid down his brush.

Another gesture from the bishop, and the painter was gone, and I found myself kneeling before the great man and kissing his ring, and he was thanking me for my long service, and my work, of late, in "calming our ill and melancholy queen." I kept my face quite still. He went on to praise my playing, which I was sure he'd never heard. He said he hoped I wouldn't succumb to vanity and pride, but that my playing had shown the northern courts the stately nobility, the purity of our native land. "They prefer to see us otherwise," he said, with the saddest of smiles.

I was asked to stay to supper. It seemed he was alone, and had more to say. And he did. As the evening went on, I learned more than a lowly musician should: that he had unrealized ambitions as a player himself; if only he had more time to practice, wasn't beset from moment to moment with conflicting claims, clawed at from below by ambitious young monks, eyed by Bishop Cisneros from time to time for traces of Jewish blood—an absurdity, he said, I am no Talavera. He swerved to music then, such a solace in dark times. Great musicians and instrument makers must be protected, he said—unless of course they shouldn't. I watched his eyes for a villain's glitter, but there was none: his eyes were watery and rimmed with red, his thin jowls shook a little as he spoke. He confided, over soup, that the crowning of Juana and Philippe had come at a terrible time (as a musician, of course, you wouldn't understand). They'd suspended the Tribunal's work while they were still at Brussels, so that they might "oversee it" once they arrived. Well, here they were, and no word at all. Paperwork had piled up, and hundreds of prisoners who should have come to trial still waited in their cells. It was a great burden—a cruelty, in fact—to all concerned.

It was the longest evening of my life. We had to have music, of course, and recall fond memories of dear Prince Juan, how nothing had gone right since his death. A tuning of Deza's new instrument, and a lesson, too. Don't ask me if he could play; the competence of such great men is not to be belittled—they have so many cares. The exercise of patience had never been my strength, but I thought of Juana, riding her mule through the night, sleeping sitting up in a chair in a bake house. I thought—but only dimly—of Inés, whose shape fit so well with mine for the briefest of dreams, and who, moments later, vanished exactly the way my father had, first whispering something tender and ordinary into my ear. From that moment to this, she had somehow found lodging in my blood and bones, but no lodging anywhere else that I could see. She might be in this very building, in a small room stripped of all comforts but furnished to extravagance with my deepest fear: unmeasured time.

I had only to think of this to launch myself into another tune, and offer the bishop a little more instruction. I was waiting for the sliver of the moment that would find him tired of playing, but just before he grew sleepy or worse, began to worry again about the foes and tangles and intricacies that mounted up around him every day. The moment presented itself in a surprising way. If Encina had been there, he would have chided me for yet again employing the deceptive cadence. I was playing a little tune in a minor key, something Prince Juan used to love, when I broke off, then shook my head as if seized by a sudden cramp.

Deza leaned forward, all fatherly concern. He gazed on me a moment more, and in this time seemed to wake suddenly to the fact that I was often in the presence of the new sovereigns of Spain, and might have some gossip or useful knowledge of courtly things.

I understood his look, and murmured that Philippe was enjoying great celebrations in his honor, and our lady Juana kept herself very quiet, because of the child, but was healthy and strong. He nodded, a little bored. "Rumors reach us," he said, and waved his hand. "That he exerted himself too much at tenys, and is at this moment lying ill in the constable's own bed."

"I've been traveling for some days," I said. "Is there any news?"

He shrugged. "If he is to govern Spain, he will have to learn first to govern himself."

I nodded, then took a little breath, as if making to speak.

He leaned forward again. "What is it? What were you going to say?"

"Nothing," I said. "Only there *is* something on our sovereign lady's mind," I said. "I am a little embarrassed to say. But as you know she has her mother's will, and I fear she will never drop the idea until it is resolved. You know how she is." I let a beat pass, and he crossed himself.

"May that will, and the grace of our Lord Jesus Christ, carry her through her present trials," I said.

Now Deza was fully awake. He bade me put the vihuela aside, and tell him what the matter was.

I did. And my elaborate effort, the intricacy, the care which I put into that small motif—came to very little; he said he would, in the course of the next day's business, instruct his private secretary to look into the case of this unfortunate lady, Doña Inés de Castro, and see what, if anything, could be done.

Then he sighed heavily. "Don't let yourself hope," he said. "They are new sovereigns, and I fear they must learn, like everyone else, that the least drop leads to a very great wave." And before I could ask him what he meant by that, he said he was very tired, and must retire for the night. He thanked me for bringing the vihuela, and all the rest, and the two of us knelt and prayed. "It has gotten very late," he said, and gestured that I might rest a while in that room before going on my way. He called for a guard, and was conducted away. I heard the door latched from the other side.

To bed down, right there? The best place seemed near—or under— the easel itself, though the sharp scent of the painter's oils still wreathed the room. Then I noticed that the chamber wasn't locked on the other side. I opened that door to get more air, and discovered, waiting on the other side, a man who called himself "the night watch of the lower floor." He admitted he'd been listening for a while. "We don't get much music here," he said, and then, in the humblest, meek- est voice, "a little tune wouldn't go amiss with the others, if you didn't mind." He took me to another room, down another hall, where three or four others stood leaning near a set of doors.

How long I played for them I cannot say, only that I watched them as I could, and after they themselves had had a chance to sing—keep- ing their voices very low—I made my voice careless and a little warm, and said, "I have always wondered what it looks like further in."

The night watch looked at his companions, who looked away.

That is how I came to see what I should not have seen, and how I was granted just enough hope to make myself more hopeless still. My guide took me first to the public rooms, the Tribunal chamber itself, its table hung with banners of richest red. A crucifix hung just behind and above its handsome central chair, with smaller chairs on either side. I was surprised to learn that in spite of such imposing gran- deur, a defendant sometimes dashed at the table, to upset the papers and inkpot lying there. So there were always three or four guards at the ready.

There were two doors in this room: one led to the office of the Secretary, and my guide spoke now in a tone of hushed respect, as if to suggest that this was where the true power lay. Then, with even greater reverence, he pointed to the other door, which I saw, now, had three locks.

"The Records Room," he said. "We've never seen it ourselves, but we hear it is carefully kept. They say the one in Barcelona has no order at all." He gave a lopsided smile, and the reverence seemed to leak from his face. "That's enough of that," he said. "Let's have another tune."

I had noticed a third door in the room. "What's that?" I said.

"Staircase," he said. "Goes upstairs, and sometimes down."

"Whatever tune you'd like," I said. "In fact," and I lowered my voice, "I could play it up there, if you like. Are there guards up there who might appreciate a little song?"

He got a candle, and told me to follow close, and say not a word until he gave the sign.

The staircase and upstairs corridor were unremarkable—you don't need me to tell you. A series of doors as in any grand building—what did I expect—though each was furnished with an extra lock, and there was a deep silence from within.

Three more guards up there, all deadly bored, playing cards by a sputtering light.

Nothing to see. Nothing to hear. I'd expected moans, wails, little shufflings of feet. There was a smell, yes. It came and went. Of fresh urine, chiefly, and a hint of stale broth. It was impossible to believe what the card players told me, when I asked: there are two hundred in this building, more than four hundred at Toro, and smaller places—for women and children—in private residences, scattered all around the town. Even we don't know where all of them are. It's better that way. But trust me, the conditions here are of the best. "Did you know," said my guide, "that your common criminals spout heresy, just to get moved from civil prison into these fine lodgings?"

"The food is better, as they pay for it themselves," said a card player. His voice was low, with a little angry edge.

"I don't suppose," I said. "I don't suppose there's an empty cell, so I could see what you mean?"

That's when my guide gave me the first wrong look, and I knew I'd gone too far. "Never mind," I said. "Shall we have that tune now?"

"Yes," said the deep-voiced guard. "And if we don't care for it, we'll find a cell for you. How does three years sound?"

"Now, now," said my guide. "Leave him be."

"Three years," I whispered. "What does he mean?"

"That's how long it usually takes," he said. "Now play."

And I took my last mad chance. "There is a Tower at the Sea."

A voice. A female voice. From somewhere deep within. Just two lines, and then it stopped.

The card players all stood up.

"Which cell?" cried one.

"Can't tell," said another.

And they all sat down again.

I confess I found myself glad to be rushed away, down the hall, down the stairs, to feel the night watch hold my arm and bring his face too close to mine. "Who's in there?" he said. "Which one is the one you know? Who is she?"

"No one," I said.

The guide kept hold of my arm. "It never happened," he said.

I agreed, and he let me go.

And so I found myself back in the library, the smell of paint and solvent still faintly on the air. The new vihuela sat in the corner among the books, the tapestry, the fine silver candelabra, all the signs of a man of learning, letters, and vision.

To say that I slept is both true and untrue. I must have, because there is no explaining the feeling of something—of someone—in my arms. I was carrying this person down a long black hall, past the card players, down the little stair. I carried her, yes. For I am no Orpheus. In my dream she didn't walk behind me. No, I carried her in my arms. This way there was no danger of turning around and losing her. I carried her in my arms. and she weighed almost nothing, and it was this—the surprise of how little she weighed—that woke me, still feeling the easy lightness of her little shape, like the body of the girl by the stream of Granada, had I carried her, or the body of the girl in the hills of Granada, had I carried her. Or the body of the love I held at Benavente one summer night, a body made for flight and kept from flight.

I woke tasting salt, my face damp with my own tears. A young man crouched beside me, his eyebrows raised in great surprise. He wore a humble friar's robe, belted by a rope, and had a friar's fringe of hair. It took me a moment to know him. But the look he gave me hadn't changed at all, nor had those eyes of his, alight with curiosity, keen to the smallest shift, the slightest move.

"You," said Pedro de Fermoselle.

"You," I replied.

Later, when I had time to think it through, I grasped how it was we had come to meet again in just that time and place. For Deza, before he ascended to these heights, had been the Bishop of Salamanca, and Pedro de Fermoselle the kind of boy you could trust to deliver other things besides shoes and music manuscripts, and in such a timely way that he quickly worked his way up the Tribunal ranks. And though his brother, the most brilliant composer of our day, could not get himself the post of Salamanca's cathedral chapelmaster, his younger brother, sleek as a fish and keeping his thoughts to himself, had risen to private secretary of the inquisitor general, Archbishop Diego Deza.

Pedro hadn't changed—or rather, he'd changed exactly as he should. He conducted his business with efficiency, with stunning gentility and smoothness, so that once again I found I couldn't speak. He gave me time to use the privy, splash water on my face, then told me to meet him in the Tribunal's public rooms. He led me into the secretary's office, and there, from behind a table, he heard my stumbling request, made on our sovereign lady's account. He replied that he would look into it, "as a favor to our unhappy queen" and also because "Archbishop Deza appreciated your music last night." Then he paused. "If," he went on, "it turns out not to be a mistake, that is, if the witnesses in the case have described Inés de Castro accurately, and aver that she has performed heretical acts alongside the pastry cook and her family, then you will understand, of course." He stood. "It is all to the good that you came forward today. You have done our sovereigns a great service, either way. Especially," he said, "if this results in removing an infection from our sovereign lady's midst"— and here he smiled—"since that *other* infection is like to spread unchecked." Was this a reference to the moral and physical condition of her spouse, who lay ill or dying one day's ride from here?

"And now you should go," he said. "She will surely have need of your playing in the days to come."

She—the way he said it gave me another, deeper chill.

Pedro's words tingled in my fists the way my brother's taunts had done when I was young. I didn't try to fight back then, nor did I now. What bothered me most was that in all that time, the Secretary never asked me what *I* had heard and seen that might be pertinent to the Castro case. He only scribbled something on a sheet of paper, then put it in a box. What had I given him? Then he said, in the old friendly voice I remembered from Salamanca, "I am so glad we met again. I may well call on you in future. In the meantime, you may go, and please tell the queen that in spite of the inevitable delays, we will put all our resources toward resolving this case."

Then he did what secretaries always do to let you know your time is up: he stirred and stacked the papers on his desk. My fists still tingled, but I busied myself by putting away my vihuela and smoothing out my wrinkled cloak. I heard myself give out the usual tripe: thank you, the queen will be so grateful, and all the rest.

Who had sung back to me upstairs, and taken false hope in the night?

"One last question, if I might," I asked.

"Yes, of course."

"I don't suppose there are women held in this building?"

He looked up from his papers then, and gave me an angelic smile. "Alas for us both, I have no idea," he said. "That information is kept in the Records Room. Even to ask would be highly irregular, and raise suspicions at the highest levels."

"Oh," I said. "I thought His Eminence Diego Deza was the highest level here."

"Not exactly, no," said Pedro, letting the dazzling smile fall and die. "No, there is always someone at a higher level. And failing that, someone at a lower level who finds the weak place in the man above."

By the next day I was back in Burgos, at the constable's great house. But I couldn't find the queen. How long had I been gone? It seemed a century had passed—even La Rue rushed past me in the hall as if he knew me not at all. But it was he who came back, and took my arm, and patted my back too many times, and finally said, "Stay close. There may be need of music sometime soon."

That's how I learned it was true. Philippe, a man of twenty-seven years, was about to die. Everyone seemed to know it but his wife, who would not leave his side, but tended him herself in the constable's own bedchamber, where they'd brought him from the hunt. As ever, some found the queen's behavior heroic, and others found it disgusting and wrong.

I took my vihuela and waited outside the door with others, as we had waited for Prince Juan. La Rue told me what he could: how *Monseigneur* had fallen ill the evening before the hunt, but didn't want to disappoint his host. A fever came on, but he wanted to "get something first," then he promised he would rest—they assumed he meant a fox or hart. His own physician was at his side, and this man said he feared poison. Still, the doctor told our lady to protect herself and stay away.

She refused to leave his side. "If it is poison, how can there be harm to anyone else?"

Who called for music I would never know. But a priest came out, and three of us went in—two lutenists and myself. "Play quietly behind this screen," he said. "It won't be long." There was some confusion with the screen, and we had a partial view of the bed. I tried not to look, but saw something shaking beneath the linens. It rose and fell, it puked into a bowl and fell back again. Juana herself leaned toward this form. "Drink this," she said. "If you can."

A new doctor came in—not one of Philippe's own. "It's not poison," he said in Spanish, very calm and sure. "There is an ague in the neighborhood that can kill a king as easily as a peasant."

He was the one who saw us standing there like fools, and put the screen to rights himself.

But it was too late. We'd seen enough, and now we heard the voice of a dying man trying not to show his fear, but wanting witnesses all the same. He invoked the Virgin. Then whispered the name "Fernando."

"Is that water clean?" he cried.

"It is," Juana said, and took a sip of it herself.

"Ask the vihuelist to taste it first—I forget his name."

My heart thrummed in my chest. Any moment he would remember my name, and call it out.

But he was raving, and his people were exhausted, and had the future on their minds. I saw it on the faces of his knights. And on the faces of the lutenists, too. They told me then, in whispers, that they hadn't been paid for several months. How in the name of God would they make their way home?

If you want to make yourself vanish, think of something that brings you peace.

But I was already hidden behind a screen. A musician's place, after all. To make music, and stay out of view.

As I stood there I wished it *was* I who had drunk first from the cup. Let its specks be poison or something else, let me disappear, so I wouldn't have to see the doors and staircases of our towns, and all the places where people are led and locked away. Thresholds not marked by fire, no. The entrance to hell is just a little door.

Much would be made of Juana's behavior with her husband's corpse, how she would accompany it, for nearly two years, across the night roads of Castile. But no one ever spoke of the way her fingers curled bravely around the basin rim as he begged her, weeping, to bury him as a King of Spain, in the royal tomb at Granada where Isabel lay, and her son and daughter and the babe Miguel. I heard Juana promise that she would.

In return, her father now made it clear he would permit nothing of the sort.

And would anyone mention the Burgundians' own extravagant ways of showing their love for their *Monseigneur*, dressing him in a king's finery and propping him upright in a chair for days? And how badly his advisers would fight to have his heart removed and wrapped for a journey north, all by itself?

The battle for the corpse began. A battle in which she proved herself as stubborn as her mother. Yet that mother was praised for her stubbornness. Not Juana, somehow.

You have the gossips' reports: that over the next two years she watched over that coffin, had it moved suddenly in the dead of night, ordered it broken open and inspected—you will even hear that she fell at the corpse's feet in their rotted wrappings and kissed them till she was pulled away.

I only know that she was trying to fulfill his final wish. And rightly trusted no one else to get him—all his parts intact—to the place he wished to lie.

That's how the Galician grandmother's prophecy came true. To be sure, his corpse never went very far: a few miles here, a few miles there—and once we halted so the queen might give birth, and rest with her infant, her dear Catalina, for the winter months. But soon enough we were on the night roads again, toiling south to Granada in a failing dream.

Always by night, as was proper, for as Juana said herself, a widow must not be seen by day. Still the roads were lined with the curious, and those who follow the curious, and there was always the envoy Luis Ferrer, Fernando's spy, watching us closely, then slipping out of view again.

And because the dead must have music, and the living, too, the organ carrier came, and three *bas* musicians too, and we pitched our tents or slept in any shed or barn through that autumn. At every bridge and crossing I looked into the faces of the women who lined the road, hoping for the one I knew. At every church, I looked up at the rows of yellow tunics and prayed I would not see her name.

Until one day, when we stopped to hear Mass at Benavente, and I saw one there that bore her name, alongside three others: Catalina Sanchez, Alonso Sanchez, and a smaller one, made for a child. Maria Sanchez.

It was the queen who saw the *sanbenitos* first, and pointed them out to me. "But it doesn't mean she's dead," she whispered.

I bowed my head. But I knew too much about the queen's capacity for hope, how she could deceive herself and keep a little light against the blackest gloom. It was a trait she shared with Inés. They refused to see the way things really stood.

The procession moved on, and stopped. Moved on and stopped. In summer her father came and took his grandson Fernando away. Only for a little while, he told his daughter as she wept. Is he not nearly six years old? He should begin to know the lands he might someday rule.

The last of the Flemish singers left us, too. Pierre de la Rue, I think, felt some regret at going. He told me that the queen had restored to him—and all the others, too—all the wages her husband had owed them, and more. Gentlemen, believe me, she was neither as mad or as foolish as Philippe's scribes would make her out to be. I think, sometimes, about the young man on board *The Julienne*, who threw so many pages overboard.

What story sank beneath the waves that day?

Pierre de la Rue, before he departed, put a hand on my arm, and said the strangest thing. "One good listener is worth a thousand bored monarchs," he said. "Stay by her side as long as you can."

In bitter February, we were at Arcos, and Fernando came again. By then little Catalina was nearly two years old. One night there was a great noise in the lodgings where we stayed, and Fernando's favorite envoy, Ferrer, the one always clinging to our side, came to us with great dignity and told us to pack our things. The king was moving his daughter, said Ferrer, and it must be done by night.

And where? we asked.

The town of Tordesillas, on the River Duero, he said. There is a small fortified palace there, beside a convent. She will be safe there, and Philippe will at last find repose. Rest at Tordesillas a while. The body will be safe there, in the convent yard. In time, we will find a way to move the body south.

Juana was tired. She begged for a day to make herself ready, and promised she would go. She ordered new candles, new wagon wheels. She knew, I think, that the people would gather to see her pass.

Catalina was old enough by then to hold a simple tune, and babbled something sweet the day we crossed the plains and saw the river just ahead.

It was February of 1509. Tordesillas on its riverbank was raw and damp and shrouded in fog. Yet the bridge was lined with people, and they bowed their heads and knelt as we passed by. Four black horses led the way, hauling Philippe's coffin on its everlasting tilt, the planks nearly rotted through by that winter's rains. Then Fernando himself, and his daughter at his side, a nursemaid just behind, carrying Catalina, who wailed in little gulps. Ferrer was also near the front, though none of us yet knew why; Fernando had chosen him as mayordomo over Tordesillas. The queen's first official jailer, you might say.

There were, at that time, five chamber musicians left, and a few singers, a drum and two trumpets. Juan de Anchieta was with us, and the organ carrier, too.

As we mounted the bridge, with all the people standing beneath their torches to watch her pass in the freezing cold, my eyes fell on one small figure, all in black in a French hood, who looked back at me as I went past. She had green eyes, and a little gap between her teeth.

But as you know, I see resemblances everywhere. Everyone looks to me like someone I once knew, now gone. Only the wrong people return.

"Where is the palace?" Anchieta cried. "I don't see anything that looks like a palace. What sort of place is this?"

The organ carrier was the one who saw it first. He was always first to see the next place he might set down his terrible load.

The Duero lay before us now. Sluggish, brown. Did its waters move at all?

"There," said the organ carrier, and pointed to something on the steep far bank. It looked like nothing but a row of broken, crooked teeth.

thirteen

Luis Ferrer: a string that breaks in the first measure of a dance tune; a loaf of bread that takes pleasure in refusing to rise. I am sorry to say I have no portrait on hand. Give him a long somber face and a long somber gown, the furrowed brow of a noble judge. He was gifted in the art of locking doors and alert to the merest breath of change or chance or light or air—anything that might stir, in a young widow, the will to live. His was a solemn task: to keep any news of the world from reaching Juana, and shield the world from any accidental sight or sound of her. God forbid the people might find her sane and fit to rule.

And one more thing: he must make all this look reasonable, wise, and humane.

He waited a while to show his hand. That first February, though a bitter wind blew off the Duero, Juana chose the one large chamber with views of the river, the bridge, and the fields beyond. "It will do me good to look out," she told him.

Ferrer blinked at her, a dumb-show of surprise. "Beg pardon, but it's drafty and cold. And the path below will be noisy. Children, mules, the smell alone. And surely you do not want to expose your daughter to the morning fog."

"A little air is a good thing."

He clasped his hands before him. "Your father wishes—"

Her face went dangerously still. She bowed her head and when she raised it, she said, "Until my father visits and tells us himself what he wishes, we will take the riverside rooms. And one more thing," she said. "I will hear Mass with the Sisters of Santa Clara."

For a few months, he let her have her way.

Once, I accompanied her to the gates. I still remember the Sisters' fine, pure unison. After mass, they sang for her in their courtyard, under arches and doorways whose curves I knew in my bones and blood: long ago the convent had been a Moorish palace—you could still see its baths. That evening, the setting sun bathed the stone until it gave off an apricot glow.

You can imagine the frantic letters Ferrer sent to Fernando that first year. Circumspect at first, then compliments slip into complaints, into requests for more funds for tapestries, wax, servants, etc. Fleeting mention of Juana's various "indispositions," and a plea for Fernando to visit soon. Alas, the king was very busy. He was newly married, and between signing treaties and trying to get himself an heir of his own, it took him until December to visit Tordesillas.

It gave his daughter hope to see him. She called for lights and music; she dressed herself well, and ordered a feast. And Fernando, in return, patted her hand and bade her do his will: to change her apartments for the smaller, inner ones, though they had no natural light or view or source of air. As for hearing Mass at Santa Clara: *We will see, we will see, perhaps at my next visit.* Then he left, taking with him a few "old things" she surely had no need of now: some silver and plate, and most of her chapel singers, too. He also took her long-time composer, Juan de Anchieta.

Anchieta, with his soaring music, his eyes sunk ever deeper in their turtly folds of skin. We'd been together so long he was like an old cousin to me now.

After Fernando and his people were gone, I stood among the courtyard stones. A few small birds hopped about in the cold, searching for seeds. If they made a sound, I don't remember it.

Three chapel singers remained besides myself. We slept in servants' quarters, in a warren of alcoves well above the street. After Fernando's visit, the smallest journey—to San Antolín across the street—was conducted under guard, and while at church, we were forbidden to speak to anyone about the queen. But it was in San Antolín that we heard the town's first grumblings: was the mayordomo Luis Ferrer mistreating the queen? And why were there so many soldiers posted at every gate and arch of the town? To all this Ferrer gave no reply, except to say that he had his orders directly from the king, and Tordesillas, besides, was dangerous and prone to plague and desperate for gossip too.

It was likely true: he made it so.

Our hours with the queen herself were just as closely watched. I played and the chapel boys sang, often behind an arras to make sure she didn't try to make some sign to us or play some other trick. Ferrer began to restrict Juana's allotment of wax: too much light would encourage the reading of wrong books and the playing of wrong music for a woman already too much under the influence of Saturn. If, on occasion, we offered something that fell into a minor key, we were banned from her presence for the rest of the day. This will sound like nothing to you, but imagine, if you will, that music is the only medicine that brings the queen relief, then take away her daily dosing. And meanwhile? We were given a lecture on the value of bright and simple things. There were a few miraculous days in which he let her out into the riverside galleries for an hour or two, and she played her monochord with us. But we were not to look at her directly, for she was "very ill and any little thing could excite her" and then "measures would have to be taken, and surely you don't want to be the cause of that."

Measures. You know exactly what I mean—don't look so shocked. For is it not well known in your pious ranks that sometimes the knotted rope is the only cure for the intractable spirit?

Seven years later, when Ferrer was at last driven out, we saw the punishing cord with our own eyes. It was kept in a cupboard far from the public rooms. Very secluded. Very hard to find. And he would claim, as he left, that he was only following the orders of Fernando himself, and if he hadn't *corrected* her, she would not have eaten or kept herself clean—did we want our lady to die? As for orders: don't you obey, without question, the orders of your superior—and doesn't he obey his, and so on, up the chain to the inquisitor general?

Never mind that Ferrer's heretic was the rightful heir to the Crown of Castile, twenty-seven years old, and a widow who had borne six children, managing to keep her last by her side.

I don't like to think about the strength that took.

Why, you might ask, were any chamber musicians kept at all? Initially, Fernando thought it best to keep up appearances, in case of noble visitors demanding a glimpse of the queen. And for the town itself. Ah, yes, and to give Catalina music lessons once she was old enough. Look, he could say, even in her illness my daughter has her favorite consolation—music—and Catalina is receiving her education precisely as befits an infanta. But there was a day when we musicians were once more told to pack our things. This time Ferrer gave us each a small purse, and thanked us for our service. Even at the time I knew it was a test: to see how far he could tame the queen without killing her outright. He was clearly nervous—clasping his hands and twisting them about—and he told us to remain in the outer corridor until, as he put it, "the danger had passed." His instincts proved correct: she stopped eating, bathing, and changing her clothes. She frightened her attendants with their own broom. She appeared to have no scruple about dying for lack of music.

So we magically reappeared, and took up our instruments, and our strange work.

Where would I have gone, had I been allowed to leave? Perhaps it is a fault in me—an old timidity—that I was content to stay. I had traveled enough to know the truth of what Pierre de la Rue had said at our last meeting: *one good listener is worth a thousand bored monarchs*. Besides, sometimes, in a quiet, out of the way place, you can hear yourself think, and new music comes. I scribbled little tunes, both light and dark: light, to fool Ferrer, but with little depths and side channels to bring solace to the broken heart. I had no ambition beyond that; no thought of sending the music further out. I wrote for her. I played for her. She, in return, wrote a musical puzzle, and played it on her monochord, by way of thanks. It slipped past all the women and all the guards. Anchieta would have caught it, and smiled, had he been with us in those years.

Oh, but I heard it, and stored it away. It was only a "thank-you" but it suggested that other news might be smuggled out through music.

There was one other thing that held me there. You remember the woman I'd seen on the bridge? The one in the French hood, with green eyes and a little split between her teeth? I liked to pretend she lived nearby, and that I might see her at San Antolín someday.

In those seven years under Ferrer we were blessed twice more with Fernando's visits. On one occasion he brought his new young wife Germaine, that she might learn the secret of fertility from Juana herself. Such a thing belongs in a play—it is too rich for life. The two ladies conversed for an hour, and came out arm-in-arm. Did Juana suggest, in general terms, that the problem might lie with the aging husband, and not the wife? And that she had heard there were remedies for old men, to make them virile once again?

I don't know. But there is a certain poetry to Fernando's fate. For not long after, young Germaine procured—and administered to him herself—an elixir made of extract of bulls' testicles and other little things. I have heard it said that a man may be killed by the thing he most desires. I don't say it myself. But *if* desire could be distilled, and taken at one gulp, it might well produce a black melody, one that would play itself on the body for the rest of time. Let's just say his hunger ate him, belly and brain, first fast, then slow, then fast again.

A music lesson of sorts, in that.

At any rate, as long as the king remained alive, Ferrer did his best to keep him informed of his daughter's own refusal to die. I overheard Ferrer once, dictating a report: "She is scarcely human . . . pissing like a beast and wearing the same gray gown day in and day out, eating on the floor." As a man, I dare not comment on such things. But I heard the laundress say, once, in a very quiet voice, that if Ferrer had borne six babes in so short a time, he might well do worse.

Of the gray gowns, nothing need be said. Except for when her father came, for whom should she dress? I did once see her make herself grand. It was on that other visit of her father's, which he made with a flock of nobles, intending to show them how poorly she lived and how ill-suited she was to rule—and how right he'd been to lock her away. The demonstration nearly failed, for during their visit she insisted on being bathed and dressed and served at table. For twenty days we had a proper court. Ferrer could not, in front of the grandees, treat her as he usually did.

And they had to hire extra musicians, since our ranks were so reduced, and there was so much demand.

Then Fernando and the nobles departed, and we fell back into silence again. And after a time the small trinkets and jewels Fernando was wont to send her ceased to come. Juana asked everyone—

the guards, the women in her chamber, Ferrer himself, if her father was still in good health. Everyone knew the truth, but no one was allowed to tell her: he had died. He had died, in fact, without producing an heir, and named Cardinal Cisneros regent in his stead. No one told her that her son Charles was anxious to be crowned king in his stead, and that only Cardinal Cisneros stood in his way, and he was feeble himself, and could not live long.

The doors of Tordesillas were firmly locked and she knew nothing, and was never, for a moment, truly alone. Where would she have run off to, if she could? I will tell you where: to the convent of Santa Clara just steps away, where her husband had been interred, and where the Sisters bowed their heads over simple soup, sang, and walked, barefoot beneath the ancient Moorish arches.

It was April of the year 1516. Chilly and bright as it is today. I woke in my alcove one morning to find the air itself one faint degree warmed. After Matins, I went as usual to the queen's chamber door. Not a single guard was there, nor any women. It looked bereft, that door, without the whispers of wool and silk and false concern.

I knocked, and a faint voice bade me come in.

Candles guttering, a foulness in the straw.

Juana was at her monochord, in one of her plain gray gowns, her hair hidden in a grimy cloth. On the floor were three bowls crusted with old porridge. In the light of one candle, down to a stub, she smiled at me. Catalina was at her feet in the dirty straw, playing with her little dolls.

"Where is everyone?" Juana asked. "Is it a mild day?"

"Very mild," I replied. "It seems all the important people are gone."

She could have been a girl in that moment, in that forgiving light. We both held still and listened hard. Then I began to play and she joined in. After a while she stopped. "They won't like it," she said lightly. "But please go on."

We must have played for an hour; even little Catalina sang. At last I stood up, and went out to the riverside passage. The child followed me there, and I lifted her up so she could see where the children played, and the horses passed along below. She squealed with joy, and squirmed in my arms, and though I feared I would be "given the rope" for such an act, I let her stand there by herself. I went down the passage in both directions, and into the courtyard too. There I met our haggard laundress, and the palace cobbler, who was picking herbs for a poultice. But not one official did I see, nor a single guard. I heard, at a distance, the sounds of shouting and cheers, of tambor and horn and drum. Only later would I learn what it was: the town of Tordesillas had had enough of Luis Ferrer. Men had assembled at the palace gate the night before, stifled the guard, and sent him packing. His lesser servants were paraded through the streets that day with placards round their necks announcing all their crimes against the queen.

But in the riverside corridor it was wondrously quiet. Just Catalina's voice as she called down freely to children on the path below, and they shouted back in great delight.

I went back to Juana's apartments to find a stranger there, a man in courtier's clothes, kneeling before the queen.

She was weeping softly.

Kindness, gentlemen. Kindness is the thing that breaks us.

Duque's spring, I call the time that followed. For no real reason. Everyone knows he was a failure. Our gentle failure, Hernan Duque de Entrada. An island, gentlemen, of eighteen months, in an ocean of forty-seven years. As I said before, it is nothing you can lay hands on. There is no record of it to speak of. That is its great beauty.

Juana was thirty-seven years old, and Catalina a somber girl of ten, her mother's comfort and companion.

Hernan Duque, as different from Ferrer as a man could be. Eyes of a greenish gray, a trim beard, a quiet voice, the sort you had to lean forward to hear. A man who understood that a small gesture can do great work. How Cardinal Cisneros found him—and what induced His Eminence to break, however briefly, from the tradition of hard masters—I will never know.

Our new mayordomo took the queen for a walk that very day, to the convent of Santa Clara. He did so for three days in a row, and many more after that. Everyone saw the effect: the color in Juana's cheeks, the beginnings of a timid smile. He ordered a window cut in her chamber wall for light and air, and she moved freely through all the rooms. Catalina was allowed to have a friend, little Beatriz, a girl from the riverbank tribe—she was made a member of court, and brought inside to play.

Even I received a gift, "for my long service," he said. A little house of two rooms on the Street of Kitchens. From its high back window I could see a corner of the palace's kitchen courtyard, and from the front window, a view of the houses across the street. I could come and go as I pleased, as long as I played at the queen's usual times, and on all great occasions, and was, of course, discreet.

I began to give lessons to gentlemen and their children in the town.

And it was not long after—late May—that the cooking at the palace improved.

You may say there's nothing odd about that. It was spring, after all, and the kitchen garden had its early peas and herbs and other greens. But what do you make of a queen who, for seven years, has made no mention of what she eats, and has refused food as often as she swallows it. What do you make of a queen glancing up from her plate to say, "I know this dish from long ago. My mother loved it, too."

Hernan Duque only smiled and said he was glad.

Juana's eyes shimmered, but she closed them briefly and straightened her spine. She turned to me where I sat waiting to play.

"Juanico," she said, "on your way home tonight, stop by the kitchens, and give my compliments to our new cook. And while you are there, let her give you a little more. You are getting too old to be so thin."

The palace, which I trust you'll take the time to explore, is so constructed that when you walk from the queen's inner apartments to the fine galleries on the riverside, you go from the blackest dark to an impossible light. I never left her chamber without putting my free hand out to steady myself against that sudden flood of light. So it was that day, and so it was that my hand was still out, like that of the old man she saw me becoming, as I made my way down and out into the street and across to the kitchens. I heard the familiar sounds: scrape and tap, a rill of notes, water pouring from a jug. Female laughter. I readied myself, for I knew the new cook and her kitchen maid would tease me as women always did: "Always underfoot, Juanico," the old cook used to say, as if I were still a scrawny boy. "Take a little taste!" I couldn't explain that it wasn't the food I hungered for, but the simple pleasure of being near women at work. She would have been insulted. But I could watch for hours the women at their kneading: the lift and fall of their forearms, the tapping of spoons. The way they bank up the last ashy coals of their cooking fires.

From the street, as I passed that afternoon, I heard the rhythmic beat of chopping—vegetables, I thought, not meat, by the clean quick thwack of it, nothing stopping the knife. As I opened the yard gate, I saw a small woman in a dingy gown, her back to me. Her elbow lifted and fell, and the clap of the knife on wood was sharp and clear, in sets of three. Two damp medallions darkened the dress beneath her shoulder blades.

That faded gown. That small square hand with its firm grip on the knife handle. So small and square, like a child's hand. A memory stirred my gut. One mushroom, in the pale light, tipped on its side like a lolling head.

Without turning, the woman said, "You have the lightest step of any man I know. You're barely here. Whereas I—"

She turned, and came down hard on one foot as she did. Then she licked her finger and touched it to the tip of my ear. "Dirty," she said. And then, in a smoky voice, "My name is Dolores and you are late for Mass."

I was trembling too much to fight with her. I bowed and turned, and was nearly to the gate when I remembered the queen's request.

"Dolores," I said. "The queen is grateful for your cooking." And then I turned on my heel. I was afraid to stay a moment more.

The next morning, in her chamber, Juana was pacing to and fro. "Well," she said. "What does she look like? Does she look like someone we know?"

"I can't really say," I replied. "She is certainly small. But she has a lame leg."

She did not look up from her work, but only nodded and said, "Ask her if she knows how to make lemon marzipan." She smiled. "Poor Juanico," she said. "All we do is order you about. Tell her to visit me, just once, so I might thank her for her work. Whoever she is, she has brought my appetite back."

At San Antolín that night, and the following, I prayed for serenity, for the grace to convince myself and the queen that Dolores Hernandez was who she said she was, and no one else. The *sanbenitos* hung along the nave flared at the corner of my eyes like flames, each with its family name shouting from the eaves. People do not return from the dead, I told myself, and as Pedro de Fermoselle himself had told me, the Holy Office does not lose people, even if they change their names and move to another town. Besides, I reasoned, Inés was light on her feet, and could move suddenly as a bird. This *Dolores* had a limp, as if one leg were shorter than the other. To watch her at her work, you'd think the earth itself arose to meet her.

As for the matter of cleaning my ear with her finger, well, maybe it was dirty. Maybe there was something about me that always made women want to clean my ear.

I stayed at church until the sun went down, then went back out into the street. Surely all the grandmothers of Tordesillas were watching me from their high windows. Look at the skinny bachelor out for a stroll along the riverbank, off to the river to commune with the biting insects!

One or two happy louts passed by. One cocked his head and winked. "Off to see a lady?"

The river was its usual secretive self, giving out only a faint lapping against the bank. I sat myself down beneath a wizened tree. On the water, only faint dimples stirred, until full dusk, when everything came alive at once: the insects, the birds and then the bats, and at last the fish who lie so wisely beneath the surface until that hour.

If I were a fish, I would never rise at all, but wait, all patience, for things to drown of their own accord.

In the dusk, I saw someone coming along the river path, and scrambled to my feet. She might be hidden in her cloak, but as she got close, the rhythm of her footfalls gave her away. She stood beside me a while and looked out, as I did, saying not a word. Then she asked if we might sit down beneath the tree. Her leg, she said, was beginning to ache.

I helped her to sit. Side by side we watched the water, and nobody spoke. The Duero is, of course, unnavigable at this spot. Did Fernando choose Tordesillas in part because of that? Did he fear his daughter capable of building a little boat, and bribing a servant to ferry her out?

What if a lullaby could come to life: a sea made of milk, and a boat of cinnamon. I would gladly fish for all our sorrows.

No chance of that here. The Duero at Tordesillas is broad across and greenish-brown. During storms it dares to ripple a little, but even then, very cautiously and evenly, lest it raise the viewer's suspicion that something lives beneath its surface: an errant rock or root, a fish, a drowning insect. But watch it at dusk, with a woman who is not in the mood to speak, and you will see all kinds of things—or imagine that you do. It occurred to me that this was why Inés had always loved dusk best: when the light softens and dims all divides, sharpening only branches against the sky, branches that hold nothing, and pull the eye away from human figures. They blur and vanish into the wavering light, and you are alone and free, and no one can hear your thoughts, or know your heart.

I waited as long as I could stand. But I lacked the patience of a fish.

"Inés," I said. "Tell me how you hurt your leg."

She gave the smallest sigh. "Don't call me that," she said. "And *I* didn't hurt it. I was one of the fortunate ones."

She pressed my hand, and warmth went through her palm into my veins, rich as some velvet broth. Let me die now, I prayed. Let me die before the next thing goes wrong.

"Tell me about the other servants," she said. "Which ones should I avoid?"

I said I didn't know, and this was true: I had learned, at Tordesillas, how to keep from knowing things. She laughed, and took away her hand. She said she was a little worried about the kitchen maid. The girl was very set in her ways, and resented any instruction at all. She had said, more than once, that she was from a fine Old Christian family that had never been given its proper respect.

We talked a little more about nothing much, and I said—and I truly believed it—that she had nothing to fear from the kitchen maid, as long as she treated her well, and didn't find too much fault. Then I stood up, and gave Dolores my hand, and helped her to her feet. She wavered and strove to right herself, like a candle flame recovering from a breeze.

"You walk away first," she said.

"No, you," I said. "Let me follow, to keep you safe."

Did her eyes fill? I don't know; it was full dark by then. But there was a kind of watery light in her voice. "Once I had a pretty leg and foot," she said, with a brief, low laugh. "And now I am of an age where my belly looks like it holds a babe inside, when in fact I have none, and fear I never will."

"Don't say that," I said, and before I could stop it, my own hand rested there, on the sweet and slightly rounded belly. I felt how warm it was through the cloth. She put her hand on mine, but it was only to move it away.

Then she said, "Do you like to walk in the country?"

I was glad it had grown dark. I told her I had not done so for many years, but would be glad to keep her company.

"On a Saturday?" she said.

"On any day," I replied.

Yes, Saturday. I only wanted to humor her. Let her scour the countryside for the old rituals of home; I was sure she would find nothing. The church eaves were dense with yellow tunics; how could there be a heretic left in the land?

She herself was full of caution, insisting that she walk ahead, at a good distance, till we were far beyond the gates of town. She wore her everyday clothes, but carried a little bag with a clean, embroidered blouse inside, "in case," she said, "we find a place where friends are gathered." Further and further we ranged out, and when her leg began to ache, we rested beneath a tree and she took from her bag some fruit and cheese and a crisp flat-bread she had, in the last few years, learned how to bake.

Sometimes we rested near a certain cottage, and she cocked her head. "Listen," she said. "Tell me if you hear singing."

I said I didn't.

"Exactly," she said. "Inside, they'll be dipping greens in salt water, and eating nuts with figs, and hard-cooked eggs." Then she pointed up at the chimney. And look, no fire, she said. And listen to how quiet it is, and how perfectly swept this little yard. She sighed as if she had found home.

She pressed my hand.

I waited, and she laughed. "Oh, I see. You are waiting for your knightly reward." Her cheeks were flushed as she kissed me, but she didn't rush. When she stopped, I drew her back to me, and she allowed this embrace for some time.

Then she put both her hands against my chest. "Wait here," she said. "Don't follow. Once I am inside, go home, and forget what you saw."

"What did I see?" I said.

"Exactly," she replied. "Nothing at all."

She stood up, and brushed off her clothes, and made me turn away while she changed her blouse. But as she got closer to their door—and away from me—a wildness poured through me, a fear that once she walked through that door, I would never see her again. "Wait," I called, and before she could answer, I was standing at her side. Her face was burning red, but it was too late: a little girl was at the door, calling for her mama, and tugging us both inside.

They're gone now, that family. Some of them are dead and some are in exile, their descendants scattered far and wide—to Amsterdam and Venice and God knows where else. It will not hurt them if I recite their names, but you could just as easily go across to San Antolín and look up at the cloud of yellow tunics. You'll find them there.

I will tell you how it went: how we were greeted with love—they seemed, already, to know Dolores, or her kin, though I think now it was just the joy of those so eager to share old customs, to make a family larger than their own. We sat in their house for a time, and though I kept quiet and out of the way, they had a vihuela and induced me to play for them, nothing religious, only folk tunes everyone loved from long ago, and they told a very long story that might have had Moses in it, and the parting of the seas. When it was over, Dolores and I walked back together, and when I offered my arm, she took it, "only because it is dark," she said, "and I don't want to fall." I waited until we reached our usual spot, under the tree, then slowed down, and turned to face her, my heart very loud in my ears. Her face was still alight with the sweetness of the day.

"Inés," I said.

She stopped and frowned. "Dolores," she said. "Say it after me."

"Dolores," I said, then slid my fingers along the side of her shawl until it fell away.

She calmly picked it up again and put it back on. "You tremble too much for a full-grown man," she said. "Walk me home."

For a week I caught only glimpses of Dolores here and there. But I had made up my mind: I would ask her, one last time, about her injured leg, and beg her to tell me what had happened at Valladolid. Surely she would tell me now. I confess I wanted something more. I wanted her to take off her shoe, unwrap the foot from its stocking, and let me hold it, feel its heft, its weight, in my palm. Did my face reveal what I wanted then? She was hard to find, and very brisk when we met.

She had asked me, in those early April days, not to talk to her beyond a passing way, in the kitchen yard, or anywhere else that people could see. I honored her request; Inés, after all, had been a lady of the court. But watching this Dolores move about, in the kitchen, I felt the old pang of watching Inés with Encina that night, the way he'd so firmly pushed back her hood, and raised her face to his.

At last I caught her alone by the riverbank, and after we had talked of other things, I said, "I tried to find you at Valladolid."

She said nothing for a long time. "I stayed in a private house there," she said mildly. "Two years. I don't know the name of the street, or where in town it stood. For a while I was kept somewhere else."

"And your trial?"

Her voice dropped. "Suspended," she said. "They never said why."

"Who was the inquisitor in your case?" I said. "Do you remember what he looked like?"

"Tell me something, Juanico," she said. "What would you do if someone asked you, someday, to tell everything you know about the woman you once knew, the heretic named Inés de Castro? What would you say?"

Well, I was properly stung. I fell silent, like a moody boy.

She sighed. "Now it is my turn. What did the queen want you to ask me?"

"If you would make her lemon marzipan," I said listlessly.

It was her turn to fall silent. At last she spoke. "Tell her this. Tell her I will gladly make anything else she loves, but never again lemon marzipan."

"And if she asks me why?"

"Tell her the truth," she said. "That lemons are prone to blight, like so much else."

The next day I dutifully passed the message along, and the queen bowed her head, and said she understood, and would never ask for it again. She sent me back with that message, and her thanks, which I was to deliver on my way to my new home.

And in this way, for well over a year, we found a sort of balance, a rhythm between what could be spoken and what must be left to dreams. Hernan Duque understood his task was to bring the queen ease and comfort, while still keeping from her the news of her father's death. Within his limited means, he allowed more music at Tordesillas, and took her walking every day, and in the spring of his second year, even began to prepare the fine riverside apartments as if, someday, she might hold royal audiences there. Tapestries were hung and carpets warmed the stone, and we had more candles than before. She must have sensed there was change in the air, but she couldn't have dreamed it was her father's death that had unclenched Ferrer's grip. As good and true as Hernan Duque was, he was forbidden to tell her that Spain belonged to her, and that her son Charles was preparing to come from the Low Countries, determined to rule our country himself.

That spring Dolores and I walked in the country again. It is true that we played and sang once for a wedding party, and that between the time the couple said their vows in church, and the time the fiddlers and drums began to play for dancing, there was some little private exchange between bride and groom, and I saw a man briefly bind their hands with a cloth, and the groom threw a wine glass in the air and let it fall to the ground and shatter. The feast itself was a strange mixed thing, which made Dolores shake her head and laugh. Yet it was sweet: they ate Dolores's unleavened bread, and I saw again the greens and salt water, the hard-cooked eggs. Again there was talk of "Saint Moses," who, they said, had been born after "our Lord Jesus Christ."

Now that it's all over, it doesn't hurt to ask: would a Jew of old recognize the rites performed that day? The thing was like a magpie's nest—something of this, something of that. And while it is true that Dolores sang and I played, our tunes were not religious at all, just good old songs, accompanied by tambor and drum, and good for dancing. I remember looking at the faces of the guests and admiring their courage. They insisted on living their ordinary lives—and for a moment, refused to show their fear.

Evening came, and the man who knew the rites came to us where we rested beneath a scrawny little tree, and asked if we were married. We looked at each other and Dolores gave a hearty laugh. "No, no," said Dolores. "He likes his bachelor life—and I do too."

"Well," said the man, "you look married, and maybe you are, under the stars and under God."

And before we could stop him, he had taken our hands and wrapped them in a bit of cloth, and mumbled some words. "What you might do together later is right and good, and no sin at all," he said. "May you bring forth life."

Dolores waited till he was gone, and then she said merrily, "Did you pay him to say that?"

I shook my head, and said I thought he'd had too much of the bridegroom's homemade wine. Then I fell very shy, and even Dolores seemed at a loss for words. We were saved by the tambor player, who came and said, "They want more dancing," and we played another hour or two, until the Compline bells, very faint from town, had rung their last. At last Dolores said she was very tired, and must rest her leg a while. And under lantern and starlight she gave me a small smile to destroy my wits and everything else. I understood the poets then, who said, give me this one night, and I will gladly die.

One more song, she said, and without consulting her, I began to play, and she to sing, "There is a Tower at the Sea." Her voice was roughened with smoke and she looked at me as a bride looks at a groom.

Give me your hand, dove
So that I might climb to your nest
You're unlucky to sleep alone
I'll come to sleep with you.

That night, we lay together in a corner of the country house, and knew for ourselves the pleasures of a bride and groom. Time itself gave us a little wedding gift, and turned modestly away while we loved. We laughed, afterward, to think that under the stars and by the law of Moses, it might be said that we, too, were married.

I am no religionist. But some things are holy to me. To watch a woman shine with calm as she lets a shawl fall from one shoulder. It wasn't until it was over that I had a sudden fear. We were resting, and I was utterly at peace, when my hands and feet went cold, and I felt her vanish beside me as if the earth were tugging her down. I pulled her close, and she nestled in—but soon enough she declared she couldn't breathe, and wriggled free.

As you may have heard from others, the Jews have a custom: to part the bride and groom after their first night together, and keep them from each other for seven days and nights. They have their reasons, I suppose, and the rabbi-who-was-not-a-rabbi, in the morning, told me two of these: First, in case the lady is in her unclean time. Second, to honor some story from the Torah—he didn't know what it was, himself. I only know about its effect, because, by virtue of what happened next, the fate of a young husband befell me too.

The morning after the wedding dance, Dolores and I parted as if nothing at all had changed. She walked back to the kitchens alone, and I took myself straight to Mass at San Antolín, and from there to my little house. I thought I might sleep for a hundred years.

But in the bright of early afternoon someone knocked on the door. It was old Anchieta himself, so long away. It seemed he'd been restored to his old position as chapelmaster to the queen, sent by Bishop Cisneros himself, he said, to keep an eye on our sovereign lady's condition. And furthermore, two important persons were about to arrive—any minute—from Valladolid. The cook and her assistants had just been told they must "outdo themselves" and Anchieta would organize the music. We were to be in our places, ready to perform, when they arrived.

That's how it happened that by afternoon, I was playing, by Anchieta's command, the music of Juan del Encina. The grand sala was bright with early summer light and a silky breeze blew from the riverside. The queen and her daughter were in the other room, putting on their best gowns. A good table was already laid.

It was Duque himself who brought the visitors in.

They were both covered in dust from their ride, and the elder of the two wore a cleric's broad black hat against the sun. When he took off his cloak, I saw his priestly garb and a portly shape. But it was not until he removed his hat that I saw his face, and recognized his eyes: still bright hazel with their lavender shadows beneath. Juan del Encina's face was flushed, and there was a heaviness to his limbs I hadn't seen before, but he still had his dark, curly hair, only a little gray, and a fine bearing that drew the eye. He held a small wooden crate in his arms, covered with a cloth, which he now set down on the sideboard, and opened with a flourish.

Then he clapped me hard on the back. "Well, Juanico," he said. "Aren't you going to welcome me in? Or are you sorry to see me again after so many years?"

"I am not sorry," I said. And I embraced my old master and took in his warm gravelly voice—a memory of my father's voice. Too long ago now. A seduction, I understood. But the man behind him cleared his throat. He wore cleric's garb too, but his robes were made of better, darker cloth, and he wore, on a chain around his neck, the medallion of the Valladolid Tribunal.

"And how long has it been for us?" said Pedro de Fermoselle.

I was struck dumb. Hernan Duque smiled graciously, that man of patience who was nearly as innocent a fool as I. But I could neither count the years nor bring out any witty words. Pedro watched me with the same bright, curious eyes he'd always had, the same light, swift glance. He was like a fisherman, alert to the water's slightest ripple, and gifted in the art of setting the hook. I remember wishing that he was fat, or had an unsightly wart, or the blazing pain of gout that afflicts so many men of status and authority. But no. He was slim and sinewy and slightly underfed, a functionary who might live—and do his duty—until the end of time. Unlike his brother Juan, Pedro was a man who could forgo his bread if there was work to be done.

Only one thing was different: his shoulders curved slightly forward as if protecting a weakness at the chest, and for the briefest moment, I saw how that curve would deepen as he aged. I confess I made a wish that it would curve him till, when he walked, his eyes met the ground.

I still had not spoken, and finally Duque stepped in. "What is this treasure you've brought from the south?" he said.

And Juan del Encina bade us look into the box.

Lemons. Perfect, unblemished lemons. Like something in a dream, demanding your attention, but meaning something other than they are.

"Shall we play for the queen and the infanta, for old times' sake?" Encina said. "We hear good reports of the music at Tordesillas. Almost as legendary as the cooking, if the rumors are true."

fourteen

Lemons in a crate. Bright as little suns. Why shouldn't we have them? Why should we distrust their color, their jostling beside each other in an ordinary wooden crate? I told myself I had lived too long among secrets, that this was a perfectly natural gift. But Pedro, wearing an inquisitor's badge and robes, was at Encina's side, and surely in the Valladolid Tribunal's *secreto*, in its Records Room with its three locks, among the papers devoted to the Castro family's persistent heretical habits, there was testimony from the pastry cook's apprentice at Benavente. Testimony concerning one Doña Inés Castro and her willingness to cook lemon marzipan over dying embers on a Friday afternoon. Nor had I forgotten what Pedro himself had told me: that the Holy Office doesn't lose people. Change of name and town might delay discovery, but never prevent it.

I stayed in the grand sala a few moments longer, discussing the June weather with Duque and the two brothers, and agreeing that the queen should have music every afternoon. How could I get word to Dolores and put her on her guard? At last the discussion turned to supper and sleeping arrangements. I went to the music table and fussed with my vihuela until it was sufficiently out of tune. "My apologies," I said. "Let me just take this away. I promise to be brief."

"I'll come along," said Encina, "and see where you live."

I murmured something about a bachelor's neglect of housekeeping. The brothers exchanged a smile, and Encina took me by the arm. "Nothing would surprise me—we are all three bachelors. We'll go together, you and I, and surprise the cook with this gift on our way."

Either I was going mad, or Juan del Encina, whose own music had always held secrets, and whose poetry mourned the necessity of deceit, was now his younger brother's ferret.

In the kitchen yard, Dolores sat on her favorite bench, shelling peas into a bowl and resting her leg on a little stool. Her shoulders and back were slumped; I had never seen her in such a tired pose. The kitchen maid who bore her no love stood nearby, chopping onions on a board. The girl's face was damp from onion tears, and set, as ever, in its sullen mold. I turned to Encina at the gate.

"We'll leave the gift here," I said. "Our poor cook is tired—we've had so many visitors this spring."

He agreed, though not without a frown at Dolores' small, aproned back, and we set the lemons by the gate. We soon stood at the door to my house. But his eagerness to see it was gone; he asked about the palace wine cellar, which was just next door. I had never gone down there myself, and believed it to be small and not well-stocked. I told him so. Furthermore, I said, the high steward kept the keys very close.

"As he should," he said. "And does the high steward have a wife?"

I was a little shocked. Encina was forty-eight years old, and wearing a cleric's robes. He laughed and said he was only testing me, glad to see I was still my old and easily affronted self. "Go up and make your repairs," he said. "I will wait for you here."

I went up alone while he waited in the street. Upstairs, my fingers were cold and clumsy on the strings, as in a dream when you can't tie a knot or thread a needle. When at last I came back down, he was just standing up, as if he'd been kneeling to look at something in the street. He scuffed at the cobbles with the toe of his boot and shook his head.

"Someone must have spilled wine," he said, taking my arm and turning away from the cellar gate. "Now, shall we try the kitchens again? Surely your little cook is rested by now."

Back at the kitchens, Dolores was on her feet. Encina insisted on taking up the box of lemons, still sitting by the gate, and bringing it in. "No excuses now," he said. "Introduce me to the other legend of Tordesillas."

I approached her, hoping my raised eyebrows would suffice as warning. But she wasn't looking at me.

"Doña Dolores," he said, with a gallant bow. "We are so looking forward to supper. Do you know your talent is spoken of in Madrid and beyond? Beware—you could be abducted by an envious grandee."

She blushed. How could she not—the compliment was so extravagant, and yet it touched a secret vanity. He had a nose for the lasting childhood trait. Now, like the girl she'd been at thirteen—the last time she'd seen him—she shyly dropped her gaze.

Never has a crate of lemons received such somber scrutiny.

"I will do something with these for tomorrow," she said. "What are my instructions from the queen?"

"Something sweet," he said. "Would lemon marzipan be too much trouble?"

She held very still—too still, if you knew her—and told him it would be no trouble at all. I watched her face as she spoke, watched it the way we watch the heavens when they cannot decide to rain or shine.

And myself? Suddenly invisible at his side.

Had I been less proud and miserable, what might I have seen? That she knew what he was up to, and was trying to thrust me out of harm's way? That he had a job to do, and no fond memory of her kisses would keep him from it? I don't know; I felt purely cast aside. Married under the stars and God! I was a poet and a fool, and shouldn't a fool sacrifice himself by walking away, and letting the lovers reunite in peace? Besides, I told myself, he was important, and could protect her in ways I never could.

I excused myself politely and turned to go. But as I went, Dolores called my name. "Why so unfriendly?" she called, and I saw the kitchen maid glance up from her work. Alas I had not quite set my own mask. I have told you enough for you to guess how Dolores might act: how quick she was to perceive, to judge, to leap.

She was at my side. The bowl still in her arms. The kitchen maid was chopping less angrily now, her face gone perfectly mild.

This is the moment I remember: so small, so apparently without consequence. She searched my face as if I'd been the one to inflict some hurt on her. The look nearly reached me where I'd burrowed in my shell.

Encina stood there, watching, waiting.

"I prefer them preserved," I said at last. "And added to chicken or some other dish, if time permits."

"Ah poor Juanico, but time never does," she replied.

To say that she smiled at me is to do her an injustice. It was a look I still find difficult to describe. Worry in the eyes, a sadness I had never let myself notice before. And something else—I saw now that crease in the brow that deepens as we age. But in the curve of her lips was still something of the old Inés, of a child's sparkling thirst for risk. A look as tart as any lemon, and one by which, as long as I had sight, I would know her in any season, by any name.

She was trying to say goodbye. And I missed that, too.

I have always thought that unending time is the place in hell reserved for me. And this may yet prove true. But first, time had to quicken, to press forward at astonishing speed. That is what time does when false justice, with its maddened appetite, hankers to be served.

She sat back down and put her hands back in the bowl. As she shelled, she kept the frown, but now it was the mild one, that of a cook who has just been told there are extra guests for dinner. As Encina and I stood there awkwardly, she seemed to come to a decision of some kind. She glanced at her assistant, so quiet at her onions. And without another word to us, she told the girl to stay and receive all deliveries, and finish the vegetables—she, Dolores, would be back soon. The girl, in turn, gave a respectful dip. It was all very worrisome. More worrisome still was the fact that as Dolores did this, she was taking off her apron and putting on her sturdiest shoes.

"I am so sorry to leave you here," she said. "But I have errands in the town, and I'm sure you gentlemen are needed at the palace."

"Not at all," said Encina. "We have the hour quite free."

But she, apparently, did not. She was already on her way up the street, her limp like some ghastly beacon for all to see and be guided by.

He wanted to wait a little, then follow her.

"That will look strange," I said. "Why would you?"

"What is strange," he said bitterly, "is how incurious you are. *Poor Juanico.*" He paused, and let me see his face: the tired eyes, the too-firm set of the jaw: a man with no love in his life for years. "A word of advice, from one who has learned the hard way. Never try to impede the Holy Office from its work. It helps no one."

"Tell me one more thing," I said. "Why is this little cook so important?"

"She isn't," he said. "She is merely easy to catch, and one fish always brings in others. Also, King Charles is concerned that too much money is spent here." He shook his head. "Now off you go to the queen's chambers, and keep our sovereign lady calm and consoled."

And he waited, with grim patience, until I obeyed.

You are aware of our church of San Antolín across the street. No need to look; its doors are perfectly blank today. We have a visiting inquisitor now and then, but he finds us dull. But that June day, you would have seen the proclamations nailed up, both there, and at Santa Clara's gates. They are ever the same, such notices. In small print, at the bottom, the necessary reminder that it is a Criminal Act to remove or deface the notice. This reverence for pieces of paper has always impressed me; not a morsel may be lost to history, praise God, except for whatever it was that the Flemish scribe threw off the *Julienne* on our voyage back to Spain. It pleases me to imagine other papers, covered in careful script, even some referring to heretical acts, that somehow get flung into water, burned, or torn up by hand.

How maddening that must be to the Holy Office. Our young scribe would never do such a thing.

At any rate, the Edicts of Faith were to be proclaimed at San Antolín the next morning after Mass. It seemed, however, the purpose of the notices had already been fulfilled: as beautiful a day as it was, there were no children playing on the riverside path, and only a lone merchant or two who hadn't heard the news, going past on his mule. You would think the town had been visited by the plague.

Juana had little idea what went on outside the palace walls: only stray bits of gossip the housemaids blurted out, and who could trust them? She did seem strangely agitated that June, however, and the next day, ordered her small corps of musicians and singers shaken out of siesta, and brought sleepily to the *grand sala*. We played from after the midday meal till just before supper, and she told us she would like to hear more that night. She would, I think, have detained us forever, so intensely did she crave music. That night at supper, with Encina and Pedro back among us, she became more insistent still. She closed her eyes a good bit of the time, but especially when Encina sang, as if she were dreaming she was a girl again, writing poetry in a garden. Later she joined us and played the small portative organ; her bellows-men pumped until their arms were sore.

Pedro excused himself before dessert, and begged the queen's leave to go to Compline at San Antolín. After that, he said, he would spend some hours with our local priests. She let him kiss her hand, and after he was gone, Encina explained that his brother had been given new responsibilities of late, and felt his duty keenly, and could not bring himself to rest. Juana seemed to accept this, and lifted her hand as her mother used to do, to signal us to resume our playing. I remember watching her face, and Hernan Duque's, and Encina's, to see if they were enjoying the meal. And to see if, at dessert, lemon marzipan candies were served.

They were not, and I felt a foolish relief. Surely it meant she understood my meaning, and was on her guard. But then I noticed something else: the way Encina watched the candles as night went on, watched them as if to will them to burn down. But he could not politely get away, and at a very late hour, the queen asked him to play something new of his own. He begged her pardon, and said that his travels for the Church had made the writing slow. For all that, he said, he was glad to be so much in service of Our Lord Jesus Christ, and Italy, in particular, had been full of wonders: he had even found himself at Venice and Rome, much in demand at the pope's table.

The queen nodded absently; she was the wrong audience for such tales. But I was glad to overhear it: this explained the high color in his cheeks, the delicate mottlings on the slope of his nose, and his great interest in our little wine cellar.

"Will you go to Rome again soon?" she asked. "And take your brother with you?"

Encina looked surprised by the sharp note in her tone, and replied cautiously that indeed, he might travel there once more before he settled down. Pedro, alas, was too busy to get away. "Your Majesty," he went on, "it has been a great joy to visit Tordesillas, and see you and the infanta so well, and to hear music and dine at your table."

"Why did you come?" she said. "To Tordesillas."

Hernan Duque put his napkin to his lips, and began to push back his chair.

But Encina was very smooth. "We were at supper with Cardinal Cisneros in Madrid," he said. "He suggested the journey. He wanted to make sure you are happy with your servants and with all things. Your son, the king—"

Juana was on her feet. "What do you mean? My son is not king." She looked warily at Duque and smoothed her gray gown with both hands, as if it were a regal robe. She called for her daughter to come stand by her side. "Juanico," she said. "Supper is over. The infanta will sing for us, and you will play. I am sure our dear brother's old tutor would like to hear how musical she is."

By which I understood I was to detain her "dear brother's old tutor" until he was ready to collapse, or pack his things and leave for Italy on the spot.

Before the lights burned down that night, she would surprise our small company once more. She waited till Encina was making his farewells, and asked him to explain once more why his brother had not honored her by staying the entire evening with his sovereign. The room went very still once more—I almost thought that Duque would take her arm and lead her away before Encina could give his answer. She had the look of a person who must be answered. Encina, looking deeply worn, gave a respectful bow. "He truly wanted to stay. But he had promised to meet with the local clergy—he had to arrange an inspection of the church and the prisons around town."

"Prisons," said the queen, her voice very clear and quiet. "Do we have Inquisition prisons at Tordesillas?"

He could not look away without offending her. "No, no, not here. I misspoke. I meant the ones at Toro, at the Tribunal there."

"Well," she said. "You would not shock me if you said we had them here. The countryside is stuffed with heretics of every kind. Is there anyone in Castile who might not be accused? I may be one myself."

Her wit was too deep, even for him. He looked alarmed, and would, I saw, report it back to Cisneros that he had seen several signs of fragility, possibly of madness—and this would suit the old cardinal and the advisers of young Charles perfectly well.

"Well," said Duque. "We'll have one more song."

The tune she asked for was one of my own. I wish she had left it in the dark. Encina leaned forward to hear it, but gave no sign of whether he thought it good. But I remember this: he was suddenly paying close attention. I recognized the look of old: he was committing it to memory. It gave me a chill, but I kept playing.

The queen was watching everything. "Juanico, you look ill," she said. "Shall I send for Doctor Soto?"

"No, no," I said.

"We will let you all go," said Duque. "It is very late."

Night in Tordesillas, even under the gentle Hernan Duque, lay under heavy guard: a hundred watchmen at the town gates, and a special militia roaming the streets. As I walked out that night, it occurred to me that between the usual watchmen, and the presence of the Holy Office in town, we had more than the usual quiet.

At the kitchens, no one was about but two boys, washing platters in a great tub, and making a great racket as they did. No Dolores. No kitchen maid.

It sank in now: Encina following Dolores up the street. He would have followed her as far as she went, to the country house itself. The populace, too, would have promptly responded to the notices at San Antolín, everyone anxious to do the right thing, the proper thing, reporting to Pedro and the local priest any little thing that seemed amiss—a clean blouse on a Friday night, the lack of smoke from a chimney on a Saturday morning.

Tordesillas has always been a small place.

The moon was bright enough for an evening walk. I went past my own house and up the way Dolores had gone. I remembered my mother's phrase, from that morning in Granada so long ago. "If only there'd been half a moon." It was about a mile out, but long before I saw the house on its little knoll, I saw the gleam of lanterns. Such is the swiftness of justice in the case of small prey.

Two guards were posted there for the night watch, to keep thieves from stealing the household goods to be confiscated in the morning. The family had already been taken away.

As I approached, they asked what business I had on that hill so late at night.

"Out for a stroll," I said. "But tell me, was it a big nest? How many were taken?"

"We don't know," said one. "We don't get into that."

"I played for the family once," I said. "Not that long ago. A country dance after a wedding."

Shouldn't that have been all it took? Shouldn't they have clapped me in irons and thrown me in their cart, so that in the morning I would at last be taken to one of these secret prisons and see for myself what happened to so many, so many who never spoke of what they'd been through, if they were ever seen again at all?

They gave me a long slow look by lantern light, then one guard drawled to the other, "I'm tired of all these people coming by with their little remarks—now they're even coming from the palace! We don't need some sad-eyed eunuch to tell us he played vihuela for the Jews. Where's the good in that—music is music." Then he turned to me. "Go back to your bed," he said. "We don't need you here."

As a small boy, I had flung myself out a doorway in a false rage, and stepped to the side of a blind girl in need of water. I had played my vihuela for heretics in Antwerp and Benavente, and now I could, it seemed, lean against a pile of dry sticks and no one would take the time to light the pyre. Let Encina use me as bait to catch a Judaizer. Let him steal my music and make it better. Let the queen declare herself to be the heretic they seek, and let her vihuelist declare himself a party to criminal acts, and somehow, the two of us, the queen and her vihuelist, would be swept to the side like two leaves in a sluggish stream, endlessly bumping against one black root.

In the morning, I dragged myself to the grand sala. Encina and Pedro were already there, dressed in their caps and traveling cloaks. Both looked quite worn, as if they had not slept well at Tordesillas. While we waited for the queen to emerge from her apartments, Encina turned to me and said, "I meant, yesterday, to ask if you happen to know how the new cook got that limp?"

"I don't know," I said. "She isn't much for talking about herself."

"That's true enough," he said, and exchanged a brief look with Pedro. "But you might like to know she said nothing but kind things about you."

"Such as?" I said, with ice in my veins. For once again Pedro's eyes were bright and watching. It was he who answered my question.

"Such as," he said, "nothing that would tie you to her at all."

The queen never came out of her room that morning, and Duque came and made excuses, and begged Encina's pardon, and signaled that I should stay nearby. She was agitated, and feeling poorly, and unable to say farewell. But the moment Encina was gone, she came out of her apartments. Her eyes were red-rimmed, her face very pale and pinched.

"The food tastes wrong today," she said. "What has happened to our cook?"

Duque's voice was quiet and full of care. "She had to go away last night," he said. "It is a family matter, and she didn't have time to make her farewells. We are all very sorry to lose her."

"But where would she go?" she said, her voice trembling. "What family does she have left?"

Duque shook his head. "I don't know," he said. "But these things happen, and you should not let it trouble you. We will find a new cook."

She did not look at me at all. She did not turn to me and say, "Go find her, find out what has happened."

She didn't need to.

What I didn't expect, when I walked home from Mass that morning, was that the kitchen maid was gone as well. There were three townswomen in the yard, plucking chickens and complaining loudly. The two boys were still there, loafing about. I asked if they knew what had become of the former cook, or even the kitchen maid.

"The girl had had enough. She didn't like being ordered about."

"And?"

"And then the cook went off with your friend, the priest who used to play music and write plays. We saw them together; he was holding her arm." He gave his friend a lewd wink. "The kitchen maid says she was a witch, and putting things in the food to make men fall in love with her, even though she's no maid anymore. My mother says the cook will pay for that sin soon enough."

The boy put his hand on his belly, and staggered as if it bore a great weight.

It was Anchieta himself who came to tell me that both Encina and the inquisitor Pedro de Fermoselle had departed. "A very short visit," he said, and waited as if I would tell him what I knew. I asked if he knew why they'd left so soon.

"Encina seemed shaken by something," Anchieta said. "He is on his way to Jerusalem, to take holy orders there. He says if he ever returns to Spain, it will be to live humbly in a quiet place." Anchieta shook his head. "He was a true genius, you know. There is no telling what he might have done."

All of July and into August I made inquiries with the queen's own confessor, and the priest at San Antolín, until finally Anchieta was sent to speak with me. He said I would harm the queen's health and reputation if I kept asking questions. I should forget all about this matter; it was being handled properly, and that the cook would be treated mercifully, especially if it turned out to be true, as she claimed, that she was with child.

"The Holy Office," he said, "will make sure the child is baptized, and removed to a good home if necessary."

If necessary. My palms sprang sweat. "And what if the child is mine?" I choked out.

"That's noble of you," he said with a sad smile. "These matters are not to be bandied about, but since you are so distraught, I will tell you that the cook has already given her testimony, under oath, and confessed everything, including the name of the child's father. It was not yours."

"She is lying to save me. What name did she give?"

He shook his head and turned to go. "Juan del Encina," he said. "Nobody believes that, either."

fifteen

That September, the Duero kept her secrets under a dark blue sky. Rumors floated past, rising and sinking at the palace doors: Fernando had been dead nearly a year, and now, they said, the old cardinal was gone too, and Charles had declared himself the King of Spain. Never mind that he was only seventeen, had never set foot in our country, and did not speak the language. Never mind that the grandees of Castile bore him no love. If Juana heard such flotsam, she could not get poor Duque to confirm it. The order to keep silence still came from Madrid, but now it was composed in Flemish and sealed with foreign wax. That's how we knew that Charles' advisers had already arrived in Spain. There was no telling how soon Tordesillas would change, and in what ways. We only knew that it would.

Encina had remarked, before he left, that Charles wanted to make changes in his mother's household, changes *befitting her royal status*. This, I suppose, explains the logic of replacing one excellent cook with three noisy, mediocre ones and explains, too, the endless hammering of workmen in distant palace rooms that began that month. The skin beneath Duque's eyes was puffed and pale, and he had taken to repeating himself in a flattened voice: *I have been instructed to make all necessary repairs.* That alone was enough to set off rumors in the street: Was Charles already in Spain? Were apartments being prepared for him, in case he should decide to come to Tordesillas to kiss his mother's hand?

Yet on the subject of the vanished cook and the people in the country house, there was a remarkable silence. In market place and kitchen yard and on a busy river path, there were only shrugs. A few people went so far as to cross themselves. Even objects were forbidden to speak: the cook's sleeping alcove in the palace was empty—even the bedclothes were gone—and the country house had been stripped of every cup and book and bit of cloth.

But silence has a body like everything else, a hunger to be heard. One morning I woke in the dark, my own name still ringing in the air. It was a woman's voice I'd heard, calling firmly, the way you'd rouse a child who'd lain too long and lazily abed. I sat up straight, every nerve alive and jangling. My mother's ghost had plucked me while I slept.

My name—no, not the one you know me by. The one my mother wrote on a slip of paper with other words to keep me safe, and hid in an amulet carried next to my heart. Until the morning Inés destroyed the paper, whispered it in my ear, and warned me to keep it to myself.

All these years I have never spoken it aloud.

I stumbled down the stairs and opened the door, trying to keep the voice in my ears as rooftops took shape against the sky. It seemed to carry memories: Of the little tree at dusk, where Dolores and I would sit, where she said so little about herself. Of Granada on a winter's morning, the taste of snow on the tongue. Does time, like music, take pleasure in repeating phrases? For as I stepped into the street, three birds burst out from the opposite eaves, as if the bells of Christian conquest had sent them forth again.

It was the soft clack of their wingbeats that made me look up. Made me notice that the small barred windows under those eaves were shuttered and fastened with locks. Other house windows further down the street were open wide to accept a breeze.

For some reason, looking up reminded me to look down. And that's when I saw, on the cobbles beneath my feet, now lit by the first pale strokes of daylight, three small rust-red stains. There, in the very place Encina had scuffed with the toe of his boot.

Someone must have spilled a little wine, he'd said. But it didn't look like wine to me. And why would he have tried to scuff it out?

By now the sun had risen, and still I stood at the cellar gate, so close to my own door. Behind the gate lay a set of descending stairs. I passed them every day and paid them no mind. They were very old and worn, older than the palace, no one knew how old. Down they led, and made a turn, beyond which I couldn't see.

My Hebrew name? There is no reason to keep it from you now. Yasque. Yasque is my given name.

To watch without being seen requires skill. It is not unlike playing: you must practice every day; you must be ready for the small surprise just at the point where you were ready to give up. There is the same brief fear of success, the desire to close the eyes, to never watch—or never play—again. This is why, at the time you most want to work on this new tune, life itself seems to play its own mad song against you.

That autumn, it was Juana and her daughter Catalina who wouldn't let me go. They seemed to have awakened from a stupor, hungry for music and visitors and all manner of dangerous things. Poor Hernan Duque, his task—of keeping the queen from knowing things—was never more difficult than on those fine autumn days.

Music, as you can imagine, is a help at such times. Our chapel-master Anchieta, if he thought he had been restored to Tordesillas to live a quiet life, was under constant commission for new work, and had to train our young singers, too. Our small consort played and sang at meals and resting times alike, and I became the master of music lessons. Even little Catalina wanted to take up the vihuela, and so did our visitors. With all this, I had little time to watch the street. Still, I never saw the high steward go near that cellar. He brought the palace wine from a smaller vault close by.

My own window was too high and small to see what happened just below, but it did admit sound, and of course the Street of the Kitchens was busy with carts during daylight hours. But between twilight and dawn it was quiet. The street guard helped keep it so, as did the emptiness of the house just across. If I strolled out with my vihuela, and played a tune or two, the guard paid me no mind. I was just the queen's vihuelist to him. If he thought me a little cracked, so much the better, and if I shared a bit of the queen's good wine with him, it was only because the days were growing cold.

That's how I glimpsed the woman who came and went, who un-locked the cellar gate just before dawn and after dusk, walked down the worn slope of those stairs, and disappeared around its little bend. An ordinary housewife, as best I could tell, she went in with a small belt of keys and a covered basket, and emerged not long after, the same basket easy on her arm, and something easier in her step as well.

Every third night she brought out a heavy covered pail, which she held straight out before her. I was quite sure, by now, it was not wine being stored below.

On those nights of the stinking pail, a grumbling man accompanied her to the gate, and took the pail away. Once in a great while, he went with her down the steps, but he never stayed for long—and sometimes he didn't come at all. It was not till late October that a third figure began to descend the stairs—a stooped and elderly one I knew: the physician, Doctor Soto, who had settled his family in town when we first arrived, and one of the gentlemen to whom I'd given music lessons.

You know what drove me now. A woman warden, a doctor visiting a cellar vault. The sound of my own name called before first light, at the hour the wardress would most naturally open the door to bring the daily ration of food, and a breath of air.

Old Doctor Soto, it seemed to me, was my best way in.

A fine family, prominent in Tordesillas for many years, until Soto's descendants found the Tordesillas air too foul, and moved away. No one guessed how illustrious he'd been; he kept it to himself. But in fact, he had been at court for many years, and was the man who'd mended my arm the day I fell from the tree. He'd attended the dying Prince Juan, and been at Queen Isabel's deathbed when that noble lady died. How slow I was to recognize the truth: that it might not be a coincidence that he lived in Tordesillas, so near Isabel's beleaguered daughter. It might have been loyalty that brought him there— and sympathy, too. Who knows but that Isabel herself hadn't begged a deathbed favor: *Watch out for my daughter. She may well need a friend.*

Isabel couldn't have known how difficult that would be. In our first seven years at Tordesillas, under Luis Ferrer, the doctor was closely watched, his visits kept brief—there were even suspicions raised as to the purity of his blood, and whether he was fit to attend the queen. But as Juana's health improved under Duque, those rumors fell away, and he came to her often, to offer conversation as well as medical advice.

As for the vihuela, his fingers were no longer supple, but he learned some simple tunes and got such pleasure from it that one night he invited me to supper at his home. He had a grown son and daughter-in-law, he said, that he would like me to meet. And Duque, that innocent, gave me leave to go.

We were on our way to his home, the doctor and I, passing my own house door, when Doctor Soto glanced up at the high window, then at the guard at the nearest street corner. "You must enjoy having your own house," he said. "After so long in the palace."

Good manners—or a subtlety woven of the finest cloth? He was like Anchieta in that way: caution and care dressed every word. But there was a crack of strange light, too—something I never heard in Anchieta's voice—and so I took a chance.

"I do, but for the quiet," I said. "Lately," I went on, "it's been almost as quiet as the palace under Ferrer. There used to be a family across the street, and one next door—I'm not sure why they left."

He nodded, and said, in a voice loud enough for the guard to hear, that this was the case in several places around the town. He believed it was the fear of plague. "Closer to the water," he said, "a worry takes root, very reasonably so."

Oh, to have seen the guard's face—a shame it was growing dark.

That's when the cellar gate creaked. The wardress stood there, utterly still, her basket on her arm, her free hand at her mouth as if we'd given her the fright of her life.

But she recovered quickly, and greeted old Soto, and said, very rapidly, that it was a miracle to meet him here, for one of her own children was feeling unwell. Could he come with her back to her house, and offer advice? In return, she would give him—at this very moment—a skin of the cellar's best wine. He had only to follow her down. Then she lowered her eyes, and the doctor gave a single nod, by which I knew I was to bid him farewell, and come to his house some other time. His bushy eyebrows contracted—I could see the poor old fellow was as sorry as I to delay the warmth of his home and fireside. But he knew his first duty, and bowed to it as he must.

Once I was upstairs again, I went to my small street window, and put myself where I could hear. But no more conversation passed between them. The gate creaked, and their footsteps faded quickly on worn stone. They were down there for an eternity—or an hour. No bells rang. The gate creaked again, and their doubled footsteps moved away.

The next day, someone thoughtfully oiled the hinges on that

gate—and I waited for the order to vacate my house and move back into the palace, for surely it would come.

All October I watched and listened as I could; I had the feeling of time running out, and a chill in more than the air. The doctor looked on me kindly, but never extended another invitation to his house. In turn, I kept my window open at all times, the merest crack, and slept beneath it, to catch the sound of footsteps, the soft sluicing of the oiled gate.

November came—the month of Queen Juana's birthday. The occasion was usually celebrated quietly, with a walk to Santa Clara for a special Mass. But the day before, the tenth of the month, three fine new iron candelabra had appeared in the grand sala, and Duque rushed about, his fine long hands fluttering in the air, his gentle temper strained to snapping. More wood on the fire! Tapestries hung here and there. The three kitchen fiends (I will not call them cooks) were at their wits' end, too, and Duque could not tell them why he wanted them to try new dishes so beyond their skills. Our consort found itself suddenly plump with musicians from Valladolid: a viol and two pipes, and two more men to play drums—even a Fleming who carried a lute. Needless to say, the laundress was busy too: everyone, down to the boy singers, must have their old clothes cleaned.

Into this splendor, one dim afternoon, dropped a Burgundian knight, who knelt before the queen while the consort played. She apologized for her old gray gown, and laughed and trembled, her face made soft and young by the surprise, and by his courtly ways. He paid her several compliments, then told her that her son Charles had arrived in Spain, and had sent him ahead to ask if he and his sister Leonor might visit. No sooner had she answered "yes" than the doors opened again.

Two young people stood there—a lady and gentleman in heavy cloaks and hats, their cheeks rosy from the cold. Then the young man removed his heavy cap, and my vihuela nearly slipped from my hands. It was Philippe who stood before us, as he had stood before Juana on their bridal day: there were his pale blue eyes, the long jaw, the small mouth, ever so slightly open.

Juana must have seen the resemblance too; she hung on the knight's arm as if she might fall.

There was great happiness, great celebration, of course. She had not seen either Charles or Leonor since they were small. But what I remember most was how Catalina, now twelve years old and clinging close to her side, watched Charles and Leonor with round, astonished eyes.

For three days we endured the jubilation, and a great flood of royal promises as to how she would live from now on. Charles even said he would raise the salaries of her composer and the lesser musicians, too. Anchieta kept his cautious squint, and later, after the palace was quiet again, he said he didn't believe a word Charles said: the higher the promises, the further our household would fall.

I thought it was his old bitterness speaking. "But he is her son," I said.

To this, Anchieta had nothing at all to say.

Then they were gone, and we were shipwrecked once more on our old river bluff. On the splintered deck a girl gazed out, imagining her brother's glittering court—oh Valladolid, oh Madrid! Where, we would later learn, he had promised her she would one day come to dance in fine gowns to her heart's content.

That late autumn was all black fog to me. I was only waiting for the cellar door to open, that I might hear, for a moment, the sound that surely must come within this month, or the next. Let it be Encina's child, I told myself, I don't care. Only let it live, and force compassion on the wardress and her employers, good Christians all. By December I was like a man at dice, forever ready to throw again. The cellar gate, the sloping stairs, the curve around which I could not see. How far did that cave extend, and did it run under my own house? How far down did it descend, how airless, how filthy and dark?

And soundless. Except for every gurgle or fart or whimper a prisoner's body makes, which would rise only as far as the damp stones and curl back on her, teasing, wheedling, doing what it liked.

Against this, surely she'd welcome the clank of the gate, the footfalls from above. I imagined how her prayer might go: "Come to me, whoever or whatever you are, even if your coming brings the taste of iron, of my baby's blood and my own, to the throat, the tongue, the lips."

Now I heard it. Silence as men use it to do their worst.

The first snow fell, and the wardress's step began to slow, her shoulders to slump beneath her heavy clothes. The grumbling husband brought a pail of wood now and then; what smoke did that produce below? Sometimes I smelled his breath long after he passed the gate—he liked his wine. I made a note of that, and stored some away for another time.

One night, when the wind blew rain sideways up the street, I fell in step beside the wardress at the gate, and offered to help her make her way home. She quickened her step, and I told her not to fear; that I was the queen's vihuelist, and Doctor Soto's friend. She faltered then, and said yes. Her poor husband would be here himself, she said, but he was worn to the bone from his own work; he could barely stay awake at meals, and had poor appetite these days.

I told her I understood, that I myself found it difficult to eat during daylight hours, but that my stomach growled late at night. "And what does your husband do?" I asked.

"He drives a special cart," she said solemnly, "between here and Valladolid."

Some women are prone to treat every grown man as a son. Especially those whose children are nearly grown. It takes almost nothing to set them to considering what is wrong with you, poor man, and how you might be cured. The seduction of such women is simple: tighten your face, ever so gently, into an expression of restrained distress, then shake your head and give a small sad smile. The next time you meet her, she will have been awake all night, considering various remedies, and if she knows where you live, there may even be a basket of culinary wonders known to soothe a troubled gut: a small clay pot of stewed chicken, and lemon-blossom candies in a fine napkin, such as Queen Isabel used to send to her son's chamber. And if you are a bachelor, a small piece of paper is enclosed, with instructions written out as if for a child or an idiot: Keep in a chest with a heavy lid, away from rats. Keep the meat somewhere cold, and only two days, or until it begins to smell.

The basket—if not its contents—was identical to the one she carried to the cellar gate.

I ate what she sent. I hoped it was something like the food she took below. I cleaned the little pots and jars and folded the napkin in a perfect square. I wrote a note of thanks on the paper she sent.

The wardress—she never told me her name—seemed surprised by the note; she said it had been a long time since she'd been thanked.

One evening, when she emerged from below with her pail, and the husband was, once more, too exhausted to help, I offered to carry it to the privies on her behalf. On my return, I said I had no desire to make trouble for her. I said I had guessed the cellar was a sick ward of sorts, for people too ill to be kept at home, and that I thought it a noble task she performed. It was important to keep such persons out of sight and hearing. Then I paused as if in heavy thought. "I used to play for our beloved Prince Juan, when he was ill, and it eased his sorrow. Our good Queen Juana, too, more recently. It occurs to me that a few little tunes as you work would do you good, and ease the sick ones. Only for a few minutes, while the door is open to let in fresh air."

She set down the empty, stinking pail where it would catch the rain. I promised to play softly and out of view of the street, perhaps down the stairs at the place where it curved around, to protect the vihuela from wind and rain.

Impossible, she said. Her employers would not permit it, and her husband would beat her if he knew. And also, the neighbors would find it strange.

"I am the only neighbor," I said. "And they would be but quiet songs. Old lullabies and things that soothe." And then I bowed and walked away.

Three days later, in the icy dawn, she knocked on my door. Her skin looked clammy, and her eyes were small and rimmed with red. "I will take your lullabies," she said. "Just for three days, before dawn and after dusk. Never say a word, nor reply to what you hear from below." Her eyes filled, and she wiped them quickly with the back of her hand.

"I am only crying because of good news," she said. "The sick ones are ready to be moved."

I suppose the question was in my face.

"Valladolid," she said. "There is room for them now, and they are fit to travel in my husband's cart."

Through the gate and down the tilting slope of stairs, around its mysterious curve. Now, I thought. Now I will see what there is to see, and know what there is to know. But around the curve was a door with a high, heavy iron grate, and behind that, a darkness so full that it swallowed the wardress's light as it dropped beneath another arch.

Three days I played at the appointed times. Three days she left the door ajar so that some breath of air and sound could travel in, and foul air might travel out. It seemed to me that her charges—how many ever there were—must be in irons, or very weak; she showed no fear of their escape.

I played as I said I would, lullabies from long ago. *"Nani, Nani,"* and "Sleep, Sleep," and if the wardress knew that they had once been sung tenderly to the babes of Jews and those who might be Jews, she said nothing, nor did she try to stop me. I played other things, too: *regret chansons* from the northern courts. I began to see how often women's love laments are sung to children late at night. The tower at the sea. The sea of milk with its boats made of cinnamon.

I heard nothing in reply. Unless you count one little cry, a hiccup of a thing.

On the third day, the wardress thanked me, her voice cracked with tears. "Your music has done me a service," she said, "and given relief where relief was needed. Tomorrow is the day."

"Tell me," I said. "I swore I heard a child's cry."

"You didn't," she said. Her eyes shone again, and she crossed herself with great gusto.

"And will you have other work?"

"There is no end of it," she replied. "The big towns are too full, so we keep them here." I could see that she held her task to be a sacred one, and deeply charitable. Then she patted me on the shoulder as if I were a small boy, and I knew she was done answering my questions.

I was ready in the morning, when I heard the sound of wheels. Her husband's "special cart" was not much better than Philippe's ruined funeral wagon with its rotted boards, but at least it had a covering made of oiled hide. The wardress and the grumbler climbed down from the front and tied up the mules, and now I saw all that I'd missed in the years before. They had an old routine: she made her way to the gate and down, while he spoke with the guard, lit his pipe, and took a walk to the privies. But to my great surprise Doctor Soto appeared in the street, looking miserable and cold, and he stood waiting at the gate, and from the arms of the wardress took a bundle of cloth. I implored the bundle to cry, to make itself known to me, but it was not to be.

Old Doctor Soto made no sign that he saw me, none at all. He went up the hill on foot, whether to his own house, or someone else's, I cannot say.

I cannot say, because I didn't follow. I stayed to watch the wardress bring up three women, heavily robed and hooded, with nothing but slippers on their feet and their hands and ankles bound. One by one, the carter and the wardress raised them into the cart, and attached them to cords within. Then the wardress stepped away, and hurried up the street.

The carter, who can blame him, was indeed a tired man, a man whose need for simple comforts went well beyond what his wife required. After the three had been loaded into the back, I stepped out of my doorway, and walked past the cart. I offered a sympathetic nod. "Very bitter out," I said. "I am no friend of early morning myself."

He squinted my way, and asked if I was the musician who had the worm. I must have scowled; he gave a brittle laugh. "My wife says you are a legend in this place: you can eat and eat and never grow fat." He sighed. "I wish *I* had the worm."

"Believe me," I said, "you are welcome to it. But I must be off—I am headed to Valladolid, to deliver the queen's good wishes to the inquisitor Pedro de Fermoselle, and must get a horse from her stable."

He frowned and sucked his pipe. "You know an inquisitor at Valladolid? How is that?"

I told him how we'd met when we were boys in Salamanca, when I played for Prince Juan's nuptials. His expression softened at the name, and he asked me what it was like to play for the prince and the beautiful Marguerite.

"It was a legendary time," I said. "A golden time." Then I added, very quietly as if I was saying something no one should overhear, "I have a confession. I have never, in all my years, had the chance to drive a cart."

He smiled now. "And I have never been entertained by a musician at such an early hour. Since we are going the same way, why not?"

And with that, he helped me up, and showed me how to hold the reins, and approved of my relaxed grip.

Could the poor man help it if he got drowsy, there in his warm cloak and the great luxury, for once in his life, of being relieved of the reins, and offered a bit of decent palace wine? He was not at fault. We jostled along toward Valladolid, and it is also not his fault that when we came to a crossroads, I failed to wake him to ask which road to take. It is hard to wake a hardworking man when he is sleeping so well.

I was as surprised as anyone when I heard the soft thump of ropes behind me, and heard a smoky voice in my ear, an alto I thought I'd never hear again.

"Don't turn around," she said. "But we all need to get down, or our bladders will burst."

I am, as you know, in great sympathy with those who need to take a piss—whether man or woman. It is a more sacred business than we know. It is why old men of a certain religion say a prayer of gratitude after pissing. But that is no matter. Good manners, gentlemen, required that I first tie up the horses, then go to the back and undo the cords that held the women to the cart itself, and then their hands and feet. There was a little shuffling in the dark as the other two got down. But the third—the only one I knew—was having some trouble, and whispered in my ear. "Juanico, I am a little weak," she said. "Will you help me down?"

If I looked at her as I helped her down, it did me no good—her face was as lost to me as the curve of the staircase and the iron-grated door. She had covered it so only her eyes showed. But our eyes met, and she said in her low, rough voice, "For God's sake please don't look at me."

She gave me her hand, as dry and rough and small as a child's, and for an instant, I held her in my arms. Held her as I'd once held her in a dream, and as in that dream, she weighed almost nothing. "Quick," she whispered. "Now set me down, and do not follow."

I did what she said. I set her down, and let her go.

This is the thing I can't forget. To come so far, and fail.

"Make sure she is called Teresa," she said. "For my mother."

And then she was gone, limping away with the two others, who had kindly waited for her: three black figures in the early light, stumbling across an open field.

"Teresa," I said, to no one at all.

After she was out of sight, I cut my forearms with some sticks, and smeared myself with dirt. And if, while I was down there on the ground, my guts began to seethe, my worm was real enough. It was the sound of my heaving that woke the carter.

"Why are we stopped?" he cried. "And what has happened to you?"

"Brigands," I said, clutching my belly. "They must have followed us from town. They took the women. You gave me no weapon, no way to defend—"

He was already on the ground beside the cart, squinting across the fields. "Which way?" he said. I shook my head and heaved again.

Poor fellow, he was awake now, and none too pleased. But what could he do? He was not made for chasing anything, robber or broken women in ropes. I spat a little more into the dirt.

Her little dry hand in mine, her smoky voice. The way she said Teresa, and not goodbye. She was gone for good this time. Let me heave my whole life into the winter mud.

And I would have, too, had we not heard, coming our way, the low rumble of other wheels, of distant trumpets and beating drums, as if an army, or some traveling troupe, was on the road. By now the carter himself was back, and what a sight: smeared in mud even more than myself, and bloodied by brambles and twigs.

"A terrible business," he said. "There were too many to fight."

And do you know, it was no small army or traveling troupe, but young King Charles himself with a great entourage, coming once again to visit pomp upon his mother—and find a way to destroy her wits for all the world to see. In a moment I will tell you how.

But first the carter and I had to come back to town, in such a sorry state that the Holy Office forgave us, and fined us both for our negligence and errors. As you can imagine, from that day forward till the day he died, the carter was accompanied, one at his side and one at the back. He was forbidden from giving rides to musicians, or drinking palace wine.

And then it was February, still cold, but with faint tight buds on bush and tree. The windows of the house across were flung open to get the biting air. The people didn't mind: they were glad to be home again, and airing out their long-closed house. And to my own side of the street came men with barrows, women with pails and rags, to scrub the cellar within an inch of its life. While it was open, I slipped down there myself—there was nothing to guard by then.

It smelled of salt. They had poured it on everything, to cover all the other smells. I took my light and went around the old curve, down and down, more flights than I had dreamed. For me to have heard the baby's cry from that corner, I now understood, the mother would have had to carry it up two steep flights of stairs.

I went to the bottom, and saw the cell in which three women—and a tiny babe—had lived for all those months. I held my light along the wall. I am a dreamer; I dreamed I would find my own name written on the wall, in blood or charcoal I didn't care. Some sign she'd heard, and answered as she could.

It wasn't there. So I took a scrap of charcoal and wrote it there myself.

Yasque.

But if I am to tell the truth, it is that everything was gone, all signs of struggle, of terror in the dark, of the blood and pain, the cries of giving birth—all forgotten, all scrubbed out.

All except the little rusty stains that gave away the entrance. No one could scrub them out, or perhaps no one tried. They are still there now, if you know where to look. The commissioner will see them soon enough, when he goes to see our excellent cellars. It's how he'll know the place.

There is nothing more to tell. Except to say that among those I played to that early spring was another of Fernando's favorites from long ago: the Marquis of Denia and his wife, a cousin of the late king's. Very well-dressed and regal in their manner, that pair. And very fertile, too, as it would turn out. What I didn't know then—what none of us knew—was just how much of this gentleman and his wife and their numerous progeny we were doomed to see. Thirty-four years were coming. Thirty-four years, in which our brief release would barely figure, barely haunt.

Oh, but changes come so slyly, don't they? Beneath bright banners, and the noise of twenty horns. First a young king must make a few small changes. First he must find a way to suggest, as did his father and grandfather, the fragility of Queen Juana's health. To show the world how dangerous it would be to let her rule.

Gentlemen, here is something useful for your records. Let us call it a recipe: how to drive a mother mad. First, commission someone to cut a hole in her daughter's chamber wall, then kidnap the girl in the dead of night. Bring her to the great palace at Valladolid, and dress her in the finest gowns. Treat her to every pleasure, every delight. And while you do all this, leave someone behind to observe how the mother takes the blow; how her cries shock the morning air. Watch how she does the only thing she can: stop eating. Stop speaking. Do her best to die.

Quickly, quickly, bring her darling back yourself. Say it was the Flemish advisers' idea, and claim the courageous role of reuniting mother and child. We're almost done. But first, while the mother is still recovering, holding her beloved *niña* close, dismiss her kindly mayordomo, Hernan Duque, and her court composer too. Yes, send old Juan de Anchieta away, though he is the great composer of the age. Send him away with the present of a decent horse, to live the last of his days in some distant country place.

Reduce the staff. Replace her servants with some of your own.

Oh, you may leave the lesser musicians there, for appearance's sake, and the shoemaker and the laundress if you like. They do no harm. But by no means let them live outside the palace gates. Send them back to their small chambers, their monkish cells. Guard their movements well.

Oh, but they may attend Mass if they are discreet and speak to no one. You may find it difficult, in fact, to stop them from attending every burial, wedding, and christening for miles around. One of these christenings, wholly unremarkable, will be that of the orphan Teresa de Tordesillas, ward of Doctor Nicolás de Soto.

I would be there myself to see her carried into church by Soto's own son. Our young scribe here makes me think of him—he was about twenty, and held the baby with a tenderness that took my breath away. He held her through it all, even as the priest sprinkled her with holy water and smeared the chrism across her brow. She was a docile child and did not cry. She was too young, of course, to gaze up where the congregants now pointed, whispering. For a whole new flock of yellow *sanbenitos* had been hung up that very morning. Some of these criminals had escaped, and others had been caught. All had been burned at the great auto-de-fé held in Valladolid the week before, whether in person or in effigy, and were never to be seen again. I kept my eyes on little Teresa. I didn't need to look up to know that among the names was one nobody in Tordesillas would claim to know: Inés de Castro.

sixteen

Forgive me, young man, if I pass quickly through the wonders of the next few years. Now that our good commissioner has at last taken my suggestion and gone to inspect the palace cellars, I feel the press of time. It's true he will be well-occupied down there for an hour or two, and pleasantly surprised by the abundance of rare old wines. How fortunate that he took a little light, and is not the sort of man to worry about ghosts.

But about Tordesillas in those years: no doubt you heard the stories as a boy. How the palace was seized by the *comuneros*, how it looked, for a time, as if the rebellion might succeed. Such tales are more enthralling when seen from afar, especially the hot August afternoon that saw the palace courtyard filled with shouting men. What a noise they made, waiting for the queen to appear on the balcony above. But she was not to be rushed, not even by these passionate rebels who came from all over Castile to free her—to free all Spain! They knelt and called her Majesty, and with her blessing, banished the man who controlled our lives—the Marquis of Denia—and all his people, too. Juana kept four servants: a woman to help her dress and wash her hair, a cook, our newest laundress, and her beloved cobbler. And yes, a certain aging vihuelist, too.

It was 1520, and she was forty-one years old.

A whole autumn of freedom was ours, if only we'd known how to use it. We kept our monastic ways while Juana paced the corridors, stunned by the army gathered on her behalf, and by so much sudden news. Were the rebels' promises real? And was it true, as they said, that her father had been dead four years, and the Emperor Maximilian for a year, and Cardinal Cisneros, too? For fully ten years she had subsisted on a handful of deceits. Is it any surprise that the stew the rebels offered now might prove too rich, with its hot vows of loyalty, and spiced with tales of her own son's dark maneuvers? Her own son? Forgive her if she caught, in her sensitive ears, the first pale notes of irritation in their voices, their soft and gentlemanly tones rising into cold male demand. Forgive her if, in the long November nights, she lay awake, beset by her mother's ghost, which complained in its old fierce way and gazed on her with somber disappointed eyes.

And of the rebels themselves: let us just say they got tired of waiting, and decided to starve her into agreeing with their plans.

Just a few days without food, nothing much.

Alas, she already knew how to fast. And her mother's voice grew louder: by saying yes, she would destroy the dreams not only of her parents, but of her own eldest son. All their efforts for naught?

Perhaps the *comuneros* would have brought us freedom, and fewer wars. Perhaps they would have tried to dismantle the very Office that brought you here to me, and that has cleansed our land of so much Jewish canker, so much Moorish blight. Then again, they might have failed. Everyone knows that if a sane, kind-hearted person arrives at a palace, he will soon be harried into leaving, or dismissed with the gift of a horse.

Let the powerful have their gestures, their theatre of pomp and righteous truth and certainty. Let them sign their treaties and stir our ordinary waters into mud so we cannot see which way to swim. It is how we live within their walls that matters. It is how we secretly console our broken hearts, and how we take the smallest steps, play the quietest notes, that will produce the odd small lift of something close to joy.

The cunning this work requires takes a lifetime to learn.

Therefore picture the queen at moments of great drama. Observe how, on that August day, she washed her hair in holm-oak ash and put on her finest gown to meet these men and listen to their pleas. And how, in December, when her son sent a delegation of grandees, nobles she had known all her life, she washed her hair and dressed again, and listened to what they had to say. In the end, it was the grandees who held sway, who got her to sign the documents that would seal her fate.

It must have felt like the proper thing to do. But did she feel a small chill when she noticed that among the kindly old faces was one so familiar over the last few years, one she'd grown to fear and hate? It was the Marquis of Denia, her own son's choice. She must listen to his counsel, and do everything he says.

We found ourselves caught once more in the sturdy embrace of the Marquis and his ever-growing family. *Dios*, he knew how to cultivate a single vine that it should send out shoot upon shoot until the palace and the town were nearly smothered by its fruit.

And as in the oldest tales, our palace life was under a spell, hidden from view for many years, with only a little glimpse from time to time. The Infanta Catalina, having tasted freedom, tried to smuggle a letter out, raising a cry against the Denias' cruelty to her mother and herself. A shock to poor Charles, of course, but his response will come as no surprise: one day, when Catalina is sixteen years old, a great procession arrives at the palace gates, and she is lifted onto a horse. Off she goes, to Portugal and marriage to a king. Who can possibly complain? Her mother, after all, was near this age when she boarded a carrack bound for a great alliance to the north. But the girl trembles on her horse, and the mother turns away from the balcony above. She cannot bear to watch her leave.

Now the palace shrinks a little more beneath its heavy vines.

How often does our lady ask to have a few minutes in the riverside galleries, from whose windows she can see the unnavigable river and imagine a boat making its way against the current up and up, carrying a young woman who speaks three languages, plays and sings and dances with grace, and writes her own verses besides. Up the unnavigable river comes the fine carrack, its great sails taut in a good stiff breeze.

After such interludes, she retreats into the old dark inner apartment, where the Marquis insists she must stay. Her daughter's side chamber is empty now, hung with heavy tapestries and useful for the hiding of female guards, who can, at the slightest sign of agitation, signal the servants to quit the queen's chamber and leave her in the dark. God, but they rustle in their hiding spots. We hear them—like insects chewing wood.

She finds ways to occupy her time. She strings rosaries and embroiders covers for the altars of Santa Clara, though to get her to attend Mass herself, even in the palace corridor arranged for that purpose, is half-a-day's work. She has become as stubborn as her famous mother, and can use words with such power that, as Denia will someday write to Charles, it would break your heart to refuse her.

But refuse her he does, for it is what her son Charles wishes, and also necessary for her health.

Sometimes Doctor Soto visits, though he is watched at all times, and very tired. He prefers, now, to listen, rather than to put his poor thick knobbled fingers to the vihuela's strings. But he brings good cheer. Little Teresa is thriving at his home. He says that when she is old enough, if the Marquis will permit it, he will send her to the palace, to help in whatever capacity she can.

Music: the queen and I write some small things together: *folias* and *ensaladas*, little nothings that sound quite simple but are alive with little jokes and clues. Sometimes we tuck in traces of forbidden tunes, just a phrase here, a phrase there, disguised by a key change, or the lift of an ending. It takes an ear, a memory, to hear the lost jewel in the pale casket, and the Denias are not gifted in that regard. And sometimes, to our great surprise, a young grandee arrives from as far away as Madrid or even Venice, to pay respects, and we play, and they write it down, and two years later someone comes again, and plays it back to us, changed yet a little more. But we know what lies inside.

Those were slow years. But the music of Tordesillas found its way, tendril by tendril, into the great world and back again. The queen sometimes turned to me and smiled faintly. "How do you think your music traveled so far, only to come home again?"

And one day, in the old musical code she learned from Agricola, she asked me to play the names of the condemned whose *sanbenitos* hang at San Antolín. Just a few, she said.

I always did as the queen asked. Always, and without question.

The truth is, nobody would have cared had she asked for it aloud. Ever since Pedro de Fermoselle's visit, and the disappearance of Dolores and the country family, the Holy Office seemed to lose interest in Tordesillas. There was no mystery here—the Holy Office was interested now in other things than secret Jews. We were, I think, understocked with Lutherans, unless you count the queen herself,

who sometimes acted like one, and worried her confessors greatly—
she had great difficulty attending Mass, and could not, for the life of
her, swallow the host or the sacramental wine. And as for Judaizers, it
was as if some thirst had been quenched, at least for a while, and the
tunics that hung above our heads, so bright in their early days, began
to fade, to tatter a little in the constant breeze. I wasn't sorry. Yellow,
once the sweet color of lemon candies, had become a shade I found
hard to love.

Blue, on the other hand. The blue of violets coming up in the mud
of early spring, and a little later, waving on fat stalks of lavender, to
bring the bumblebees. A lovely, delicate color, that kind of blue—
I am thinking of certain early violets that found themselves woven
into the single dark-brown braid of a little girl. A child too young
and insignificant to be kidnapped or betrothed or useful to anyone
except as a pair of small hands to knead dough or stir a pot. Hardly
big enough to be noticed at all.

That is the way to be in this world. Invisible.

It was Good Friday of the year 1525—the spring after Catalina
left for good—and the violets were up. I remember them very well,
because I was sitting on Dolores's old bench, having a bit of bread and
soup, when the child came inside the kitchen yard gate. I will confess
that I had, a few days before, found an occasion to speak with Doctor Soto, and suggested that the time was right. Might he suggest to
Denia that Teresa come work in the kitchens? He agreed, and presented the idea to the Marquis—such a harmless thing, and of no
cost to anyone—and so it came about.

The child carried pale-blue eggs in her apron, and stepped delicately to keep them safe. Our latest cook, an elderly woman, bent
stiffly down and let Teresa hand her the eggs, one by one by one. Forgive me, there was something about those hands—a certain swiftness
and decision—that caught at my heart. Hands that knew what to do
in a kitchen, and didn't waste a gesture.

I encouraged the cook to employ the girl in any way she could. I
explained that she was an orphan, and had been raised by the family of Queen Isabel's own physician. Born and raised in Tordesillas,
I said.

So Teresa took her place beside the cook, doing all the small
things that save an old back: picking oregano and wild thyme, slip-

ping eggs from beneath sleeping hens, and other delicate, if tedious, tasks. The Marquis was pleased, for she cost him only food and a place to sleep, and was far too young to gossip. When, in that bitter spring, she took the occasional lesson on vihuela, or was brought in for an hour to bring solace to the lonely queen, she was well watched by the Denia women, who, as I may have said before, were not well trained in music.

It was Teresa herself who came one day to tell us that her dear *abuelo*, old Doctor Soto, had died in his sleep. I was given leave to attend the burial, where I met the doctor's wife and his two grown children, and gave them the queen's deepest condolences.

A good family. A generous one. I came back from the burial a weary man.

But Teresa was not weary, and it gave me pleasure to watch her grow. Once in a while I brought her to see the queen, though a dozen ladies watched us through the door. And if I watched her, as she grew, to see if she had my mother's eyes, or my father's curly hair, is it any crime? It seemed my proper fate—or a kind of penance—that she was so purely her mother's daughter, with no sign of either Encina or myself, that she might as well have sprung from no father at all.

Her ear for music, you see, might have come from us all.

She worked in the palace kitchens for nine years, and when she was seventeen, I was among the company who gathered to see her marry Soto's son, a doctor now himself, and the one who'd brought her to the baptismal font and looked at her, a scrawny babe, with such tender care. She left us then, as of course she should, but she sent little notes, and was pleased to tell me—and would I tell the queen?—that she was now with child.

This was around the time the plague threatened Tordesillas, and Denia moved the household of the queen up the Duero to a safer place, where we spent the late winter and early spring. That journey is worth recalling, if only for the remarkable sight of Juana, still slim and upright in her fifty-fifth year, seated upon a royal mule in the hour before dawn, moving along the Duero's banks like some stately ghost of her lost and girlish self.

In my dreams she spurs the mule and makes one last—and spectacular—escape.

We stayed at Tudela del Duero and Mojados from February to April of that year. The Duero moves no faster there than here, but there is another little river, the pretty Cega, not far away, and sometimes it sang a little over its stones. There were times I thought I saw surprise on Juana's face and even once, something like a frightened joy to be so far from home. But the Denias were as careful there as they were anywhere else. No windows. No direct passage from her room. Everything arranged for watching.

On our return, we got a glimpse of Tordesillas from the distance of the bridge: it still had its old look of a row of broken teeth. The town gate was so quiet we thought the whole populace had fallen to the plague. But then we saw children playing on the riverside path, and heard the market in progress in the plaza. A woman told me that only a few souls had succumbed in the end: some elderly folk, and one young woman who had recently given birth.

I feared I knew who that young woman was. I felt it in that way we do sometimes: a coldness in the limbs, the body knowing the truth before the messenger arrives. I begged Denia to let me go to the Soto house before they had time to send for me. He was so busy with the household's return that he let me go.

Teresa had already been buried, and the house was consumed by quiet. Her widower bore himself with dignity but privately told me he could not forgive himself or find any comfort in prayer. "I am a doctor," he said. "How did I lose her?" And later, he said it again. At last I begged his pardon, and said I would come back another time. That's when he and his sister looked at each other, and exchanged a nod. "Before you go," he said, "please come with us. We have a favor to ask. We promise not to keep you long."

They took me into a small chamber at the back of their house. A mirror on the wall had been turned around, and a few family members sat on the floor, eating a simple meal on an overturned rug. These were customs I had not seen since childhood. "Is it safe?" I whispered, and young Soto said to me, "We trust you. Our father would have wanted this for her. He used to tell us about her mother's family. He knew them in their happy days, when they were the Castros of Toledo. A mighty family once, close to the kings."

There was something else. The favor. On her deathbed, Teresa had asked if the queen would do her the honor of choosing the child's name. "It would be the greatest gift to our family," said the doctor, his voice catching, then lost in a quiet sob. His sister came to his side. "Will you ask on our behalf?"

And so, in May of 1534 I attended another christening at San Antolín: the baptism of Teresa de Tordesillas' daughter. I sat beneath the yellow tunics, and saw a child smeared with the chrism, and heard a newborn's Christian name pronounced, a short, simple name chosen by the queen herself.

No one raised an eyebrow, least of all me. Nor did I make a sound when the queen sent a message to the grieving widower, that when the little girl was old enough, she would be most welcome at the palace, in whatever capacity she seemed best suited for, and that she would, while she was here, receive music lessons in return.

It was such a small thing. Denia could not say no.

Juana did not say who would give those lessons to the young girl called Inés de Soto. It went without saying.

The original vine must die, but who will notice if, by then, new green shoots have sprouted at its side? I speak here of the Marquis of Denia, who died the same year as Teresa. I had foolishly hoped we might have a change at the palace once he was gone. But he had left a diligent wife and numerous offspring, and one of these, don Luis, inherited the post. You can imagine Emperor Charles' great relief. Nothing was to change at all.

Except for one thing. I began to notice a dimming of the world, a faint yellow sheen across everything I saw—it seemed a kind of penance I was glad to take. But I could still see on the late May afternoon in the year 1546, of which I wish to speak. It was warm outside, of course, though you couldn't tell what season it was in the queen's apartments. The winter chill always clung there until late June, and it was only when three doors were opened at once that you got a taste of the real air outside, the mud-and-fish scent of the Duero on our tongues, some hint of spring. Juana was, that year, sixty-six years old. She could still sit up and read, or play her monochord, and on that day, as she sat before her instrument, she stopped playing and lifted her nose to the air.

"It is a beautiful day outside," she said. "Even I can tell. Go see what it's like, and bring back a report."

I was slow to move. She laughed at me for it, and I took pleasure in her laugh.

I was writing out the melody for a set of variations to console her in the winter months. But when I stood up from the table, my leg gave out. It felt as if all my strings had broken at once. The queen looked at me sharply, a sheen of fear in her eyes.

"You still look like a boy," she said, her mouth trembling a little.

"What would you like to play?" I said quickly. Because I knew the signs. She was counting, in her mind, all the musicians she had lost.

I accompanied the queen as long as I could, until I thought her spell had passed. My own misery was rising, in its special way, crowding my eyes with dry heat, hollowing out my chest. It was as if the *meseta*, so vast and flat, had taken up residence inside me. I knew that only walking would help, stiff as I was. To go outside and walk along the river, its muddy scent seething up from the bank, somehow always eased my pain. I've been told that this smell isn't anything you can take up in your hands, that it is the earth eating its newest self, letting off the odor of its body. Everyone else hated it: our cooks were forever rinsing the fish to get rid of it. But it consoled me. It carried me away.

Without meaning to, I'd shaken my head. The queen looked up as if I'd said her name out loud.

"Go for a walk. Your leg will be a boy's leg again in no time."

"Are you warm enough?" I asked.

She nodded. Although it was May, she was still wearing her little fur-collared jacket over her gray linen, and I put some new coals into the brazier. I was already imagining where I would walk when someone came to the door. The guards stood aside to let in a kitchen maid.

"There's a visitor at the kitchens," she said. "For the musician Juan de Granada."

Setting down my vihuela, I noticed my shoulders had gone tight with cold. I smiled at the maid, preparing to tell her that I was feeling unwell, and unable to see anyone just now. I was sure it was some old acquaintance's son, a young man so desperate for work he would come to the last place on earth. For it was the great joke of Tordesillas that there was always work to be had at the palace of the melancholy queen; that it took a staff of two hundred to keep her there, though she never ate, drank, slept, or bathed. There was always someone marching out the palace gates, his dignity wounded. The Denias were not easy masters, after all.

What made me relent and go to the kitchens I don't know. That little breeze coming in, softening me; after all, I was on my way to the river. I could say "no" at the kitchen gate as easily as here. I stepped out into the passage. What surprised me first was the warmth of the day; even in the passage I felt it.

And the light, too. So brilliant that when the guard opened the great doors to let me out, there was a long moment where I saw nothing.

It was not one visitor who stood at the kitchen gate, but two. The first was the late Doctor Soto's son, the widower, and beside him, a young girl of about twelve, very neatly gowned, her head-cloth snowy-white. Dark curls had slipped out in wisps around her face, as if they refused to be contained, and her eyes, a lovely green, picked up every glint of light.

Soto asked the girl to explain what she wanted. "It was all her idea," he said, in a voice full of wonder.

"I want to serve the queen," she said. "And also learn to play the vihuela and sing."

Soto was a kind fellow, very like his father; he was helpless before his daughter's request. Elegant like his father, already beginning to stoop a little, to keep others from feeling badly about being short.

But I couldn't look at him for long. Because I couldn't stop looking at the girl. The dark curly hair. The bright green eyes.

"She could be a comfort to our sovereign lady," her father said. "And her love of music is beyond anything we can help at home." Then he paused. "I never told you this before," he said. "But long before you came to our house, my father told me who you were. 'There is a great musician hidden inside the walls of Tordesillas,' he said. 'A man not without courage.'"

I blushed and shook my head, but he went on. "My father would have wanted you to teach her the old songs."

"The old songs?" I repeated.

"From the time before this one," he said, without meeting my eyes.

As for young Inés, she had inherited her grandmother's squint. Did it come from too much glancing toward the sun, from a witty nature, or an unwarranted delight in ordinary things? Perhaps all three. And she had, too, her grandmother's sweet sturdiness, however small her frame. If I lifted her up in my arms, I was quite sure she would have that strange lightness, as Inés did, the last time I held her in my arms.

"She's an alto," said her father. "And already adept at the baking of bread."

I looked at Inés. "Your grandmother ruined her voice in smoky kitchens," I said. "My advice is to sing more, and bake less."

"Tell me more about my grandmother," she said.

And I promised I would, when she was a little bit older.

"I'm old enough now," said the squinter.

"Soon," I said. "I promise."

"You won't forget?"

"No," I said. "I won't forget."

The shape of our palace, long and narrow like a lozenge with its outer passages, the inner room without windows, has always made for difficulties. It suited the Denia family perfectly. The women could keep an eye on the queen, and hear her footfall with ease. Juan del Encina had remarked on it during his visit, for they had shown him the little hole Hernan Duque had cut in the passage wall for Juana, so she could look out and see the water, and the children playing on the riverside path. When everything had gone so wrong, the Denias had the hole plastered over, so she could not look out at the slightest thing. What was it that drove them all? I never understood it. They had created, in their minds, a towering monster out of their prisoner. They believed that a breath of air, or a morning's hour among the Sisters of Santa Clara, would somehow result in mayhem. But the more they enclosed her, the more they invited the world's suspicion. Only Hernan Duque had understood how much easier it is to treat someone well.

After young Inés had been with us half a year, I asked Don Luis if the girl could spend more time with the queen. He hemmed and hawed. What if Juana coerced the girl into carrying messages out into the world? No, it could not be risked. But the queen, elderly now, and tough as old meat, refused her meals, refused to bathe, and curled up in her bed until Don Luis gave up in despair. He was under more pressure these days, as the Empress Isabel and her daughter Maria had paid a visit, and cast an eye on things. Was Juana being treated in a manner befitting a dowager queen?

Nor could Don Luis risk another thing: Juana's sainthood among the people of Castile, if she starved to death.

Juana went further still: she requested more candles on the days of Inés's visits, so that we could more easily play our instruments and sing. This soothed Denia a little: he did not like the extra expense, but at least we were playing music, and not speaking.

The girl was impatient when it came to reading music; she preferred to take a melody and pick out variations her own way. But in the afternoons, after Terce, and before the cook needed her, I taught her how to play the vihuela. *You hold the instrument like this. You move your fingers thus.* In playing and everything else, she moved quickly, like a bird on the branch, her ear and eye caught by everything that went past. Her beauty worried me more than all. I feared she would spend her love too soon, on someone not her equal. But she kept to herself. She was only hungry for music, and loved to cook. I tried to explain that some songs are better kept hidden in the heart, just as some dishes are best left uncooked until one is older, and living somewhere else. "Wait," I told her. "Wait until you leave Spain. Then you may play and sing and cook whatever you like."

"But I don't want to leave Spain," she said.

"Maybe I will go with you, when the time comes," I said. "How would that be?"

"That would be fine," she said. "But I like our river. And I love the queen and her music."

Ten years of being watched; ten years of little tricks. I taught young Inés to open the queen's door swiftly from the inside, so the Denia women, crowded all around it in the passage, would stumble in and look like fools. I taught her how to look very grave, and watch their eyes light up with hope that our sovereign lady had finally died. These were small pleasures. But we needed those pleasures, for poor Juana was entering a new and troubled time. A demon-cat came into her dreams, and devoured her mother and father, devoured her Philippe too. And then she began to murmur to her confessor that her servants were worshipping the devil in her own apartments. If they were removed, she promised she would hear Mass, and try to take the sacrament.

But when Inés flitted into the room, Juana's eyes filled with tears, and we had to stop playing while she gathered herself again. Each time it was the same: she always thought, at the first sound of the girl's feet, that her own dear Catalina had returned from Portugal to be with her once more. The tales you have heard of the queen's morbid love for her dead spouse are fantasies; they matter not at all. It was the absence of her lost niña that broke her in the end.

One day, while the Denia women kept their watch, the queen sent for Inés. While we waited, she turned to me. "Tell me," she said. "Is this girl as stubborn as her grandfather?"

"You mean the good Doctor Soto?" I said. "Or do you refer to the composer Juan del Encina, whom they say—"

"No," said the queen, a sharp glint in her eye. "No, not Encina. He was never the one." Then she laughed and shook her head. The Denia women looked alarmed. One began to ring the small bell they kept there, to summon extra guards in case of an outburst.

"She is only teasing me," I said, and the women shook their heads in disgust. Then Inés arrived, and I was saved.

That day, in the queen's apartments, Inés played Pierre de la Rue's lovely *pavane*, and brought our sovereign lady to tears. I worried that it had been too much. Then the queen spoke up. "But are you also teaching her the older songs?"

I pretended not to understand.

"She tells me you are supposed to teach her the old ballads. The ones her grandmother Inés used to sing. 'The Nightingales.' And 'There is a Tower at the Sea.'"

"You used to sing them too, Your Majesty," I said.

"Oh, but I first learned them from Inés and her mother, when we were very small. I believe these are songs you learned yourself when you were young."

"Let's wait a while longer," I said. "The *pavane* was difficult enough."

Then Inés, who had kept her arms around the vihuela all this time, spoke up. "Could Her Majesty teach them to me herself?"

There was no shock on the queen's face, no hesitation or distress. Just a small, secretive smile that only Inés and I could see.

And that's how it happened that a kitchen maid named Inés de Soto became the music pupil—and the last confidante—of the mad Queen of Spain.

Yes, a tune or two might have come from me.

Yes, I taught her chords. But one day, when she was nearly eighteen, she sang me two tunes I could not have taught her. Tunes that, in her rich and husky voice, made the hairs on my arms stand up. I knew the songs. I knew the voice. But I never could have sung them myself. I would never be such a fool, and put her at such risk.

seventeen

In one note many are hidden.

So it follows that in a palace there are many rooms, and in one room there are many cupboards and crannies, one of which contains an old box or jewel casket, and used to contain something else, too. But about the jewel casket: have you never seen, among the confiscated goods of heretics, a small chest with a latch on one side, which releases a false floor, and reveals another compartment you never suspected was there?

Why do I mention these things so late in the day, and at a moment when the commissioner, apparently fascinated by our old wine cellars, hasn't yet returned from his inspection? Never mind, my testimony is nearing its end, and if you find, when I am done, that you are, yourself, in a hurry to depart, fear not, I will go fetch him myself, and offer myself to him in irons. It may well be that I am the heretic the Holy Office seeks. There is no other left in Tordesillas.

The poor fellow may, in fact, be trying to get out as we speak: the cellar door has a habit of swinging shut behind a person, then appearing to be locked. It is simply very old and warped, and tends to stick. The Emperor Charles himself discovered this once, just last year when he came to visit. He had arrived to inspect the expanded cellars—oh, yes, and to pay respects to his mother. The expansion had been a difficult business: they had to knock down the house next door. You remember. My own little house during Duque's Spring, of which I was so fond.

Well, the cellars were at last finished, and the emperor insisted on going to see them by himself, and he was down there for a long time.

Whether the door had slammed shut by itself, or someone had played a joke on the great man, we will never know. There were guards nearby the whole time, smoking lazily as they are wont to do. He was never in any true danger, for someone eventually missed him, and the high steward recalled that he'd gone to inspect the cellars, and they found him clawing at the door in a less than dignified manner, his fine clothes soaked in sweat.

You really can't hear a person calling out from below unless they stand right behind the door. And even then, sound gets swallowed at that little bend in the sloping stair.

The local women have stories—how do these things start? But you will hear them say that it took an astonishing amount of scouring with salt and lye to remove the unsightly stains down there—the blood of childbirth, they say, is particularly stubborn. I've also heard it said that at certain moments, if you sit there long enough, you'll taste salt and something of iron on your tongue. There is idle talk of a ghost.

I hope none of this spoils the commissioner's sampling of the emperor's wine.

I hope he holds his lantern to the wall as I once did. If he does, he'll find, in a certain undisturbed corner, the name of a heretic scrawled there in charcoal. Yasque.

Inés de Castro, or the cook named Dolores, left nothing behind at all.

But anyone who goes down there now, whether a king or a commissioner or an ordinary musician who cannot let go of the dead, will find nothing but his own fear. Silence and solitude—the terror of never being heard from again. The thing we're always running from, but that never gives up the chase, until we turn to meet it.

I am almost ready. Very close.

Where was I? Ah, the jewel casket. I only meant to suggest that our prison palace at Tordesillas, and a stretch of nearly fifty years, might yet be capable of a small surprise or two.

No one could get the queen to make a full confession, there at the end. Not even the great Jesuit priest Fray Francisco de Borja, whom she had known when he was just a boy. I saw it all, for she was determined to have music day and night, and because she was dying, Don

Luis dared not refuse her any wish. So I saw Fray Francisco come in. Beneath his cleric's cap his fringe was gray, and I noticed the heaviness of limbs I had seen in my old master Encina. For all that, Fray Francisco had a light touch on the clavichord, and went to it now and played a little thing he still remembered from his visits here so long ago. Juana's eyes shone, and he went to her bedside and took her hand and said, "I would not have you go to the Lord so sadly," and she pursed her lips and nodded as if she might relent.

Don Luis left them alone—and took me away too. "Let him do his work," he said.

And so for three days Fray Francisco went in and out of the queen's dark apartments. Three days of listening. By God, old people can test a man's patience.

He told us later that she allowed him to open his Missal, and read to her, and put his own rosary into her hands. She seemed very interested and curious about the whole business, he said, as if it was all new to her, a foreign custom she'd never seen before.

For three days he went to her. And everyone waited and believed that she would, in the end, make confession, and there would be an end to the absurd idea that the queen was herself a heretic, a secret Lutheran.

But the last time Fray Francisco came out, he looked as if he'd aged ten years. She had, it seemed, allowed him to confess her generally. But she insisted she had nothing particular to say. "She says she is done with priests and if any of Denia's 'demon-women' come near she will scream loud enough for all the town to hear." But it seems she did have one last request. She wanted to bid farewell, in private, to her long-time servants. She named, in particular, the washerwoman, the kitchen maid, the cobbler, and the old vihuelist.

The cobbler went in first. Juana was always absurdly fond of him, scrawny old fellow, for all she could not wear out a single pair of shoes. Nearly as old as I, the man had always kept himself very quiet. Because of this, and also because he practiced the ancient trade of the Hebrews, I had always wondered if his parents, or grandparents, had been Jews in the time before. I wish I knew what he and the queen spoke about. He came out of her chamber with tears in his eyes, and I could swear his pockets looked heavier than when he'd gone in.

Catalina the washerwoman was called in next. Our last laundress. By the time she joined us, in Juana's last decade, my sight was too dim to see her face, but everyone said she was a funny old bird, a real hag, and it's true that even I cannot miss her when she comes down the corridors, for both her ankles click with every step, and she has a downbeat on one side that puts me in mind of a Moorish dance. She was not much of a laundress, either, they said; that is, she couldn't, at her age, lift the linens once they were soaked, and had to have a team of young boys to help her in the yard. At any rate, the queen's great attachment to her was a source of merriment among the servants— she had twenty well-born Denia ladies to choose from, but she batted them away as if they were biting insects, or worse, and was forever calling in the laundress.

In the courtyard they called the old laundress the queen of rags, for she was forever telling people what to do, and truly, Juana's clothes had gone dingier than anyone could believe. But even Denia didn't dare remove the laundress, for no one else would touch Juana's old gowns and underthings. But the queen loved the laundress as if she were a friend, and even Don Luis was powerless to do anything about it—it wasn't worth the wild scene to send her packing. Some said the reason Juana loved her so was simple enough: she had the same name as her own lost niña, long since married and worlds away.

You could hear them from the door: they murmured together in a mad, incomprehensible duet, of such trivial matters that it might have been a cipher for all we knew. They sounded like two mockingbirds high in the trees, and when I thought of this, I remembered something from so long ago it took my breath away: two young girls on mules bedecked in crimson and cloth-of-gold, chattering away beneath a Nasrid gate. For a moment I felt my pulse beating madly in my throat. I was a boy again, and everything was about to begin.

At last Catalina left Juana's bedside and came to the chamber door. She started to shuffle-and-click her way past me. She paused, and I felt her warm old breath in my ear. "You're next," she said. God knows which way she meant it. But it was her smoky voice, deep in my ear, that raised the hairs on my neck. So husky and deep. There was only one voice in the world like that.

But surely it was only my old-age madness. I have told you before: I have a kind of illness. I seem to see—and hear—resemblances everywhere. As if those lost to me keep coming back—the ones I dread, and the ones I miss. This has gotten worse with age.

Fray Francisco was telling me to go in.

Juana was sitting up among her pillows, a fine brocade coverlet and a matted old fur drawn up together under her chin. Her face looked flat and gray, as if the light beneath had flickered out. "Sit here," she said, patting the edge of the bed. I had never sat there before—I was a little afraid, and there was a smell—of some scented oil poured over sweat and other foul human things. "I have a gift for you, Juanico," she said, and raised her chin a little. "Over there, in my niña's old sleeping place. The wardrobe has a secret back. Our good Hernan Duque had it made for me before he left." And she raised her chin again.

I crossed the room in its flickering light, everything ringed by that yellow veil across my sight. At the end of the room, I found the thickness of the arras: Catalina's small chamber. A few steps further, and I was at the wardrobe itself. In its depths, my calloused fingertips found the little latch.

It is dangerous to do such a thing. Easy, with such old wood, to catch a splinter in your thumb. And if you are a vihuelist, a cut to the thumb may spell your end. But I received no injury, no sliver. I confess I would not have minded if I had. I was ready to be done.

Almost ready. But not quite.

I reached into those depths and my fingers curled with ease around a wooden neck. I let my hand drift down to the delicate filigree of her central rosette. I plucked a string—but what a nightmare, so wrecked and out of tune. I felt her rounded back once more. The bruise was still there, from the day it fell out of the little holm-oak. A rough spot that could never be sanded down.

I brought the oud back to Juana's bedside. "Play me something," she said, and closed her eyes.

"The strings—"

"Play," she said.

I plucked it once and she gave a little shudder. Then the whole bed seemed to tremble. I stood up, sure that this was the end. But it wasn't. The wretched noise had made her laugh.

"It seemed dangerous to have it tuned," she said, without opening her eyes. "But I kept it for you, in case the world should change." She sighed.

I thanked her, and we sat a while in silence. It was in that silence that my stomach gave a mighty grumble. She opened her eyes then, and gave a little smile. She lifted one hand off the coverlet, very naturally, as if that bed were the throne so many had kept her from.

"Leave me now," she said. And I heard the last bit of warmth in her voice begin to fade. "Your appetite, Juanico, gives you away. See if the cook will give you a scrap, a bite of something. You're wasting away." And she turned her head away.

At the chamber door, the old laundress Catalina was still hanging about, bothering the guards with her chatter. As I started to move past her, holding the oud, she didn't seem surprised at all, but gave me a sly little smile of her own. I had the wretched feeling, as I often do around women, that by the time they let a man in on things, they have long since discussed and decided his fate.

Nor were the women done with me yet. Catalina took me by the arm, as if I were completely blind and could not get to the Street of the Kitchens, let alone out of the palace, without her help. As we shuffled along the corridor, a swift shape went rushing past the other way, toward the queen's apartments.

"Not so little anymore, our Inés, but somehow still a child," said Catalina. We were out on the street by then, squinting together in the bright April light. "I suppose you can find your way to the kitchens from here?" she said. And then she gave my arm a squeeze, and was gone.

My legs were suddenly like water, my hands like water too. I couldn't let go of the dream. The touch of her soft dry fingers on my withered arm, her husky old voice in my ear. The past not the past at all. In the kitchen yard, the April sunlight bloomed yellow behind my eyes. I sat down on Dolores's bench and closed my eyes, the warm yellow of lemons behind my lids.

That's how I missed the queen's final breath. Because she sent me, by the lift of her hand, to the kitchens.

I wonder, young man, if you'd be willing to take me back there now—to the kitchen yard. You'll have to carry me, and I will hold the oud aloft. It won't be hard. We weigh almost nothing.

What a fine day it is. When did the snow melt, and the air go so mild? There is the place where my house used to stand. This old wall was always here, protecting the kitchen yard with its bread ovens, its old hearth.

On Good Friday, as I sat right here on Dolores's bench, the sun was setting, the air as mild as it is now. A faint breeze; one or two wisps of cloud. That softness in the air that makes you think winter's back has been broken once and for all.

Not unlike a deceptive cadence in music.

The cook brought me bread and salted fish, a little broth in a bowl, a wooden spoon. I remember being surprised that I still had my appetite. Over seventy, and my appetite was as strong, or stronger than when I was a boy. It felt like a wrong thing, but I could not refuse what lay before me. As I dunked my bread in broth, I thought of all the times the queen had resisted her masters by refusing to eat. I myself was never good at fasting. Not even on that one day of the year, so long ago now, when our family used to fast and make atonement. I used to hide a few figs in my pocket the night before, and devour them in secret behind our house.

It seemed that I was still that boy. But as I lifted the bread to my lips, my stomach simply changed its mind. No more. Done, it said. I let the crust fall to the ground. I looked in wonder at the wooden spoon, lying quietly on the bench. I would never pick it up again.

The spoon lay in a shadow all its own. How strange, I thought, the spoon has its own shadow—and then I realized someone was standing just in front of it, blocking the light of the setting sun. "Master Juanico, are you feeling unwell?" said a voice.

A voice surprisingly deep and rich for a young girl. That's my Inés. The queen used to close her eyes when our lovely kitchen maid began to sing. Was Juana pretending that a young man stood there— a young man with your own tender gaze—singing to her of love everlasting? We'll never know.

Our spring sunset at Tordesillas: the insects struggling to stay above the water, and drawing the attention of the swallows from above, who come a-diving and swooping with their own avid cries, and the fish from below, who rise to sip or slash, each as they are made. I sat on my bench that early evening, wishing such a fish would come for me. I had lived too long.

But Inés was still standing there, waiting for me to answer her simple question.

Before I could reply, the bells began to ring. It was still too early for Vespers, and they rang and rang. I thought they would never stop. But at last they did, and a little silence held sway.

Some find such a silence, at such an hour, the most melancholy thing, but I am soothed by it. I am soothed by the gathering blue, by the bushes and trees at last gone black against the sky. The swallows are done, and now the bats come swooping.

That Friday night, no bird sang, nor bat swooped. No rustle of leaf. Everything stopped, and I heard it. The one pure silence beyond all our faiths. A voice but no voice.

Inés was kneeling now at the bench, tugging my sleeve. Was I unwell? Did I need her help?

I had forgotten I was not alone.

She helped me to stand. I remember listening to the old spoon wobble on the bench as I rose. We waited for it to still. Then she helped me back into the palace, to the passage where you and the commissioner found me this morning, after the snowfall and the thieves.

If I have failed to describe Inés de Soto as she looks at twenty-one, it is only because my sight is not what it used to be. Besides, we are nearly out of time. The poor commissioner is trapped in the wine cellar just up the street, and your inkpot is nearly empty. I suspect that the last words you write today, should you choose to write them, will leave no mark on the paper. May I suggest that you lift your pen away now, and only listen, and commit to memory what I am about to tell you? For there is one last thing I wish to say.

But first listen: here is a portrait of a young woman. It may or may not be accurate. I know she is a very small, slender person, with lovely green eyes and dark curly hair. She has a beautiful singing voice and way of darting here and there. Little bird on the branch, she never alights for long.

That Friday evening, after she helped me back inside, Inés would not leave me for some time. She sat down beside me and started to cry. She still wore her kitchen apron, and wiped her tears on it. She told me how the queen had asked her to come sit on the great bed—and then had asked her to come nearer, and nestle just a moment at her side. I know this is difficult to believe, and I am sorry, in one way, that there was no courtier there to worry over it. Should such a thing be set down for history, or left out? So demeaning to the Crown!

I love, sometimes, to think of all the gaps and holes that fill our histories, all the stories that must be guessed at, invented, hoped.

The palace was already half-empty by then, its galleries and passages ringing with absence. The queen had outlasted dozens of servants, and several masters too. They kept her so well that she outlived them all; there was no one left to write to her father or her son and make one last dark report: *I am sorry to say that to the last our lady lacked judgment, and allowed a household maid to have access to her royal person, while the respected persons set by her own father, and her own son the emperor, were abused and sent away.*

Such pomp. Such outrage. Let it be recorded in the wrong place, at the wrong time, in the records of the Holy Office of the Inquisition, in ink so faded it cannot be seen, that the rightful Queen of Spain breathed her last with a kitchen maid nestled at her side, a kitchen maid whose identity she shielded to the last.

The girl was still weeping quietly at my side. "She gave me her little ruby," she said. "Should I wear it, or hide it?"

"Wear it," I said. "No one has seen it for years. But I have something for you too."

And from my pocket, with a trembling hand, I brought out my mother's key to our house in Granada. I put the key into that small warm hand and closed the fingers tightly over it. "This trinket has no value in the world," I said. "But I want you to keep it, and remember me when you are far away from here."

Her lip trembled, but she wasn't weeping any more. "But what does it open?"

"A house in Granada. A house that might not be there anymore. But it once belonged to your great-grandmother."

She fell silent. "I don't understand," she said.

"It's just a little trinket," I said. "Don't try to understand. I am an old fool, anyway."

"Do you want me to go there?" she said.

I laughed and said no. But it pleased me that she had asked. That's the way Inés is made. Always offering the impossible, and wanting to leap ahead. I know her; if she should chance to meet a good man such as yourself, she will be drawn to you, and love you well. She needs someone like you at her side. Someone calm, a person who moves steadily and has been out in the world.

Then I told her what I wanted her to do. "Make your way north, not south," I said. "Take the chapel singers with you. Go to the port at Laredo, and board one of the ships bound for the city on the river Scheldt. In Antwerp is a family by the name of Castro. Tell them an old vihuelist sent you, one who remembers their parents' kindness, and all they were able to do. They will help you get to safety."

Inés. It is a common enough name. And many young people nowadays look younger than they are. Some, it's true, might find her beautiful, if you like a small person built for swiftness, a little hard to catch. Another trait by which to recognize her: she is always hungry. Not only for food, but for stories and songs—the kinds of songs that tell stories, and the longer the better.

What a look she gave me as she left. Such eyes. I wish I could describe them to you. But you have stopped writing—have you run out of ink at last? Or do you at last understand me? Are you like the young scribe I mentioned earlier, the fellow who threw those papers over the side of the *Julienne*?

Soon enough it will be night. Let the commissioner linger below for a few more hours, and come to appreciate the dark, and a prisoner's unreasonable fear of doors and walls. Do you want to hold the oud a moment, see how it feels? Very like a lute, that's true, but it has no frets, and you can run your hand along here and make a thousand tones where a lute, as lovely as it is, makes only one. Before you go, leave me at the cellar gate, and when, just before Matins, the commissioner finds the door miraculously unstuck, I will hand the oud to him myself. He may carry me away to Valladolid with it in my arms, and put us on a shelf marked *Tordesillas, April, 1555*.

After all, the oud doesn't really belong to me. Who knows where my father got it. Who knows how many stories lay in it before this one, for it is very old. It was old before it fell from a tree and got its little bruise. Who knows but that it belonged to the famous Blackbird himself, Ziryab, who gave *al 'ud* its fifth string—its soul—and knew that it would keep getting lost, that we would be forever rediscovering the notes between the notes, the sound we can never fully hear.

It is still dusk. The hour that knows how to move slowly and swiftly all at once—it needs no bells to make itself known. At last we have it: the little quiet, the square of pale blue that speaks of peace. No bells now till Compline.

Go north. On the road to Laredo you will find a consort of four musicians: three singers and a vihuelist. This last will look like a boy, but he will have a very delicate face and bright green eyes. Ask this one if you may see the key to the house in Granada, and say the old vihuelist sent you. And once she reveals herself to you, you may ask to see the ruby given to her by the queen. The royal jewel box looked empty, but *Dio*, it had a trapdoor, and was as full as a young girl's heart.

Remember, she looks younger than she is. It is a quality of the Castro family from long ago, and from my family too. Did I say that in her heart I have hidden an amulet of sorts, two or three songs without paper, those my own mother taught me?

Some things are hard to pack, she said, *but we carry them anyway.*

As for Tordesillas, all will be well. Once you are away, I will sing a tune and play this old cracked thing to the poor commissioner where he lies among the barrels and casks, and when Matins is rung at San Antolín, I will bring him above ground. Together we will ride in the cart to Valladolid. I will be very docile, and submit to everything.

My hunger is gone. It's as if I am already inside the Valladolid Tribunal's *secreto*, seated on the defendant's stool, hearing the tiresome litany of my life of crime. Or perhaps I am still waiting in a solitary cell, in a depth of human silence I have never known. And if the inquisitor who, in time, examines me is not the one I hoped for—if it is not Pedro de Fermoselle—I can always imagine that it is. Whoever he is, my questioner will have to play the brother I left behind so long ago. And all brothers ever since.

If I could see better, I would guess that you look like a young knight in *Tirant lo blanc*, gazing out across the plain, where, it is said, a beautiful girl moves swiftly along in disguise. You'll have to follow one ocean, and perhaps another. You will have to smear the pages of your official documents, and tear out a page or two before you go. Tear them all out, tear them to bits.

Smear your signed name, too, for safety's sake.

I never asked your name. Never asked if you had brothers, or family, or anyone to worry about you, or send notes to your employer. Nor will I now, though the grandfather in me would like to know.

Dusk—it lingers so. Flat, those fields, both north and south. May it make your walking easy. It gives an old man hope to think that you might find her. Set out soon, and alone, and with any luck you will recognize her gait, and then her voice. In time, she will show you the key that opens no door known to man. Find her, find her, go with her across the sea. Wait one more moment, and let me put my hand on your head, and let my fingers drift over your brave young face. Such an ancient blessing. May the two of you, someday, be the subject of a song far from here, a legend, a ballad, a romance all your own.

acknowledgments

My first thanks go to Kris and Rich Daniels for a candlelit Hallow-een evening in 2000, and the music coming from their living room: *Music for Joan the Mad*, by the contemporary Canadian ensemble La Nef. It was this album, with its re-imaginings of Sephardic ballads and 16th-century Spanish court music, that caught at my ear—what were these two musical traditions doing on the same album?

As the question evolved into a story, several scholars and musicians gave generously of their expertise and guidance. I am grateful to Marc Vanscheeuwijck and David Wacks at the University of Oregon, to Bryan Johanson of Portland State University, to Mary B. Quinn at the University of New Mexico, and to Rachelle McCabe at my home institution of Oregon State University. Luthiers and lutenists such as Andy Rutherford, Pat O'Brien, and John Schneiderman shared their time and expertise, and welcomed me to their studios. Thanks also to Douglas Alton Smith, whose scholarship helped me understand the place of the vihuela in 16th-century Spanish culture.

My deep thanks go to Israel J. Katz, among other scholars of the Sephardic ballad tradition, for encouraging me to imagine the unknown stories of *converso* musicians in Inquisition Spain. Henry Sullivan's biography of Juan del Encina, with its brief but fascinating speculation about the composer/dramatist's possible *converso* back-ground, helped me create a more complex fictional character. Back home in Corvallis, Irene Bakalinsky shared the work of her late father, Leon Algazi, on Sephardic ballads, and alerted me to the doc-umentary *Diaspora*, about the *conversos* of Belmonte, Portugal, whose forbidden religious traditions were kept alive through many centuries by mothers, daughters, sisters, and aunts.

Eternal thanks to Jordi Savall, for the inspiration of his music, and for the encouragement he unknowingly gave when he answered "yes" to a stranger's question one evening at Lincoln Center.

Thank you to the Center for the Humanities at Oregon State University, as well as to the School of Writing, Literature and Film and College of Liberal Arts and to the board, staff, and my fellow writers at Hawthornden International Writers Retreat near Lasswade, Scotland, where I wrote the final chapters.

I'm grateful to Dr. Nora Gold and *Jewishfiction.net* for publishing the second chapter of this novel, in slightly different form, in the September 2018 issue.

For translation help, I owe a great debt to Julia Malye, who pored over 16th-century French accounts of Philippe le Beau's *Journeys d'Espagne*, and to Christina Léon, who translated key passages of scholarship on 16th-century palace life at Tordesillas.

Many dear friends lent their ears, imaginations, and expertise to this project, and I am grateful to them all. To name but a few: Andrea Barrett, Linda Bierds, Rosellen Brown, Patrick J. Clarke, Scott Nadelson, Susan Jackson Rodgers, Martha Lewis, Margot Livesey, Nick Lyons, Phillip Lopate, Lia Purpura, Steve Stern, and Bob and Mary Jo Nye. Thank you to *all* my dear friends, colleagues, and students at Oregon State University and the Rainier Writing Workshop.

I am grateful to my agent and friend, Colleen Mohyde, for her faith in this project.

I owe an enormous debt to my dear friend, the novelist Suzanne Berne, for her years of patient, engaged listening, and for asking a particularly galvanizing question: "Why just one inquisitor? What if there were two?"

My thanks to Debra Leigh Scott, founding publisher of Hidden River Press, for establishing the Tuscarora Award in Historical Fiction, and for taking a chance on this novel, and to the book's designers, Douglas Gordon and Andrea Marks.

My big love to my family, and especially to my daughter Hannah and my son-in-law, Arlo.

Finally, my greatest debt of gratitude goes to my husband, Tracy Daugherty. It is because of his extraordinary capacity for reading, rereading, and nurturing all-things-quixotic that *The Secret Music* has a life in the open air.

A Brief List for Further Reading and Listening

BOOKS

Hispanic Costume 1480–1530 by Ruth Mathilda Anderson
Juana the Mad, Sovereignty and Dynasty in Renaissance Europe
  by Bethany Aram
Seek the Darkness by Amarie Dennis
The Jews of Spain by Jane Gerber
Secrecy and Deceit by David Gitlitz
A Drizzle of Honey by David Gitlitz and Linda Davidson
The Expulsion 1492 Chronicles by David Raphael
Musical Repercussions of 1492, ed. Carol E. Robertson
The History of the Lute from Antiquity by Douglas Alton Smith
The Mad Queen of Spain by Michael Prawdin
*The Dream of the Poem: Hebrew Poetry from Muslim and Christian
  Spain 950–1492* by Peter Cole
Isabel the Queen by Peggy Liss
Wine, Women and Song, ed. David Wacks
Arte y Vida Cotidiana a Tordesillas by Miguel Zalama
Splendours of Court and *Feast*, both by Ray Strong

MUSIC

Music for Joan the Mad, La Nef
Music for the Spanish Kings and *Court Music and Songs from the Age of
  the Discoverers 1492–1553*, Hespèrion XX and Jordi Savall
Isabel I, Reina de Castilla, Hespèrion XXI and Jordi Savall
Ballads of the Sephardic Jews, Sarband
Sephardic Romances, Ensemble Accentus, Thomas Wimmer
The Echo of Orpheus, John Griffiths (vihuela)
Música cortesana en la Europa de Juana I de Castilla (1479–1555),
  Música Antigua, Eduardo Paniagua

about the author

Marjorie Sandor's previous books include the linked-story collection *Portrait of My Mother, Who Posed Nude in Wartime*, winner of the 2004 National Jewish Book Award in Fiction, and two essay collections, *The Night Gardener: A Search for Home*, and *The Late Interiors: A Life Under Construction*. She is also the editor of *The Uncanny Reader: Stories from the Shadows*, an international anthology of short fiction. A member of the MFA faculty at Oregon State University and the Rainier Writing Workshop, she lives in Corvallis, Oregon with her husband, the writer Tracy Daugherty. This is her first novel.

CPSIA information can be obtained
at www.ICGtesting.com
Printed in the USA
LVHW050821050620
657418LV00004B/640